Dedication

To Roy and Dale for their unconditional love and continuous support.
And in memory of Bruce who, for too short a time,
shared with me his joy of life and adventurous spirit.
—*Joanne*

To Samantha for the inspiration and to Don for his exuberant
enthusiasm and contagious creative energy.
—*Nancy*

Special thanks to

Joy Morgan Dey, whose computer graphics skills and artistic vision are gloriously evident in every page of *Quilts from The Quiltmaker's Gift*. Her patience is not so visible, but equally valued.

Barb Engelking and her staff at Fabric Works in Superior, Wisconsin—a contemporary quilt shop with an old-fashioned attitude of enthusiastic welcome for quilters of all skill levels. Barb was a staunch supporter during the creative evolution of *The Quiltmaker's Gift* and an invaluable technical consultant during the development of this book. She advised us on patterns and construction techniques, provided space and free classes for testing patterns, and encouraged us every step of the way.

The many quilters from Minnesota and Wisconsin who first loved *The Quiltmaker's Gift*, generously made mini-quilts for the traveling trunk show, created full-size quilts for this book, tested and retested the pattern instructions, and oohed and aahed over the results. They are model quiltmakers and quiltmentors.

Barbara Brackman for her systematic cataloguing and differentiating of quilt patterns by block construction in her *Encyclopedia of Pieced Quilt Patterns*. Gail and Nancy pored over this volume for months, searching for patterns and names to fit the story line and illustration possibilities of *The Quiltmaker's Gift*.

Lila Taylor Scott, technical editor for *American Patchwork & Quilting* magazine, who painstakingly reviewed all the fabric requirements, cutting instructions, and piecing diagrams for accuracy.

Susan Gustafson and Jennifer Isley, whose keen eyes and orderly minds have caught our errors and kept the grammar police at bay.

Jeff Brumbeau, whose charming fable inspired the creative energies of so many.

Gail de Marcken, whose incredible imagination is abundantly evident in her artwork and the secret stories behind her illustrations.

Contents

Quilts from The Quiltmaker's Gift

20 traditional patterns for a new
generation of generous quiltmakers

Joanne Larsen Line
Nancy Loving Tubesing

illustrations by Gail de Marcken
story text by Jeff Brumbeau

SCHOLASTIC INC.

New York Toronto London Auckland Sydney
Mexico City New Delhi Hong Kong

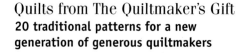

Quilts from The Quiltmaker's Gift
20 traditional patterns for a new
generation of generous quiltmakers

©2000 by Joanne Larsen Line and Nancy Loving Tubesing
©2000 watercolors by Gail de Marcken
©2000 story text by Jeff Brumbeau

ISBN 0-439-30909-3

All rights reserved. Published by Scholastic Inc.
SCHOLASTIC and associated logos are trademarks and/or registered trademarks of Scholastic Inc.

The illustrations, written instructions, photographs, designs, projects, and patterns are intended for the personal noncommercial use of the retail purchaser and are protected under federal copyright laws. No part of this publication may be reproduced, or stored in a retrieval system, or transmitted in any form or by any means, electronic mechanical, photocopying, recording, or otherwise, without the written permission of the publisher. For more information regarding permission, write to Permissions Department, Scholastic Inc., 555 Broadway, New York, NY 10012.

The information in this book is presented in good faith, but no warranty is given nor results guaranteed. Since Scholastic Inc has no control over choice of materials or procedures, the company assumes no responsibility for the use of this information.

The authors and publisher have made concerted effort to ensure the accuracy of pattern instructions, but inadvertent errors are inevitable. Check the website **www.quiltmakersgift.com** for an updated list of corrections. Please notify the publisher if you discover any additional errors so they can be corrected on the website and in future editions.

Illustrations by Gail de Marcken and text by Jeff Brumbeau from *The Quiltmaker's Gift* are used with permission.

Diagrams for Trip Around the World, pages 46-48, are adapted with permission of C&T Publishing Inc from the book *Tradition with a Twist* by Blanche Young and Dalene Young Stone, illustrations by Kandy Peterson. Available at your local quilt, fabric, or book store, or order from C&T Publishing at 800-284-1114 or http://www.ctpub.com.

Quilt term glossary (page 144) adapted and diagram (inside back cover) reprinted with permission of Martingale & Co–That Patchwork Place, from the books *Simply Scrappy Quilts* (1995) and *Two Color Quilts* (1998) by Nancy J. Martin.

Art Director: Joy Morgan Dey
Cover Design: Joy Morgan Dey
Book Design: Joy Morgan Dey
Editorial Director: Nancy Loving Tubesing
Quilt Photography: Steven Tiggemann, Jeff Frey & Associates Photography Inc, Duluth, MN

Printed in the U.S.A.

First Scholastic paperback edition, March 2001

10 9 8 7 6 5 4 3   02 03 04 05

Library of Congress Cataloguing-in-Publication Data

Line, Joanne Larsen. 1937-

   Quilts from The Quiltmaker's Gift: 20 traditional patterns for a new generation of generous quiltmakers / Joanne Larsen Line, Nancy Loving Tubesing; illustrations by Gail de Marcken; story text by Jeff Brumbeau.

      144 p. 28 cm.

      ISBN 0-439-30909-3

      1. Patchwork—Patterns.   2. Patchwork quilts.   I. Tubesing, Nancy Loving
   II. de Marcken, Gail, ill.   III. Brumbeau, Jeff.   IV. Title
TT835.L   2000
746.9'7—dc20   00-102128
                              CIP

5

Introduction

*T*his book began as a companion to *The Quiltmaker's Gift,* an inspiring fable about a mythical quiltmaker who made the most beautiful quilts in the world—then gave them away to the poor and homeless.

When the greedy king demands a quilt of his own, imagining it will make him happy as none of the many treasures in his castle have, the quiltmaker refuses. For this impudent rejection, the king throws her to a hungry bear and strands her on a tiny island, but each time the quiltmaker's kindness thwarts his plans.

Ultimately she relents and agrees to make a quilt for the king, but only on one condition— he must first give away all his possessions to the poor. Eventually he does so, and *The Quiltmaker's Gift* concludes with a powerful message about the joy of giving.

Why did we write this book?

So many quilters asked for information on the quilts Gail incorporated into her illustrations that we decided to create a book of patterns offering quilters of all skill levels the joyful challenge of making quilts featured in *The Quiltmaker's Gift.*

We especially wanted to help beginners, including children, gain skill in the art of quiltmaking. We have included several very easy patterns and provided lots of diagrams and pictures to make the learning process as friendly as possible.

All the blocks are constructed from squares, rectangles, and triangles that are easy to cut with a rotary cutter and easy to assemble. Novices may need some support from an experienced quilter when tackling the three-bird (most difficult) patterns, but instructions for all patterns are clear enough for beginners to follow successfully.

We also hope this book inspires seasoned quilters to share their expertise through quiltmentoring—teaming up with new quilters to pass on the traditions, techniques, and the

kindhearted attitudes of the craft that Jeff Brumbeau captured so splendidly in *The Quiltmaker's Gift.*

What's inside?

Quilts from The Quiltmaker's Gift provides everything you need for successful construction of twenty different quilts—historical background on quilt blocks, step-by-step cutting and piecing instructions with color-coded, easy-to-read diagrams, tips and techniques, as well as suggestions for creative adaptations.

For your pleasure and inspiration, samples of the whimsical illustrations and delightful story line from *The Quiltmaker's Gift* are scattered among the pages of this book.

Don't miss the unusual reference features: visual glossaries inside the front and back covers, mini-lessons in every pattern, simple self-care routines for ergonomically-challenged quilters, suggested print, on-line, and service resources, and information about ongoing Quiltmaker's Gift Generosity Projects. Check the website (**QuiltmakersGift.com**) periodically for announcements of contests, challenges, and projects featuring patterns from this book.

Meet our model quiltmakers

Quilts from The Quiltmaker's Gift was created with one additional goal: to celebrate the creative and philanthropic efforts of the millions of quilters worldwide who quilt just for the joy of making something useful and beautiful to give away. They would never expect to win a contest or have one of their quilts chosen for a quilting book. These generous everyday quiltmakers also deserve their moment in the limelight. So we have chosen to feature typical quiltmakers of our region.

In these colorful pages you'll find quilts made by people of all experience levels and ages: beginners and seasoned quilters, children, young adults, middle and golden agers. Many were made by intergenerational teams. One was the product of three generations—a boy, his

In Quilts from The Quiltmaker's Gift, *we invite you to—*

Celebrate the joy of quilting—for beginners and experts alike.

Celebrate the time-honored tradition of sharing and mentoring which is the heart of quilting—passing on the passion from generation to generation, neighbor to neighbor, coworker to coworker, classmate to classmate.

Celebrate the rich quilting resources of our community and region.

Celebrate the generosity of quiltmakers everywhere who live out the message of *The Quiltmaker's Gift.*

mother, and his grandmother. Others were made by veteran quilters sharing their skills and knowledge with first-time quilters.

Sharing—in a word, that's the essential joy of quilting. This same sense of sharing inspired quiltmakers throughout our region to help with a host of projects related to *Quilts from The Quiltmaker's Gift*—making mini-quilts to match the book illustrations, testing patterns, and creating contemporary interpretations of forgotten historical quilt blocks.

The joy of sharing is also revealed in a heart-warming, true-to-life story from our home town. A medical student at the University of Minnesota–Duluth created a Children's Delight quilt with her landlady-quiltmentor. She began encouraging her med student colleagues to join in the fun of learning to quilt by making tiny quilts for the neo-natal unit at the hospital. As other quilters heard of the group, they offered lessons, fabrics, and supplies for the project. Quiltmentors at work!

Our challenge to you

Now it's your turn for quiltmaking and quiltmentoring. Celebrate the rich tradition of quilting and the generosity of quiltmakers. Find a seasoned quilter to learn from. Team up with a novice—make a friend and a quilt at the same time! Offer your expertise to a middle school or Cub Scout den or prison facility or Alzheimer's home. Join forces with friends to create a generosity project in your community. The projects in *Quilts from The Quiltmaker's Gift* will make a perfect starting point for beginners, experts, and all those in between.

Joanne Larsen Line, MBA
Nancy Loving Tubesing, EdD
Gail de Marcken, BA

After finishing a mid-career masters degree, **Joanne Larsen Line** took up quiltmaking at the persistent encouragement of her elderly neighbor who knew she needed a creative focus for her spare time at nights and on weekends. Now an expert piecer and enthusiastic mentor to new quilters of all ages, Joanne teaches classes year round at quilt shops, guilds, and gatherings. She firmly believes that with just a few basic guidelines and clear pattern instructions, anyone can make beautiful quilts.

Inspired to quilt by the poetry of a teenager, **Nancy Loving Tubesing**, took a quilting class at Fabric Works and discovered a whole new world of generous quiltmakers, eager to share their expertise. Curious about the names and construction of traditional quilt block patterns, she has done extensive research on quilting history and block design. Nancy enjoys sharing her entertaining, educational, and inspirational perspectives on quilting and creativity with quilt groups nationwide.

Self-taught quilter and globe-trotting spouse of a Peace Corps administrator, **Gail de Marcken**, made several quilts as warm-ups for painting her watercolor illustrations for the award-winning book, *The Quiltmaker's Gift.* Gail's gifts as an artist are evident in her exquisite Rosebud, Bear's Paw, and Hen & Chicks quilts, as well as her stunning illustrations. Look for her *Artist's Secrets* in each quilt pattern.

How to Use this Book

The twenty quilt blocks that form the heart of *Quilts from The Quiltmaker's Gift* are organized in four sections.

Easy Squares and Rectangles (pages 10–49)
Easy Squares and Triangles (pages 50–73)
Challenging Squares and Triangles (pages 74–101)
Flying Geese & Beyond (pages 102–123)

Blocks are arranged in order of difficulty within the section and through the book. Patterns are presented in two or three page-spreads, each organized in the same manner, with the same easy-to-use features, including two or three example quilts.

The remainder of the book provides reference materials that will be of interest to quilters of all levels: ergonomics and wellness strategies, basic quilting tools and techniques, suggested reading, resources, and glossary/index. Reference charts and diagrams are located inside the front and back covers for easy access.

Bird Ratings

Quilts are rated for difficulty from one to three birds, based primarily on complexity of the block.

One bird: Simple construction, minimum number of pieces. Easy enough for beginners with little or no sewing experience if they study the Quilting Basics on pages 130–139.

Two birds: Blocks with more pieces and fabric placement options or more complicated construction techniques. Easy enough for beginners who are experienced sewers.

Three birds: Blocks with numerous pieces, tricky construction, and/or complex design choices. Beginners will probably need a quiltmentor for consultation. Ask for volunteers!

Brackman/BlockBase Number

All blocks in this book were chosen from Barbara Brackman's *Encyclopedia of Pieced Quilt Patterns,* which catalogs blocks based on the construction type, date and source of first publication, alternate names, and similar blocks. This same number is used by Electric Quilt's BlockBase computer program which will print out templates for the block pieces at various sizes.

Block Illustration

Gail de Marcken's illustrations of the quilt pattern in *The Quiltmaker's Gift* provide a springboard for your inspiration.

Artist's Secrets

Illustrator Gail de Marcken reveals some of the intriguing stories behind her choice of nineteenth and early twentieth century quilt patterns included in *The Quiltmaker's Gift.*

Quiltmaker's Design Challenges

For beginners and experts alike, this column offers stimulating ideas for fabric choices, plus suggestions for borders, quilt design, and settings.

Story Excerpt

Text from *The Quiltmaker's Gift* by Jeff Brumbeau graces every opening page-spread.

Meet the Quiltmaker

Wherever a butterfly appears in the text, expect some interesting description of the quiltmaker whose creative efforts are pictured nearby.

Block Construction and History Narrative

This column focuses on interesting aspects of the pattern, including historical settings and colorings, significant elements of the block construction, adaptations and interpretations of the pattern by contemporary quiltmakers. Look for the special challenges presented by this block's construction.

Step-by-Step Piecing Instructions

Written instructions explain and color-coded diagrams show every step of the block construction process. Watch pressing arrows carefully. If seams are pressed in the direction indicated, intersecting seams will nest together nicely and the final block should be nice and flat.

Quilt Information Chart

Look here to find important details for three quilts in three different sizes: dimensions with and before adding borders, block size, number of blocks needed and their layout, and a diagram for cutting the backing fabric for that size.

Quilt Diagram

Shows block layout and borders for three quilt sizes.

This friendly bird signals caution with special warnings and construction tips throughout the pattern. Watch for helpful hints on cutting, piecing, pressing, and design elements.

The Quiltmaker Says . . . Box

Each pattern begins with a gentle reminder of essentials for success from the Quiltmaker.

Fabric Requirement Chart

Lists fabric by fabric, piece by piece, how much fabric is needed for the different size quilts. Measurements assume 42"–45" fabric that has been prewashed. Calculations allow for shrinkage and the trimming of selvages before measuring and cutting. For each fabric, 6"–9" extra fabric is included as allowance for uneven yardage and/or cutting errors.

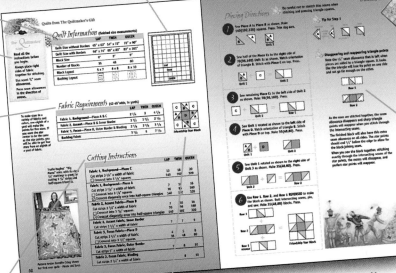

Tip Diagrams

Especially for beginners, tip diagrams expand the step-by-step instructions to show positioning of units during construction and highlight tricky spots.

Cutting Instructions Chart

Fabric-by-fabric, piece-by-piece instructions for cutting and crosscutting strips into shapes needed to construct the block. Number of strips and number of final pieces needed are noted for worry-free cutting.

Block Diagrams

Show the quilt block components with pieces color-coded and alpha-labeled to coordinate with the fabric requirements and cutting charts, and to match the step-by-step block construction instructions that follow. The Brackman/BlockBase number is below the diagram. Some patterns show alternate historical colorings for the block.

More Features

This spread may also include step-by-step photo sequences, tidbits of interest, or additional sample quilts with stories of their makers.

Take time for a break. Check out the Wellness for Quilters section (126-129).

Quilt Assembly

This section gives instructions for setting the finished blocks in a pleasing arrangement and sewing them together. For some patterns, diagrams show challenging assembly techniques and give advice for special settings that go well with specific blocks.

Photo Essays

Show hints or critical steps of the block construction process so you can see how the diagrams translate into cloth.

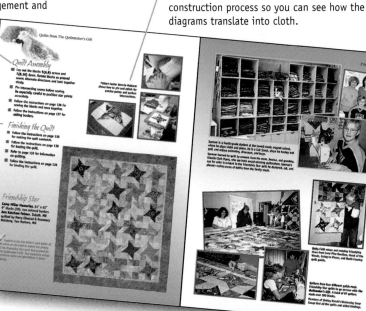

Finishing the Quilt

Outlines the final steps of quiltmaking with references to more in-depth instructions.

Watch for the helpful bird who offers reminders of good techniques or potential hazards.

More Quilts

Many patterns feature an additional quilt on this spread, along with a caption about its makers.

Meet the Quiltmakers

Look for photo collages showing the stories of novice and experienced quilters like you joining forces to make beautiful quilts.

Setting Options

For creative inspiration, photographs or diagrams of alternate settings for the block are included in patterns with light/dark diagonal blocks.

Puss in the Corner

Hot Tin Roof, 45" x 57"
12" blocks (12)
two borders with corner blocks

Michelle Bowker, Duluth, MN
quilted by Marcia Bowker, Duluth, MN

Artist's Secrets

I chose this block because it allowed me to repeat the pattern visually by putting the cat in the "four-patch" window. It also gave me an excuse to paint cats in the corner of nearly every page. Much later, the block helped me solve the dilemma of where to put the king's blue cats. I put them in the corner, too—and then let them escape from the king's treasure trove.

Puss in the Corner

Brackman/BlockBase Number: 1603
Earliest publication date: 1931
Alternate name: Pussy in the Corner

The name Puss in the Corner or Pussy in the Corner has been used historically for a whole host of quilt blocks. This X- and O-block nine-patch version is a perfect quilt for beginners to learn basic quilting skills: strip piecing, cross-cutting, nested seam construction, and efficient pressing. For those with short attention spans or limited patience, try an alternate block setting, substituting a plain 12" block of background fabric for the O-blocks.

We have updated the original four-patch unit with a more efficient rectangle and two-patch construction in the first three steps. This same beginning process is used in the Log Cabin block—an excellent next step quilting project.

Quiltmaker's Design Challenges

◆ Use a novelty fabric or large print as the "background" fabric and for an alternating block with the Pussy in the Corner X-block.

◆ An overall scrappy quilt, paying attention to value rather than color, has exciting possibilities. Imagine the whole universe of cat-types in a variety of surroundings.

◆ For a colorwash effect, experiment with florals of different scales, combined with accent fabrics in the corner.

◆ Design a two-block quilt using a more complex 12" alternate block (like Corn and Beans) with Puss in the Corner X-blocks.

◆ Incorporate a miniature version of the block into a pieced border.

Next the king fetched a hundred blue waltzing cats . . .

Fifth grade teacher Michelle teamed up with her sister, Marcia Bowker, an occupational therapist specializing in hand rehabilitation, to update the Puss in the Corner pattern with contemporary fabrics and funky quilting, using her Legacy long arm.

Quilt Information (finished size measurements)

	CRIB	TWIN	QUEEN
Quilt Size without Borders	36" x 48"	60" x 72"	84" x 96"
Quilt Size with Borders	45" x 57"	69" x 81"	93" x 105"
Block Size	12"	12"	12"
Number of Blocks	12	30	56
Block Layout	3 x 4	5 x 6	7 x 8
Backing Layout	← / ←	↑ ↑	↑ ↑ / ↑

The Quiltmaker says...

Read all the instructions before you begin.

Always place right sides of fabric together for stitching.

Use scant $\frac{1}{4}$" seam allowances.

Press seam allowances in the direction of arrows.

Fabric Requirements (42-45" wide, in yards)

	CRIB	TWIN	QUEEN
Fabric 1—**Background**, Piece A	1	2	3 $\frac{3}{4}$
Fabric 2—**Focus**, Pieces B, C & Border Fabric	2	3 $\frac{3}{4}$	6
Fabric 3—**Accent**, Piece D, Inner Border & Binding	1	1 $\frac{3}{4}$	2 $\frac{1}{3}$
Backing Fabric	2 $\frac{7}{8}$	4 $\frac{7}{8}$	7 $\frac{3}{4}$

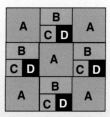

**Puss in the Corner X-Block
#1603**

Cutting Instructions

	CRIB	TWIN	QUEEN
Fabric 1, Background—Piece A			
Cut strips 4 $\frac{1}{2}$" x width of fabric	6	15	28
☐ Crosscut into 4 $\frac{1}{2}$" squares	54	135	252
Fabric 2, Focus—Piece B			
Cut strips 2 $\frac{1}{2}$" x width of fabric	6	15	28
▭ Crosscut into 2 $\frac{1}{2}$" x 4 $\frac{1}{2}$" rectangles	54	135	252
Fabric 2, Focus—Piece C			
Cut strips 2 $\frac{1}{2}$" x width of fabric	4	9	16
Fabric 2, Focus—Outside Border			
Cut strips 4 $\frac{1}{2}$" x width of fabric	5	7	9
Fabric 3, Accent—Piece D			
Cut strips 2 $\frac{1}{2}$" x width of fabric	4	9	16
Fabric 3, Accent—Inner Border			
Cut strips 1" x width of fabric	4	7	9
Fabric 3, Accent—Binding			
Cut strips 2 $\frac{1}{4}$" x width of fabric	5	8	10

**Puss in the Corner O-Block
(uncatalogued)**

Brackman's *Encyclopedia* documents only the X-block nine-patch as Puss (or Pussy) in the Corner. The original block used a four-patch for the corner and center squares. It was probably set with an alternate plain block.

When we were making mini-quilts for each block in *The Quiltmaker's Gift*, a quilter from Pengilly pointed out the need for a corresponding O-block to make the pattern look as Gail had painted it. So we created a logical companion for this historical block, which makes Gail's painting correct.

No doubt this is one way quilt patterns evolve over time—quilters make mistakes that turn out to be lovely new interpretations.

Piecing Directions

Pay close attention to the direction of pressing arrows in each step.

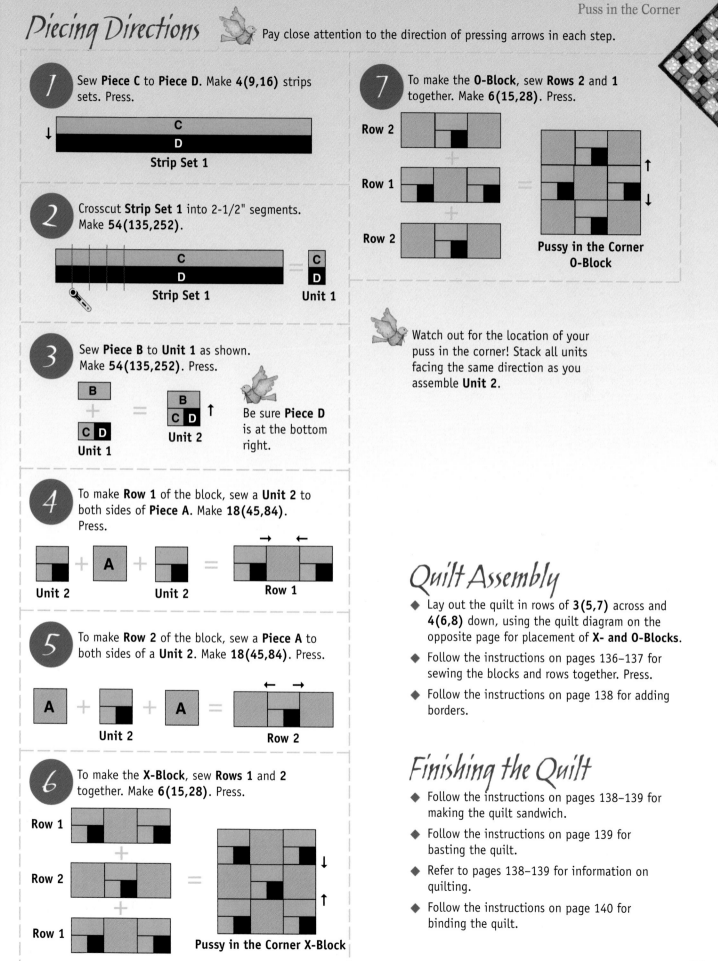

1 Sew **Piece C** to **Piece D**. Make **4(9,16)** strips sets. Press.

C
D
Strip Set 1

2 Crosscut **Strip Set 1** into 2-1/2" segments. Make **54(135,252)**.

C
D
Strip Set 1

C
D
Unit 1

3 Sew **Piece B** to **Unit 1** as shown. Make **54(135,252)**. Press.

B
+
C D
Unit 1

=

B
C D ↑
Unit 2

Be sure **Piece D** is at the bottom right.

4 To make **Row 1** of the block, sew a **Unit 2** to both sides of **Piece A**. Make **18(45,84)**. Press.

Unit 2 + A + **Unit 2** = **Row 1**

5 To make **Row 2** of the block, sew a **Piece A** to both sides of a **Unit 2**. Make **18(45,84)**. Press.

A + **Unit 2** + A = **Row 2**

6 To make the **X-Block**, sew **Rows 1** and **2** together. Make **6(15,28)**. Press.

Row 1
+
Row 2
+
Row 1

=

Pussy in the Corner X-Block

7 To make the **O-Block**, sew **Rows 2** and **1** together. Make **6(15,28)**. Press.

Row 2
+
Row 1
+
Row 2

=

Pussy in the Corner O-Block

Watch out for the location of your puss in the corner! Stack all units facing the same direction as you assemble **Unit 2**.

Quilt Assembly

◆ Lay out the quilt in rows of **3(5,7)** across and **4(6,8)** down, using the quilt diagram on the opposite page for placement of **X- and O-Blocks**.

◆ Follow the instructions on pages 136–137 for sewing the blocks and rows together. Press.

◆ Follow the instructions on page 138 for adding borders.

Finishing the Quilt

◆ Follow the instructions on pages 138–139 for making the quilt sandwich.

◆ Follow the instructions on page 139 for basting the quilt.

◆ Refer to pages 138–139 for information on quilting.

◆ Follow the instructions on page 140 for binding the quilt.

Michelle Bowker teaches fifth grade at Nettleton math/science magnet school. She regularly incorporates quiltmaking into her math and U.S. history curriculum. Students hand piece and tie quilts, which are then given away for school fund-raisers.

During Operation Desert Storm the fifth graders made a quilt from patriotic colors and raffled it off.

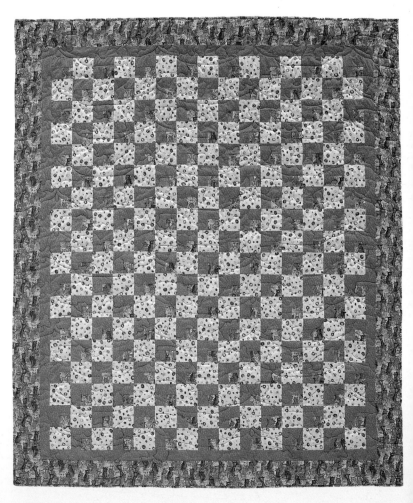

Puss in the Corner

The Cat's Meow, 72" x 84"
12" blocks (30), two plain borders
Kim Hoffmockel Wells, Duluth, MN
quilted by Debra Lussier Quinn, Superior, WI

Kim owns the Creations Unlimited quilt store in Duluth. The shop brings in nationally known quilt teachers several times a year for classes, workshops, and retreats. Kim particularly enjoys making small quilts for newborns in neonatal intensive care.

Steph Gudmunsen shows off her first quilt while Paige Louise Davis lounges on *her* first quilt made by her grandmother, Carol Jean Brooks. Both quilts use alternate plain block settings with Puss in the Corner.

Puss in the Corner

Where's Peanut?, 46" x 55"
12" blocks (12), three borders
Jeanette Christensen, Duluth, MN
quilted by Pam Stolan, Duluth, MN

Puss in the Corner

Tiger Tiger Shining Bright, 35" x 47"
12" blocks (6), two plain borders
Jeanette Christensen, Duluth, MN
quilted by Pam Stolan, Duluth, MN

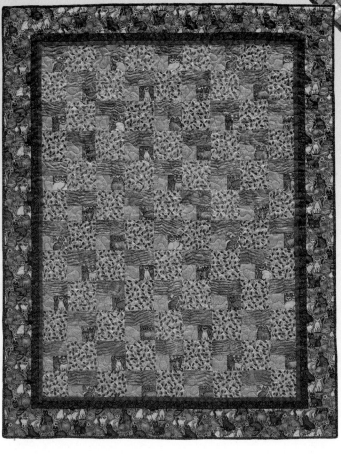

Jeanette is a public health nurse for the second largest county in the U.S. Member of three different quilt guilds in northern Minnesota, she is an enthusiastic missionary for quilting and loves teaching newcomers the joys of piecing (and surviving the north country winters) in her quilt retreats called Pieceful Dreams.

Children's Delight

"Q" is for Quilt, 51" x 51"
7" blocks (36), two plain borders

**Elizabeth Benson Johnson
& Sarah Elizabeth Anne Johnson** Duluth, M
quilted by Karen McTavish, Duluth, MN

Children's Delight

Children's Delight 🕊️

Brackman/BlockBase Number: 1070
Earliest publication date: 1898
(Ladies Art Company #319)

This block has two components: an uneven nine-patch (Pieces C-D-C, A-B-A, C-D-C) and a built in sashing on two sides (Pieces F-E). Once the asymmetrical blocks are assembled in rows, a finishing F-E-F sashing is added to the top and right sides, restoring the symmetry.

Using only rectangles and squares, this is an easy quilt for beginners and a perfect choice to make with a child. Be sure to let the child choose fabrics that appeal to her/him. This pattern is flexible enough to incorporate nearly any fabric combination if you choose a sashing that holds the whole creation together.

The speed-piecing instructions highlight making and cross-cutting multiple strip sets and following an efficient pressing plan.

Since Children's Delight makes its own sashing, you may want to wait until the quilt is finished to decide what type of border will frame it best. Notice the secondary design that develops when the four segments of the block are sewn together.

The Ladies Art Company published the first mail-order patchwork pattern catalog in 1889. These pamphlets, with their small drawings and captions, helped standardize quilt patterns and names.

🦋 *Eight-year-old Sarah teamed up with her mom, Liz, to create her first quilt. Sarah helped pick out the fabrics and sewed the strip sets together. This is their first mother/daughter quilt.*

Professional machine quilter Karen McTavish incorporated the focus fabric theme into her design by repeating ABCs in the border quilting.

Quiltmaker's Design Challenges

◆ Show off juvenile prints or novelty fabrics in the center squares.

◆ Use the center square as an appliqué block.

◆ Geometrics (stripes, polka dots, plaids) make smashing sashings.

◆ Make a "Children's Delight at Christmas" quilt featuring seasonal fabrics.

◆ The double sashing effect of this block makes excellent photo frames for a memory or celebration quilt.

◆ This is a perfect gift quilt for a teacher. Each student can create a center block with fabric markers, crayons, or computer-generated designs or messages. All the pieces of this quilt are easy for kids to cut and sew.

◆ Experiment with creating depth in each block by color combinations and value placement.

◆ For an elegant look, try this quilt in Civil War reproduction fabrics. Or use many different florals with scrappy green sashings.

◆ Transform the center square of each block into a different miniature block (Friendship Star, Pinwheel, Hourglass, Square in a Square) and create a sampler quilt framed by the uneven nine-patch block.

◆ Create a contrasting pieced border of miniature nine-patches.

Then the king ordered his merry-go-round with the real horses to be brought out. Children cried with delight . . .

Quilt Information (finished size measurements)

	CRIB	LAP	TWIN
Quilt Size without Borders	28" x 35"	35" x 49"	49" x 70"
Quilt Size with Borders	38" x 45"	45" x 59"	59" x 80"
Block Size	7"	7"	7"
Number of Blocks	20	35	70
Block Layout	4 x 5	5 x 7	7 x 10
Backing Layout	← / ←	← / ←	↑ ↑

The Quiltmaker says . . .

Read all the instructions before you begin.

Always place right sides of fabric together for stitching.

Use scant $\frac{1}{4}$" seam allowances.

Press seam allowances in the direction of arrows.

Fabric Requirements (42-45" wide, in yards)

	CRIB	LAP	TWIN
Fabric 1, **Light 1**—Piece A & D	$\frac{3}{4}$	1	$1\frac{3}{4}$
Fabric 2, **Focus**—Piece B & Outer Border	$1\frac{1}{8}$	$1\frac{1}{2}$	$2\frac{1}{4}$
Fabric 3, **Medium 1**—Piece C & Inner Border	$\frac{5}{8}$	$\frac{3}{4}$	$\frac{7}{8}$
Fabric 4, **Light 2**—Piece F	$\frac{1}{3}$	$\frac{1}{3}$	$\frac{1}{2}$
Fabric 5, **Medium 2**—Piece E & Binding	1	$1\frac{1}{4}$	$1\frac{3}{4}$
Backing Fabric	$2\frac{1}{2}$	$2\frac{7}{8}$	$4\frac{7}{8}$

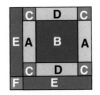

Children's Delight Block #1898

Cutting Instructions

	CRIB	LAP	TWIN
Fabric 1, Light 1—Piece A			
Cut strips $1\frac{1}{2}$" x width of fabric	6	8	16
Fabric 1, Light 1—Piece D			
Cut strips $4\frac{1}{2}$" x width of fabric	2	3	6
Fabric 2, Focus, Piece B			
Cut strips $4\frac{1}{2}$" x width of fabric	3	4	8
Fabric 2, Focus, Outer Border			
Cut strips $4\frac{1}{2}$" x width of fabric	4	5	7
Fabric 3, Medium 1—Piece C			
Cut strips $1\frac{1}{2}$" x width of fabric	4	6	12
Fabric 3, Medium 1—Inner Border			
Cut strips $1\frac{1}{2}$" x width of fabric	4	5	7
Fabric 4, Light 2—Piece F			
Cut strips $1\frac{1}{2}$" x width of fabric	2	2	4
☐ Crosscut into $1\frac{1}{2}$" squares	30	48	88
Fabric 5, Medium 2—Piece E			
Cut strips $1\frac{1}{2}$" x width of fabric	9	14	26
☐ Crosscut into $1\frac{1}{2}$" x $6\frac{1}{2}$" rectangles	49	82	157
Fabric 5, Medium 2—Binding			
Cut strips $2\frac{1}{4}$" x width of fabric	5	6	8

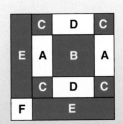

Children's Delight Block Historical Size & Coloring

Piecing Directions

Be sure to square up strip sets before cross-cutting. See page 134.

1 Sew **Strip A** to both sides of **Strip B**. Make **3(4,9)** strip sets. Press.

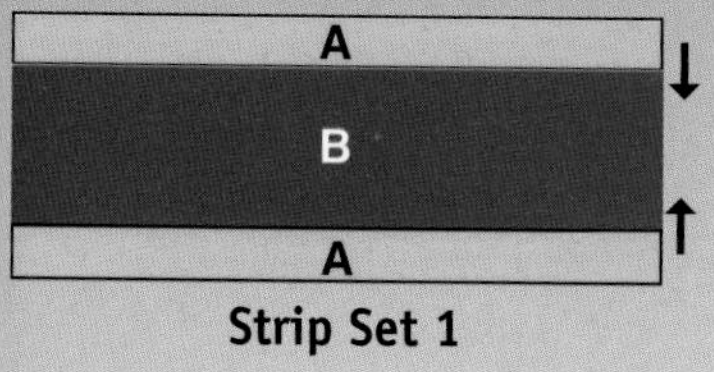

Strip Set 1

2 Crosscut **Strip Set 1** into 4$^{1}/_{2}$" segments. Make **20(35,70)**.

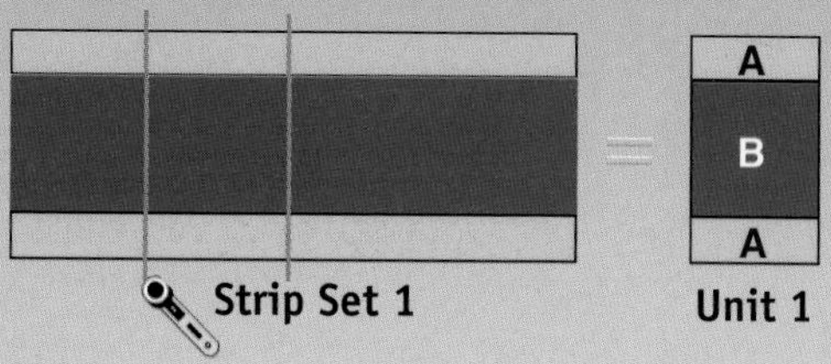

Strip Set 1 = **Unit 1**

3 Sew **Strip C** to both sides of **Strip D**. Make **2(3,6)** strip sets. Press.

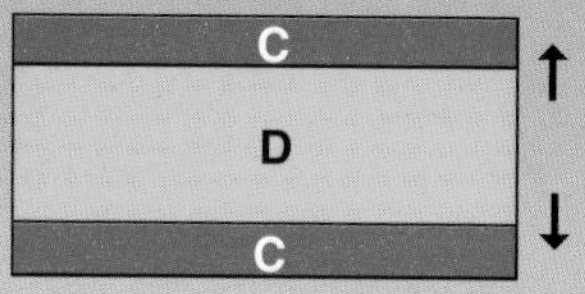

4 Crosscut **Strip Set 2** into 1$^{1}/_{2}$" segments. Make **40(70,140)**.

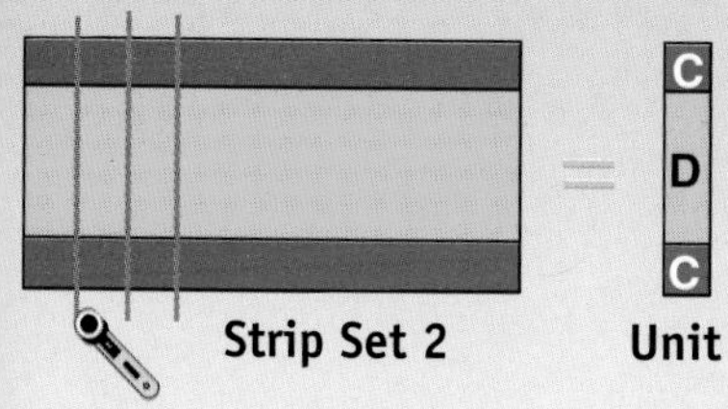

Strip Set 2 = **Unit 2**

5 Sew **Unit 2**s to both sides of **Unit 1**. Make **20(35,70)**. Press.

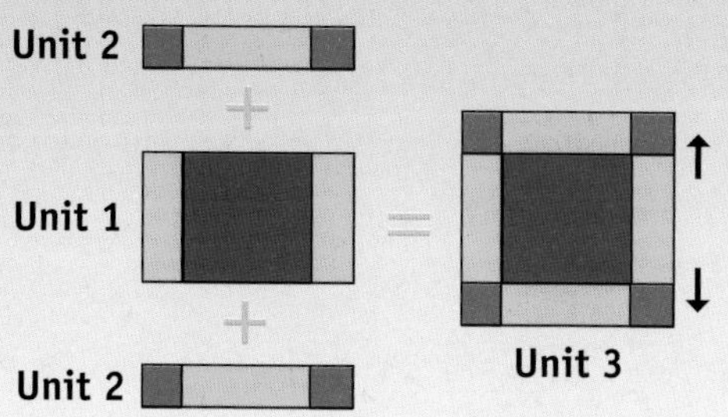

Unit 2
+
Unit 1
+
Unit 2
= **Unit 3**

6 Sew **Piece E** to the bottom of **Unit 3**. Make **20(35,70)**. Press.

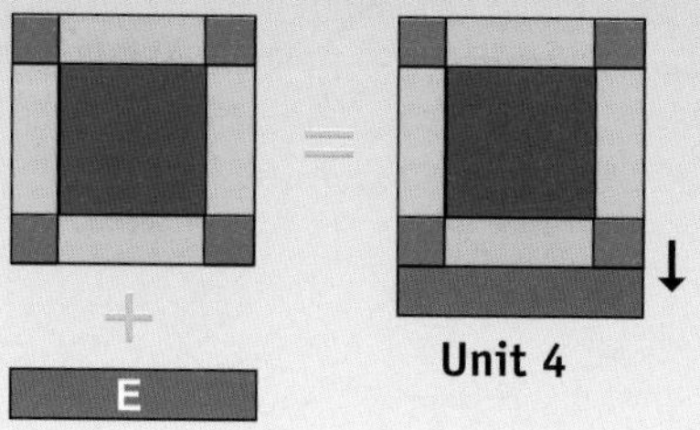

+
E
= **Unit 4**

7 To make **Unit 5**, sew **Piece F** to **20(35,70) Piece E**s. Press.

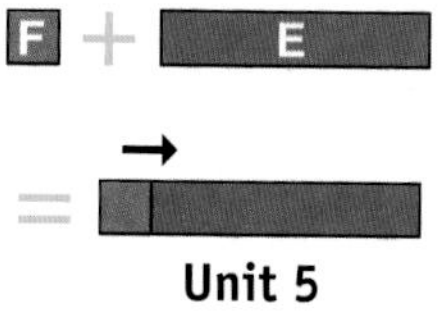

F + E
= **Unit 5**

8 Sew **Unit 5** to the left side of **Unit 4**. Make **20(35,70)** blocks. Press.

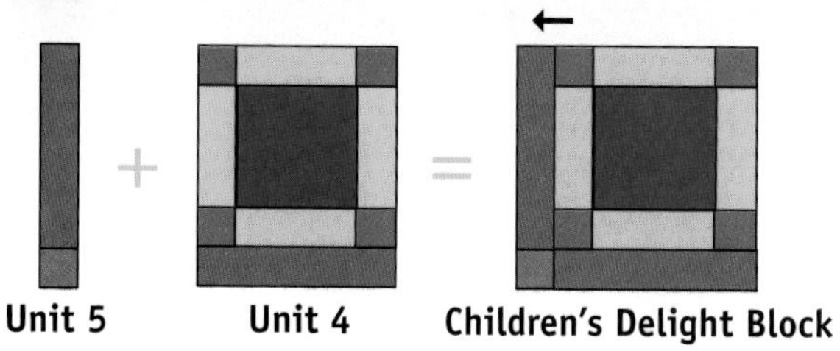

Unit 5 + Unit 4 = **Children's Delight Block**

To speed crosscutting in **Step 2** and **Step 4**, lay 3–4 strip sets on top of each other with seam lines parallel and staggered about $^{1}/_{2}$" apart. Cut through all layers, first squaring off the end and then cross-cutting the needed width.

Press after each seam so intersecting seams will nest and lock tightly. See page 134.

9 To make the final **right** sashing, sew **5(7,10) Piece E**s and **5(7,10) Piece F**s together as shown below. Press.

E + F + E + F + E + F + E + F + E + F

= **Sashing Strip 1**

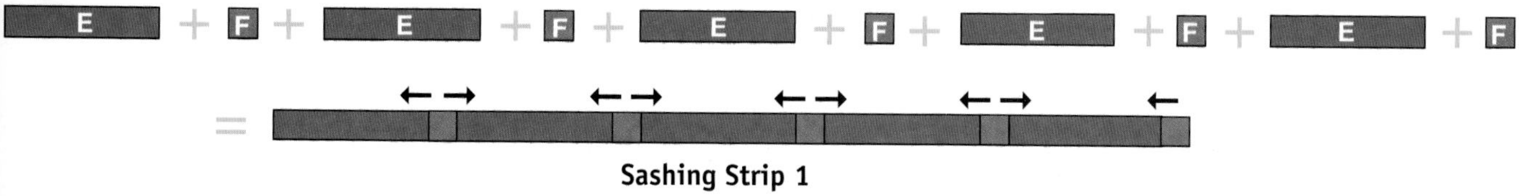

10 To make the final **top** sashing, sew **4(5,7) Piece E**s and **5(6,8) Piece F**s together as shown below. Press.

F + E + F + E + F + E + F + E + F

= **Sashing Strip 2**

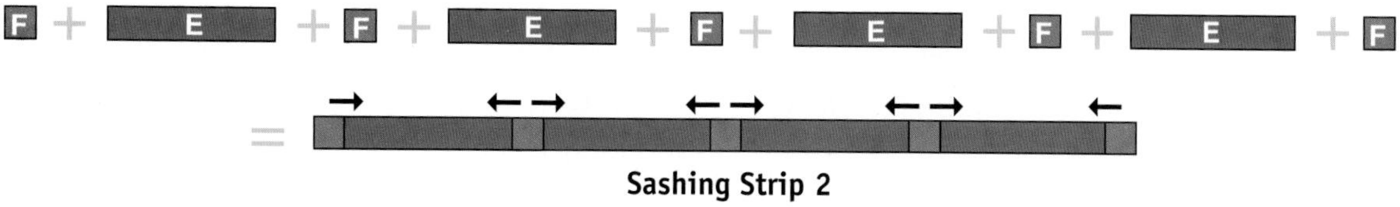

Quilt Assembly

◆ Lay out the blocks **4(5,7)** across and **5(7,10)** down. All blocks should be oriented in the same direction, with **Piece E** to the left and at the bottom.

◆ Follow the instructions on pages 136–137 for sewing the blocks and rows together. Press seams as you go.

◆ Sew **Sashing Strip 1** to the **right** edge of the quilt. Press toward sashing.

◆ Sew **Sashing Strip 2** to the **top** edge of the quilt. Press.

◆ Follow the instructions on page 138 for adding borders.

Finishing the Quilt

◆ Follow the instructions on pages 138–139 for making the quilt sandwich.

◆ Follow the instructions on page 139 for basting the quilt.

◆ Refer to pages 138–139 for information on quilting.

◆ Follow the instructions on page 140 for binding the quilt.

Busy medical student Kelly Sauer caught the quilting bug from her landlady, Minnesota Quilter of the Year 2000, Shirley Kirsch. Between studying anatomy and learning bedside manner, during her first year as a quilter, Kelly made a quilt every month under Shirley's tutelage—including this safari version of Children's Delight—using a borrowed featherweight machine.

Shirley hosts the Wednesday Soup Group, which meets weekly to make quilts for charitable causes. She has nurtured hundreds of novice quiltmakers with her patient teaching style and contagious enthusiasm for quilting.

Children's Delight

On Safari, 65" x 81"
7" blocks (80), one plain border
Shirley Kirsch, Duluth, MN
& **Kelly Saue**r, Sartell, MN
quilted by Helen Smith Prekker, Duluth, MN

Sarah's mom, Liz Benson Johnson, is Assistant Director of the University of Minnesota-Duluth Library. They have already started on another mother/daughter quilt.

Sarah Johnson is a third grade student at the Nettleton math/science magnet school, where she is a member of the Spanish club. She is also a member of 4-H and is currently raising two rabbits, Cinnamon and Ginger. Sarah enjoys cross-country skiing, swimming, and sailing. In the winter, she loves to skijor with her dog, Oreo.

Show and tell at Fabric Works.

21

King's Hiway

King's Royal Highway, 57" x 73"
15" blocks, mitered border

Diane Nyman, Proctor, MN
quilted by Pam Stolan, Duluth, MN

King's Hiway

Brackman/BlockBase Number: 1835
Earliest publication date: 1930s (Nancy Page)

Before the invention of the sewing machine, youngsters learned to quilt by stitching small squares into nine-patches, then combining the blocks with plain squares to make a final quilt in what we call an alternate block setting. The large (19 1/2") King's Hiway block is constructed of nine-patches alternated with plain blocks. Actually, the pattern is a double-nine-patch—small nine-patches in the corners and center of a larger nine-patch. With sashings between and around the blocks, a complex design is created from simple components.

This interesting adaptation of a very easy block offers beginners an opportunity to play with different fabrics in designing the quilt and lots of practice with stitching and crosscutting strip sets, pressing, and nesting seams for precise intersections. At the same time, it provides experienced quilters with intriguing design challenges.

Nancy Page was a syndicated mail-order column written by Florence LaGanke Harris. Quilt block patterns were published under this name in many periodicals from the late 1920s to the 1940s.

Artist's Secrets

Ah, this was one of my favorite finds when searching for quilt blocks whose names would help tell the story. You have to look closely, but the "hiway" in the pattern veers off to the left. The king has found his path by going off the cobblestone road and up over the hills instead. He makes his own highway to venture out and interact with the world.

Quiltmaker's Design Challenges

◆ Since the king takes off around the world to give away his treasures, international fabrics would be a natural choice.

◆ Experiment with unexpected fabrics for the sashings: cobblestones, railroad tracks, botanicals, stars, checkerboards, woodgrains, border prints.

◆ For a child's quilt, update the King's Hiway with bright fabrics featuring construction equipment, trucks, race cars, motorcycles, and traffic signs.

◆ Jewel tones fit both the theme of royalty and the many nine-patches.

◆ Alternate plain squares offer an opportunity to showcase focus fabrics. Try fancy batiks, fussy-cut large novelties, color-coordinated florals.

◆ In keeping with the highway theme, make a memory quilt with snapshots from a family trip incorporated as the alternate plain blocks.

◆ Use this large block as a medallion center for a quilt. Surround the center with other blocks related by construction (nine-patches) or theme-name.

◆ To make a large quilt (97 1/2" x 97 1/2") quickly, alternate the King's Hiway block with plain blocks of the same size in a 5 x 5 block setting. This was probably the traditional treatment for the block.

◆ For an especially professional look, create a pieced border of nine-patches on point to frame the king's journey.

In keeping with the name of the quilt, surgical nurse Diane Nyman chose fabrics that give a truly regal look to the final product. Alternate squares were fussy-cut for placement of the medallions. Pam Stolan used free motion quilting, incorporating quilting designs developed by Australian Keryn Emmerson.

Morning, noon, and night, the wagons rolled out of town, each piled high with the king's wonderful things.

23

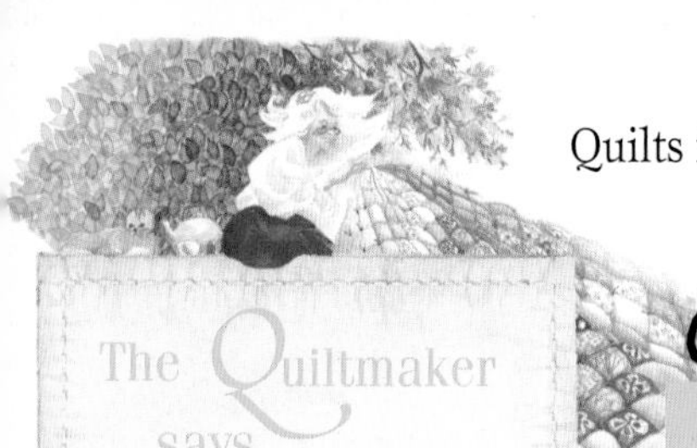

The Quiltmaker says . . .

Read all the instructions before you begin.

Always place right sides of fabric together for stitching.

Use scant 1/4" seam allowances.

Press seam allowances in the direction of arrows.

Quilt Information (finished size measurements)

	LAP	TWIN	QUEEN
Quilt Size without borders	39" x 58 1/2"	58 1/2" x 78"	78" x 97 1/2"
Quilt Size with Borders	52" x 71 1/"2	71 1/2" x 91"	91" x 110 1/2"
Block Size	19 1/2"	19 1/2"	19 1/2"
Number of Blocks	6	12	20
Block Layout	2 x 3	3 x 4	4 x 5
Backing Layout			

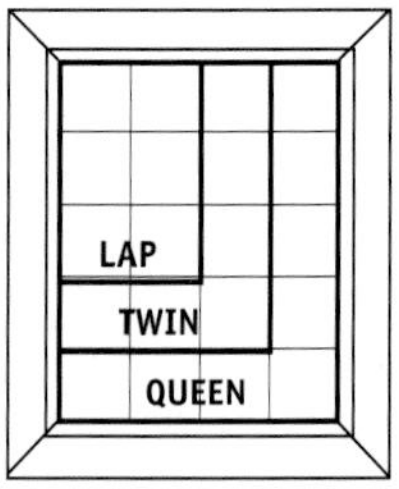

Fabric Requirements (42-45" wide, in yards)

	LAP	TWIN	QUEEN
Fabric 1, **Light**—Pieces A & D	7/8	1 1/4	1 1/2
Fabric 2, Chain 1, **Dark**—Piece B & Inner Border	7/8	1 1/2	2
Fabric 3, Chain 2, **Medium**—Piece C	5/8	7/8	1 1/8
Fabric 4, **Focus**—Piece E & Outer Border	1 3/4	2 1/2	3 1/3
Fabric 5, **Lattice**—Piece F & Binding	1 7/8	3	4 1/3
Backing Fabric	3 1/4	5 1/2	8 1/8

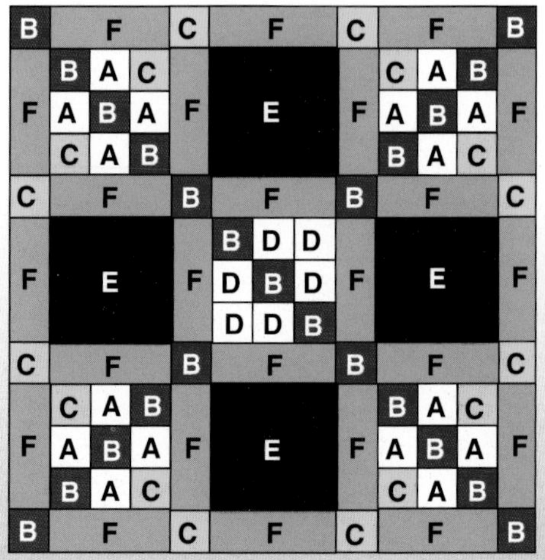

King's Hiway Block #1835

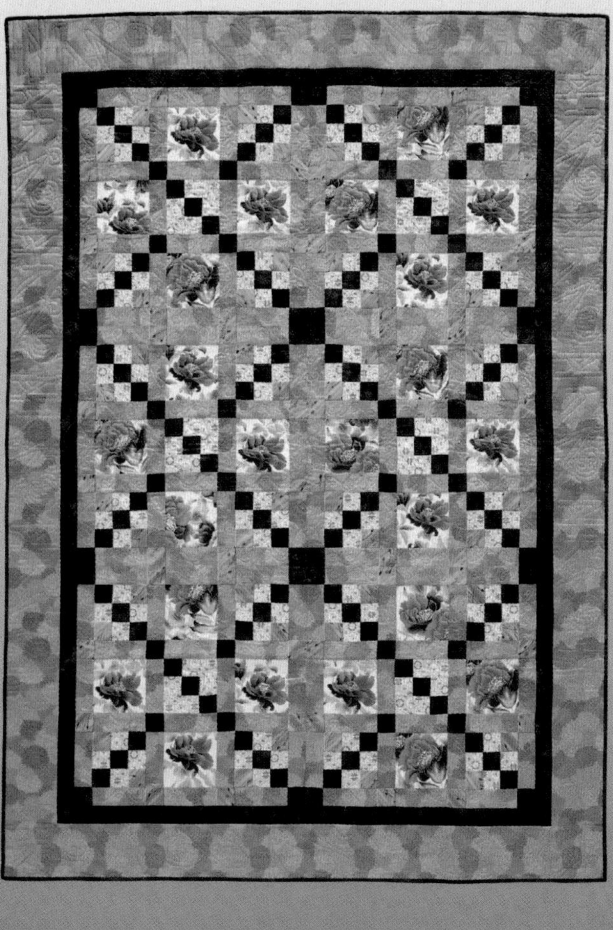

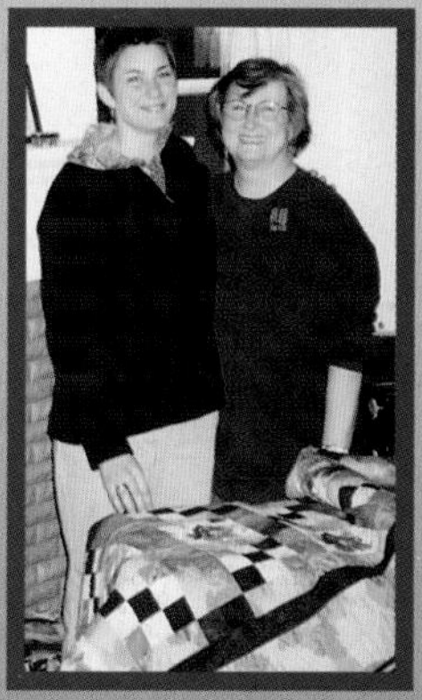

Mentor Judy assisted her soon-to-be daughter-in-law in creating this elegant quilt. Christa had never run a sewing machine before embarking on this project, which she completed in about six weeks.

King's Hiway

Christa's Quilt, 67" x 93"
24" blocks (6), two plain borders
Christa Knudsen & Judy J. Timm, Duluth, MN
quilted by Karen McTavish, Duluth, MN

Cutting Instructions

	LAP	TWIN	QUEEN
Fabric 1, Background—Piece A & D			
Cut strips 2" x width of fabric	11	17	22
Fabric 2, Chain 1, Dark—Piece B			
Cut strips 2" x width of fabric	10	16	23
Fabric 2—Inner Border			
Cut strips 2" x width of fabric	5	7	9
Fabric 3, Chain 2, Medium—Piece C			
Cut strips 2" x width of fabric	6	10	16
Fabric 4, Focus—Piece E			
Cut strips 5" x width of fabric	3	6	10
☐ Subcut to 5" x 5" squares	24	48	80
Fabric 4, Focus—Outer Border			
Cut strips 5 1/2" x width of fabric	7	9	11
Fabric 5, Lattice—Piece F			
Cut strips 5" x width of fabric	8	15	24
☐ Subcut into 5" x 2" rectangles	96	192	320
Fabric 5, Binding			
Cut strips 2 1/4" x width of fabric	7	9	11

This block is constructed in three rows with lattice strips set between. Some fabrics are used in more than one part of the block. Follow quantities carefully in each step.

Piecing Directions

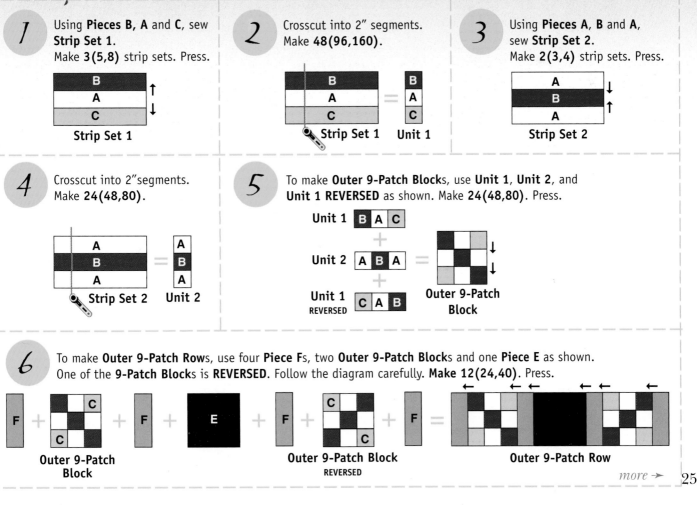

1 Using **Pieces B, A** and **C**, sew **Strip Set 1**. Make **3(5,8)** strip sets. Press.

Strip Set 1

2 Crosscut into 2" segments. Make **48(96,160)**.

Strip Set 1   Unit 1

3 Using **Pieces A, B** and **A**, sew **Strip Set 2**. Make **2(3,4)** strip sets. Press.

Strip Set 2

4 Crosscut into 2" segments. Make **24(48,80)**.

Strip Set 2   Unit 2

5 To make **Outer 9-Patch Block**s, use **Unit 1, Unit 2,** and **Unit 1 REVERSED** as shown. Make **24(48,80)**. Press.

Unit 1   B A C
+
Unit 2   A B A
+
Unit 1 REVERSED   C A B
=
Outer 9-Patch Block

6 To make **Outer 9-Patch Row**s, use four **Piece F**s, two **Outer 9-Patch Block**s and one **Piece E** as shown. One of the **9-Patch Block**s is **REVERSED**. Follow the diagram carefully. **Make 12(24,40)**. Press.

F + [Outer 9-Patch Block] + F + E + F + [Outer 9-Patch Block REVERSED] + F = Outer 9-Patch Row

Outer 9-Patch Block

Outer 9-Patch Block REVERSED

Outer 9-Patch Row

more →

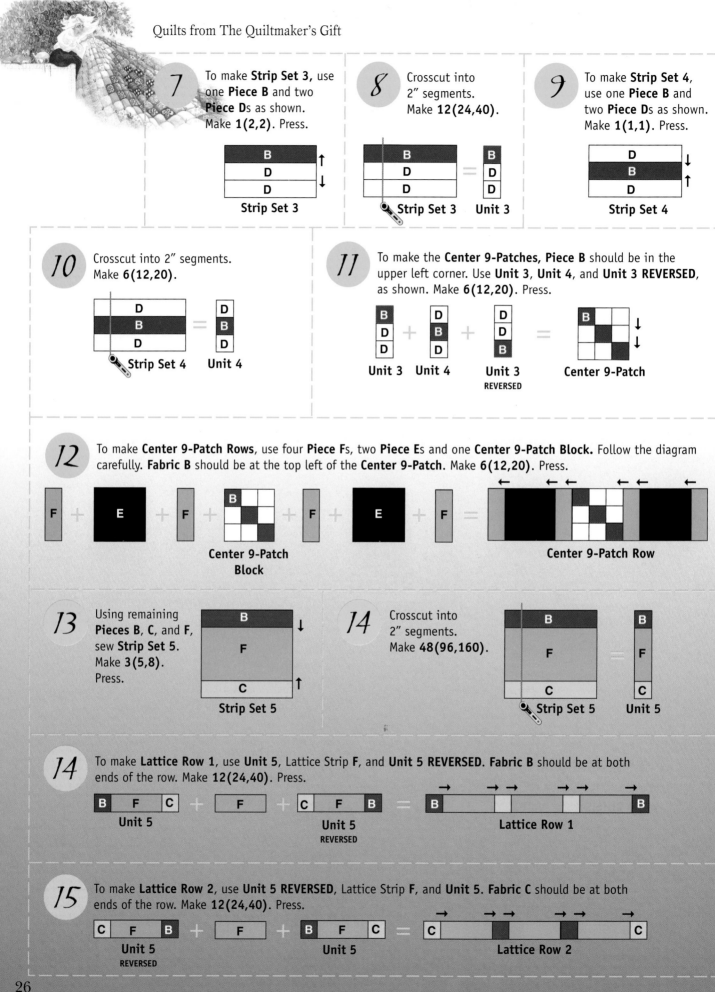

7 To make **Strip Set 3**, use one **Piece B** and two **Piece D**s as shown. Make **1(2,2)**. Press.

Strip Set 3

8 Crosscut into 2" segments. Make **12(24,40)**.

Strip Set 3   Unit 3

9 To make **Strip Set 4**, use one **Piece B** and two **Piece D**s as shown. Make **1(1,1)**. Press.

Strip Set 4

10 Crosscut into 2" segments. Make **6(12,20)**.

Strip Set 4   Unit 4

11 To make the **Center 9-Patches, Piece B** should be in the upper left corner. Use **Unit 3**, **Unit 4**, and **Unit 3 REVERSED**, as shown. Make **6(12,20)**. Press.

Unit 3   Unit 4   Unit 3 REVERSED   Center 9-Patch

12 To make **Center 9-Patch Rows**, use four **Piece F**s, two **Piece E**s and one **Center 9-Patch Block.** Follow the diagram carefully. **Fabric B** should be at the top left of the **Center 9-Patch.** Make **6(12,20)**. Press.

F + E + F + Center 9-Patch Block + F + E + F = Center 9-Patch Row

13 Using remaining **Pieces B**, **C**, and **F**, sew **Strip Set 5**. Make **3(5,8)**. Press.

Strip Set 5

14 Crosscut into 2" segments. Make **48(96,160)**.

Strip Set 5   Unit 5

14 To make **Lattice Row 1**, use **Unit 5**, Lattice Strip **F**, and **Unit 5 REVERSED. Fabric B** should be at both ends of the row. Make **12(24,40)**. Press.

Unit 5 + F + Unit 5 REVERSED = Lattice Row 1

15 To make **Lattice Row 2**, use **Unit 5 REVERSED**, Lattice Strip **F**, and **Unit 5. Fabric C** should be at both ends of the row. Make **12(24,40)**. Press.

Unit 5 REVERSED + F + Unit 5 = Lattice Row 2

16 To make the quilt block, start and end with **Lattice Row 1**. Follow the diagram carefully. Butt all intersecting seams and pin before sewing.

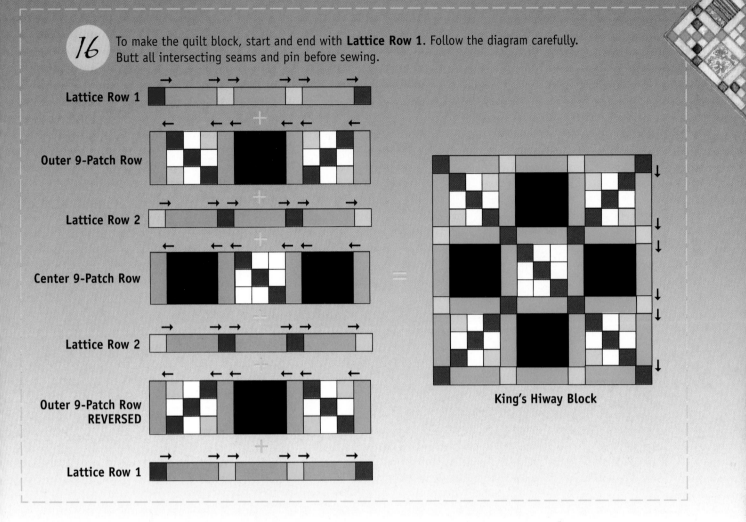

Lattice Row 1

Outer 9-Patch Row

Lattice Row 2

Center 9-Patch Row

Lattice Row 2

Outer 9-Patch Row REVERSED

Lattice Row 1

King's Hiway Block

Quilt Assembly

◆ Lay out the blocks **2(3,4)** across by **3(4,5)** down. Rotate adjacent blocks 180° in each row so horizontal pressed seams alternate directions and intersections butt nicely. Pin intersections.

◆ Follow the instructions on pages 136–137 for sewing the blocks and rows together.

◆ Follow the instructions on page 138 for adding borders.

Finishing the Quilt

◆ Follow the instructions on pages 138–139 for making the quilt sandwich.

◆ Follow the instructions on page 139 for basting the quilt.

◆ Refer to pages 138–139 for information on quilting.

◆ Follow the instructions on page 140 for binding the quilt.

Log Cabin

Aubergine Abode, 61" x 78"
8" blocks (48), 2 mitered borders
barn raising setting

Joanne Larsen Line, Duluth, MN
quilted by Angela Haworth, Superior, WI

Log Cabin

Brackman/BlockBase Number: 2576
Earliest published example: 1869
Alternate names: Pioneer Block
For similar block 2573: The Log Patch, American Log Patchwork

Perhaps the most traditional of all quilt patterns, Log Cabin was especially popular in the U.S. from 1870–1920. This easy block is constructed from narrow strips of fabric sewed clockwise around a center square, alternating values so the block is split diagonally, light and dark. Piece by piece the structure grows, resembling the pioneer building for which it was named.

Early Log Cabin quilts were pieced from scraps of fancy fabrics, such as silk, velvet, and woolens, using a cloth or paper foundation. The center square of Log Cabin is often made from red or yellow fabric to represent the hearth or a lantern in the window.

Since value, not color or texture, gives character to the versatile Log Cabin, this is a great teaching quilt for kids.

◆ Cut strips from all kinds of fabrics.

◆ Sort light and dark in paper bags.

◆ Draw out strips at random, one at a time.

◆ Cut the appropriate length and add to the block.

Once blocks are pieced, use a design wall (see page 131) and experiment with placing the blocks in traditional and innovative combinations. Kids come up with amazing designs!

Once again, Joanne has managed to include purple fabric in her quilt. No surprise to her quilting buddies from the Bag Ladies, the Ladies of the Evening, North Country Quilt Guild, and the Fabric Works Thursday Night Gang, who appreciate Joanne's purple passion, as well as her patience as a teacher and her precision cutting techniques.

Artist's Secrets

This pattern was an obvious choice. I have made many Log Cabin quilts across the years, and where else would the quiltmaker live? I imagined her in a log cabin from the very beginning.

Quiltmaker's Design Challenges

◆ Log Cabin is a natural choice for using up fabric leftovers and "uglies" from your stash. Mix and match fabric scale, color, pattern, and texture.

◆ Nearly any fabric except large scale prints will work in a Log Cabin quilt. Stretch your comfort zone with flannels, reproductions, geometrics, country prints, calicoes, florals.

◆ Make a vivid Amish-style Log Cabin using highly contrasting solids or hand-dyed fabrics. Experiment with various color schemes that accentuate the contrast and vibrancy.

◆ Combine Log Cabin blocks with 9" blocks of a different pattern, in an alternate block setting. Then set the blocks on point using pieced setting triangles from yet another block.

◆ Try an unusual setting or design your own.

◆ Use Log Cabin blocks as border cornerposts.

◆ Make borders from leftover strips pieced side by side or end to end.

◆ Piece a fancy inner border, such as a three-row checkerboard.

There was once a quiltmaker who kept a house in the blue misty mountains up high.

Quilt Information (finished size measurements)

	LAP	TWIN	DOUBLE
Quilt Size without Borders	36" x 54"	54" x 72"	72" x 90"
Quilt Size with Borders	49" x 67"	67" x 85"	85" x 103"
Block Size	9"	9"	9"
Number of Blocks	24	48	80
Block Layout	4 x 6	6 x 8	8 x 10
Backing Layout	←/←	↓↓↓	↓↓↓↓

Fabric Requirements (42-45" wide, in yards)

	LAP	TWIN	DOUBLE
Fabric 1, **Lightest**—Piece B & C	1/4	1/3	1/2
Fabric 2, **Light**—Piece F & G	3/8	5/8	7/8
Fabric 3, **Medium Light**—Piece J & K	1/2	3/4	1 1/4
Fabric 4, **Dark Light**—Piece N & O	5/8	1 1/8	1 5/8
Fabric 5, **Red** Center—Piece A	1/8	1/4	1/3
Fabric 6, **Medium**—Piece D & E	1/3	1/2	2/3
Fabric 7, **Medium Dark**—Piece H & I	1/2	2/3	1 1/8
Fabric 8, **Dark**—Piece L & M	1/2	1	1 1/2
Fabric 9, **Darkest**, Piece P & Q	2/3	1 1/4	1 7/8
Fabric 10, **Inner Border**	1/2	2/3	3/4
Fabric 11, **Outer Border & Binding**	1 1/2	1 5/8	2 3/8
Backing Fabric	3	5 1/8	7 3/4

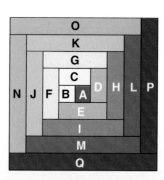

**Log Cabin Block
#2576**

Cutting Instructions continued next page

These instructions are written for a planned, graduated colorwash effect in the block—but a random placement of darks on one side and lights on the other also works well.

	LAP	TWIN	DOUBLE
Fabric 1, Lightest—Piece B			
Cut strips 1 1/2" x width of fabric	1	2	4
Fabric 1, Lightest—Piece C			
Cut strips 1 1/2" x width of fabric	2	3	5
☐ Crosscut into 1 1/2" x 2 1/2" rectangles	24	48	80
Fabric 2, Light—Piece F			
Cut strips 1 1/2" x width of fabric	3	5	8
☐ Crosscut into 1 1/2" x 3 1/2" rectangles	24	48	80
Fabric 2, Light—Piece G			
Cut strips 1 1/2" x width of fabric	3	6	10
☐ Crosscut into 1 1/2" x 4 1/2" rectangles	24	48	80
Fabric 3, Medium Light—Piece J			
Cut strips 1 1/2" x width of fabric	4	7	12
☐ Crosscut into 1 1/2" x 5 1/2" rectangles	24	48	80

Cutting Instructions continued from previous page

	LAP	TWIN	DOUBLE
Fabric 3, Medium Light—Piece K			
Cut strips 1 1/2" x width of fabric	4	8	14
▢ Crosscut into 1 1/2" x 6 1/2" rectangles	24	48	80
Fabric 4, Dark Light—Piece N			
Cut strips 1 1/2" x width of fabric	5	10	16
▢ Crosscut into 1 1/2" x 7 1/2" rectangles	24	48	80
Fabric 4, Dark Light—Piece O			
Cut strips 1 1/2" x width of fabric	6	12	20
▢ Crosscut into 1 1/2" x 8 1/2" rectangles	24	48	80
Fabric 5, Red Center—Piece A			
Cut strips 1 1/2" x width of fabric	1	2	4
Fabric 6, Medium—Piece D			
Cut strips 1 1/2" x width of fabric	2	3	5
▢ Crosscut into 1 1/2" x 2 1/2" rectangles	24	48	80
Fabric 6, Medium—Piece E			
Cut strips 1 1/2" x width of fabric	3	5	8
▢ Crosscut into 1 1/2" x 3 1/2" rectangles	24	48	80
Fabric 7, Medium Dark—Piece H			
Cut strips 1 1/2" x width of fabric	3	6	10
▢ Crosscut into 1 1/2" x 4 1/2" rectangles	24	48	80
Fabric 7, Medium Dark—Piece I			
Cut strips 1 1/2" x width of fabric	4	7	12
▢ Crosscut into 1 1/2" x 5 1/2" rectangles	24	48	80
Fabric 8, Dark—Piece L			
Cut strips 1 1/2" x width of fabric	4	8	14
▢ Crosscut into 1 1/2" x 6 1/2" rectangles	24	48	80
Fabric 8, Dark—Piece M			
Cut strips 1 1/2" x width of fabric	5	10	16
▢ Crosscut into 1 1/2" x 7 1/2" rectangles	24	48	80
Fabric 9, Darkest—Piece P			
Cut strips 1 1/2" x width of fabric	6	12	20
▢ Crosscut into 1 1/2" x 8 1/2" rectangles	24	48	80
Fabric 9 Darkest—Piece Q			
Cut strips 1 1/2" x width of fabric	6	12	20
▢ Crosscut into 1 1/2" x 9 1/2" rectangles	24	48	80
Fabric 10, Inner border			
Cut strips 2 1/2" x width of fabric	5	7	9
Fabric 11, Outer Border			
Cut strips 5" x width of fabric	6	8	11
Fabric 11, Binding			
Cut strips 2 1/4" x width of fabric	7	8	10

Log Cabin—Barn Raising Setting

Neighbors, 53" x 79"
13" flannel blocks (24)
Betty Firth, Duluth, MN
quilted by Joan's Quilting, Clinton, MO

Betty took mandatory retirement in 1987 at age 70 and returned to quilting. She turns out ten or more quilts every year—and gives them all away. She claims responsibility for introducing her neighbor, author Joanne Line, to quilting.

Beauty shop owner Fay Hanenburg proudly displays her first quilt. She invented this adventurous Log Cabin setting in a pattern-testing introductory class taught by Joanne Line.

Piecing Directions

Watch orientation of blocks carefully as you add strips.

The **Q**uiltmaker says . . .

Read all the instructions before you begin.

Always place right sides of fabric together for stitching.

Use scant ¼" seam allowances.

Press seam allowances in the direction of arrows.

1 Sew **Piece A** to **Piece B**. Press.

Strip Set 1

2 Crosscut **Strip Set 1** into 1½" inch segments. Make **24(48,80)** segments. Press.

Strip Set 1 **Unit 1**

3 Sew **Piece C** to the top of **Unit 1** as shown.

Unit 1 Unit 2

4 Sew **Piece D** to the right side of **Unit 2**. Press.

Unit 2 Unit 3

5 Sew **Piece E** to the bottom of **Unit 3**. Press.

Unit 3 Unit 4

6 Sew **Piece F** to the left side of **Unit 4**. Press.

Unit 4 Unit 5

7 Continue to sew the log pieces clock-wise until you have four rounds on each side of the center red square. Press away from the center each time you add a log.

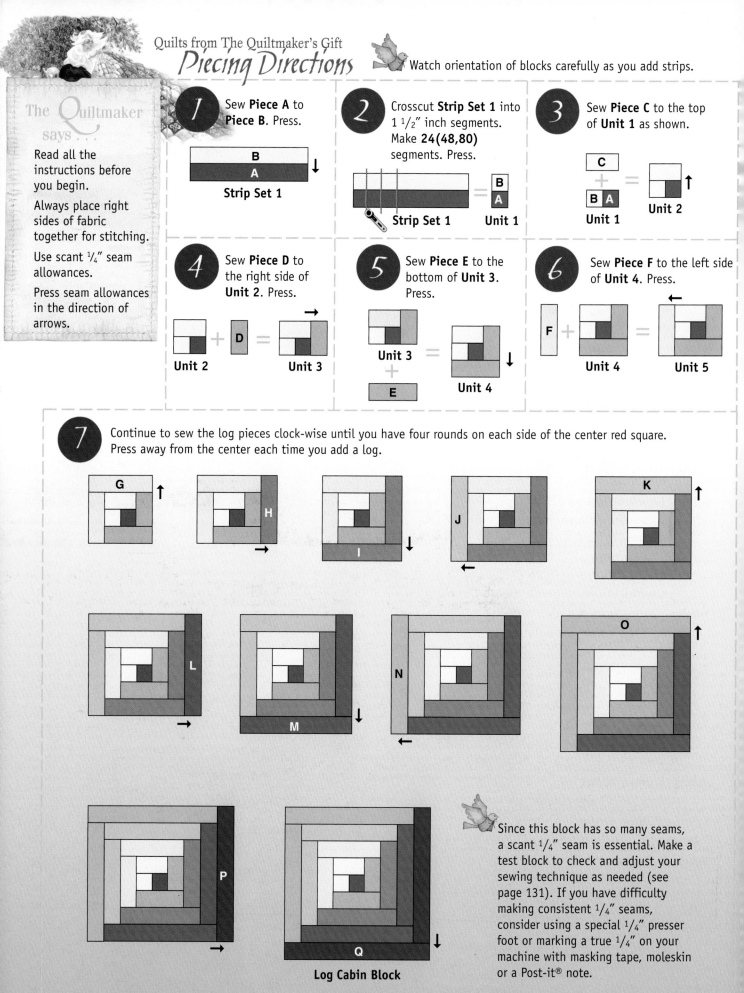

Log Cabin Block

Since this block has so many seams, a scant ¼" seam is essential. Make a test block to check and adjust your sewing technique as needed (see page 131). If you have difficulty making consistent ¼" seams, consider using a special ¼" presser foot or marking a true ¼" on your machine with masking tape, moleskin or a Post-it® note.

Quilt Assembly

◆ Choose a setting. Setting options for other diagonal light and dark blocks (Flying Birds, Northwind) will also work for Log Cabin. See pages 84, 91.

◆ Lay out the blocks **4(6,8)** across and **6(8,10)** down.

◆ Follow the instructions on pages 136–137 for sewing the blocks and rows together.

◆ Follow the instructions on page 138 for adding borders.

Finishing the Quilt

◆ Follow the instructions on pages 138–140 for making the quilt sandwich, basting, quilting, and binding.

Hang a flannel-backed tablecloth to make a temporary design wall for experimenting with different block settings. Blocks will stick without pinning to the flannel. Keep repositioning the blocks until you like the effect. Then assemble the quilt row by row.

Log Cabin—Light and Dark Setting

A Simple Gift, 72" x 88"
8" blocks (120), plain inner border, pieced outer border
Lonnie Rossi Randall, Canyon, MN
quilted by Sue Munns, Duluth, MN

Four years ago Lonnie traded the hectic business world for the wonderful world of quilting. Her great eye for color is evident in all her quilts. Lonnie credits her parents for her organizational skills and artistic talents, which find satisfying expression in quilting.

Log Cabin—Straight Furrow Setting

Autumn Furrows, 64" x 84"
8" blocks (63), plain borders
Ferne Liberty, Duluth, MN
quilted by Joan's Quilting, Clinton, MO

Ferne grew up on a farm during the Depression, when making quilts was a necessary way of life. Beginning at age ten with a Grandmother's Flower Garden, Ferne has made hundreds of quilts and has hand quilted over fifty. She averages piecing two tops a week.

Log Cabin—Barn Raising Setting, Light Center

Cabin Fever, 72" x 72"
13" blocks (16), two plain borders
Lynne Chilberg, Duluth, MN
quilted by Debra Lussier Quinn, Superior, WI

Lynne has been sewing for over thirty years, but is new to quilting. A dentist by day, she's become an avid nocturnal quilter.

33

True Lover's Knot

Victorian Rhapsody, A True Lover's Knot, 54" x 64"
6" single-knot blocks (63), two mitered borders

Judy J. Timm, Duluth, MN
quilted by Angela Haworth, Superior, WI

True Lover's Knot

True Lover's Knot 🕊

Brackman/BlockBase Number: 1429B
Earliest publication date: 1895 (Ladies Art Company #262)
Alternate names for four bows arranged in a circle (1429A):
Magic Circle, Dumbbell Block, Bow Tie

This double-four-patch block is constructed from four smaller Bow Tie blocks made of four large squares with corner triangles that meet in the center to form the "knot."

Simple enough for beginners, True Lover's Knot introduces the diagonal-corners method of turning squares into corner triangles by stitching one diagonal seam, pressing, and then trimming away the excess layers. Although the historical block used a square in the center, we have substituted this more reliable technique that simplifies sewing and reduces the risk of stretching long bias edges. The same stitch and fold technique is used in making flying geese units for Wild Goose Chase (page 102) and the patterns that follow.

The name True Lover's Knot applies only to the block with four single Bow Ties facing in the same direction. Like Log Cabin and Corn and Beans, the symmetrical diagonal nature of the block lends itself to intriguing effects when blocks are rotated in different arrangements. See pages 33, 84, and 91 for setting ideas that dramatically change the overall look of the quilt. Varying the placement of light and dark values within the block will also alter the visual impact.

Judy loves picking out fabrics for quilts, and the transparency effect of this scrappy True Lover's Knot proves it. Her job at Fabric Works puts Judy in seventh heaven, examining the goods at leisure while acting as consultant to customers who seek her advice on colors for their quilts.

Artist's Secrets

I put the True Lover's Knot quilt around an old man and woman whom the king happens to pass on his way back to the palace after leaving the quiltmaker out on the island. I wanted to show his frustration that these poor folks had one of her quilts—but he didn't. The king was supposed to see their love and contentment and feel his own loneliness and unhappiness. Imagine—they were happy with just one quilt for two people!

Quiltmaker's Design Challenges

◆ Experiment with optical illusions by creating transparencies in the center knot where two fabrics visually overlap. Karen Combs (*Optical Illusions for Quilters,* American Quilter's Society, 1997) suggests four methods:

  ◆ Pick any two colors for the outside squares. Use a darker shade of one of the colors in all four triangles of the knot.

  ◆ Select three analogous colors (next to each other on the color wheel, see page 133). Use the two outside colors for the squares and the middle color for the knot.

  ◆ Use a blended color (green) as the knot for its parent colors (blue and yellow) in the squares.

  ◆ Create a sheer knot by choosing a lighter, paler, or grayed version of one of the square colors.

◆ Choose fabrics and placements so your blocks will make a colorwash rainbow or other pattern.

◆ Use a design wall to test setting options from medallion to streak of lightening. Then invent your own.

◆ Try making huge X- and O-blocks from nine True Lover's Knot blocks and alternate them across the quilt top.

  ◆ Mix and match block sizes (4", 6", 8", 12") as well as block orientations for a one-of-a-kind quilt.

  ◆ Make a zigzag pieced border using single Bow Ties in an alternating setting.

"And how is it that this person has never given me one of her quilts as a gift?" the king demanded. "She only makes them for the poor, Your Majesty," the soldier replied.

Quilt Information (finished size measurements)

	LAP	TWIN	QUEEN
Quilt Size without Borders	48" x 60"	60" x 84"	84" x 96"
Quilt Size with Borders	56" x 68"	68" x 92"	92" x 104"
Block Size	12"	12"	12"
Number of Blocks	20	35	56
Block Layout	4 x 5	5 x 7	7 x 8
Backing Layout			

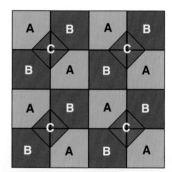

The Quiltmaker says...

Read all the instructions before you begin.

Always place right sides of fabric together for stitching.

Use scant 1/4" seam allowances.

Press seam allowances in the direction of arrows.

Fabric Requirements (42-45" wide, in yards)

	LAP	TWIN	QUEEN
Fabric 1, **Medium Light**—Piece A	1 2/3	2 3/4	4 1/4
Fabric 2, **Medium**—Piece B & Inner Border	2	3 1/8	4 5/8
Fabric 3, **Knot**—Piece C, Outer Border & Binding	2 1/3	3 1/4	4 1/2
Backing Fabric	3 1/2	5 1/2	7 2/3

True Lover's Knot Block #1429B

Cutting Instructions

	LAP	TWIN	QUEEN
Fabric 1, Piece A			
Cut strips 3 1/2" x width of fabric	15	26	41
☐ Crosscut into 3 1/2" squares	160	280	448
Fabric 2, Piece B			
Cut strips 3 1/2" x width of fabric	15	26	41
☐ Crosscut into 3 1/2" squares	160	280	448
Fabric 2, Inner Border			
Cut strips 1 1/2" x width of fabric	6	8	9
Fabric 3, Knot—Piece C			
Cut strips 2" x width of Fabric	16	28	45
☐ Crosscut into 2" squares	320	560	896
Fabric 3, Outer Border			
Cut strips 3 1/2" x width of fabric	7	8	10
Fabric 3, Binding			
Cut strips 2 1/4" x width of fabric	8	9	11

True Lover's Knot

Romance in the Pansies, 57" x 66"
12" blocks (20), two plain borders
Vonn Wien Wells, Duluth, MN

Vonn Wells works in a quilt shop owned by her sister-in-law. She does her own machine quilting on a regular sewing machine with a darning foot. Vonn has encouraged her daughters to quilt, and her 14-year old recently finished her first quilt.

Piecing Directions

Follow pressing arrows carefully.

1 Draw a diagonal pencil line on the wrong side of all **Piece C**s.

WRONG SIDE, PIECE C

2 Make **Unit 1** by placing **Piece C** on one corner of **Piece A**. Stitch on the pencil line. Make **160(280,448)**. Trim seam allowance to 1/4". Press.

Unit 1

3 Make **Unit 2** by placing **Piece C** on one corner of **Piece B**. Stitch on the pencil line. Make **160(280,448)**. Trim seam allowance to 1/4". Press.

Unit 2

4 Make **Unit 3** by sewing **Unit 1** to **Unit 2**. Make **160(280,448)**. Press.

Unit 1   Unit 2   Unit 3

In each block, press the seams of the corner triangles toward the large square for the darker fabric and toward the small triangles for the lighter fabric.

5 Sew two **Unit 3**s together as shown below. Make **80(140,224)**. Press.

Unit 3

Unit 3

Unit 4

Quilt Assembly

◆ Lay out the blocks **4(5,7)** across and **5(7,8)** down. Rotate adjacent blocks 180° in each row so long horizontal pressed seams alternate and intersections butt nicely. Pin intersections.

◆ Follow the instructions on pages 136–137 for sewing the blocks and rows together.

◆ Follow the instructions on page 138 for adding borders.

Finishing the Quilt

◆ Follow the instructions on pages 138–139 for making the quilt sandwich.

◆ Follow the instructions on page 139 for basting the quilt.

◆ Refer to pages 138–139 for information on quilting.

◆ Follow the instructions on page 140 for binding the quilt.

6 Sew four **Unit 4**s together as shown in diagram below. Make **20(35,56)**. Press.

True Lover's Knot Block

In a classic quiltmentoring process, illustrator Gail de Marcken is using this pattern to pass on the quilting tradition to her daughter's future mother-in-law. They plan to make a collaborative hoopah (wedding canopy) for the lucky couple.

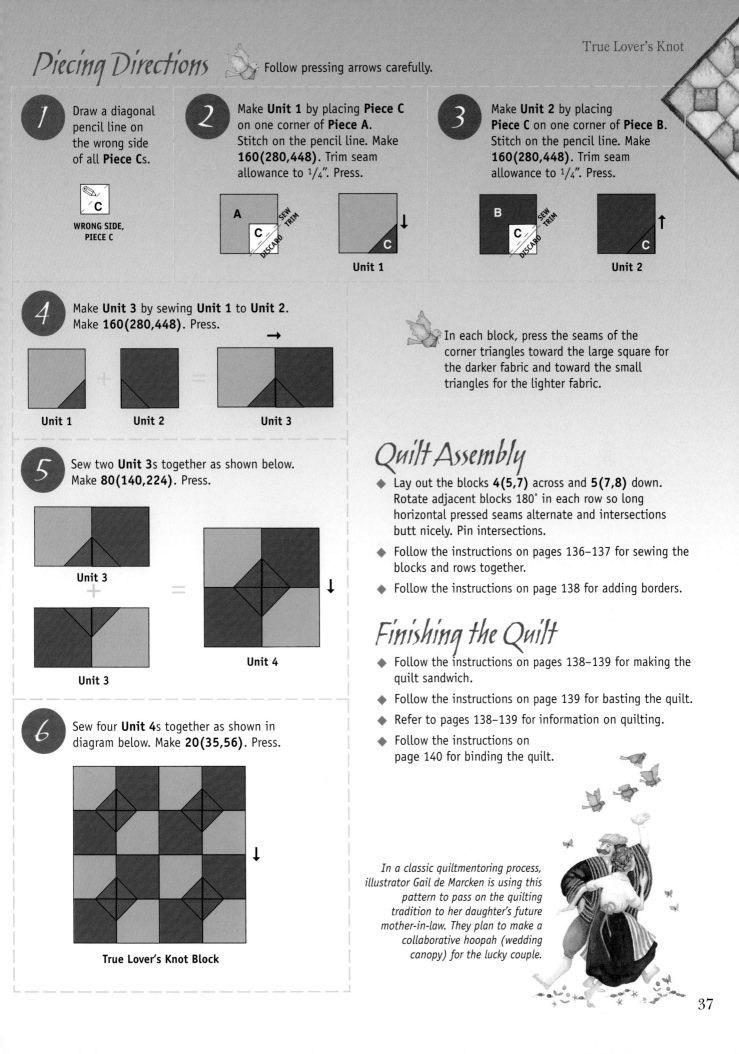

Double Irish Chain

Sally White's Party, 75" x 92"
10" blocks (63), one plain border

Nancy Loving Tubesing, Duluth, MN
quilted by Karen McTavish, Duluth, MN

Double Irish Chain

Brackman/BlockBase Number: 1013
Earliest publication date: 1895 (Ladies Art Company #60)
Alternate names: Irish Chain, Cube Lattice

Blocks in the Irish Chain family of quilts actually consist of two adjacent blocks placed side by side to create an interlocking pattern over the whole quilt top. One block is a 5 x 5 grid checkerboard, the other is an uneven nine-patch. The large, light center of the nine-patch block provides an ideal opportunity for hand quilters to show off their skills with fancy medallions, feathers, or flowers.

Although the historical Double Irish Chain was a two-color block, we have presented it here in its more common three-color version.

This quilt is easy enough for beginners and offers lots of practice in chain-piecing strip sets, crosscutting, pressing, and nesting seams for precise intersections. We recommend trying one block set before cutting all the strips.

◆ Cut only enough strips to sew one Block A and one Block B.

◆ Compare the result with the diagrams to make sure yours matches and you like the effect.

◆ If so, go ahead and cut all the indicated strips, stack them in order, and start piecing!

Many experienced quilters make a sample block like this before starting every quilt, so they are confident that they understand the instructions and like their fabric placement choices.

A relative newcomer to quilting, Nancy persuaded a young friend to join her in an introductory class at Fabric Works taught by quiltmentor Shirley Kirsch. This quilt was the result—Nancy's first finished product!

Never one to follow the rules, Nancy reversed the placement of light and dark in her quilt to show off the beautiful floral flannel.

Quiltmaker's Design Challenges

◆ Recreate this classic design in vintage fabrics or reproductions from your favorite era.

◆ Switch values so that the center of the nine-patch block is dark, and one of the chain segments is light. Or switch the dark and medium fabrics in the chain.

◆ Make a baby quilt with cute pastel flannels or vibrant juvenile primaries with polka dot chains.

◆ Try a funky novelty with large images as your "light" fabric. Imagine moose heads or zebras or comic book characters imprisoned by color-coordinated chains.

◆ Consider extending the Irish Chain design into the border.

No one had ever been so kind to the bear before. So he broke the iron bracelet and asked her to spend the night.

The Quiltmaker says . . .

Read all the instructions before you begin.

Always place right sides of fabric together for stitching.

Use scant 1/4″ seam allowances.

Press seam allowances in the direction of arrows.

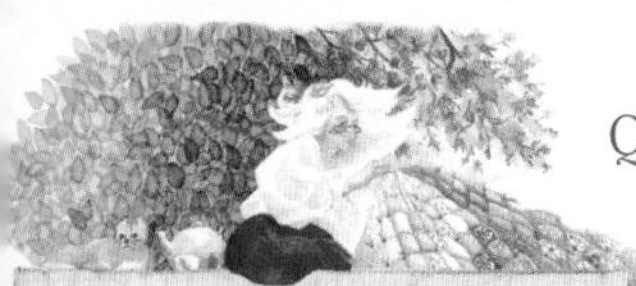

Quilt Information (finished size measurements)

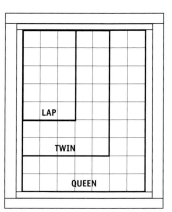

	LAP	TWIN	QUEEN
Quilt Size without Borders	30″ x 50″	50″ x 70″	70″ x 90″
Quilt Size with Borders	44″ x 64″	64″ x 84″	84″ x 104″
Block Size	10″	10″	10″
Number of Blocks	15	35	63
Block Layout	3 x 5	5 x 7	7 x 9
Backing Layout			

Fabric Requirements (42-45″ wide, in yards)

	LAP	TWIN	QUEEN
Fabric 1, **Background, Light**—Pieces A & B	1 1/3	2 1/4	3 1/2
Fabric 2, **Center Chain, Dark**—Piece D & Inner Border	1	1 3/4	2 1/8
Fabric 3, **Outer Chain, Medium**—Piece C	7/8	2	2 1/2
Fabric 4, **Outer Border & Binding**	1 1/2	2	2 1/2
Backing Fabric	2 7/8	5	7 3/4

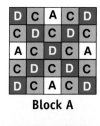

Block A

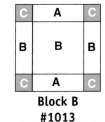

Block B #1013

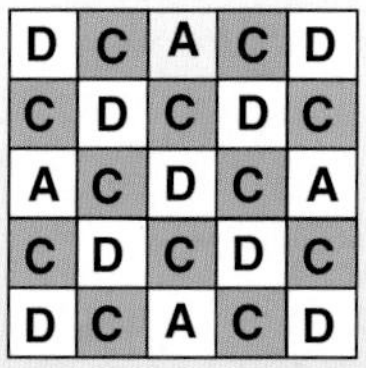

Block A #1013 Traditional Coloring

Cutting Instructions

	LAP	TWIN	QUEEN
Fabric 1, Background—Piece A			
Cut strips 2 1/2″ x width of fabric	7	13	20
Fabric 1, Background—Piece B			
Cut strips 6 1/2″ x width of fabric	3	6	10
Fabric 2, Center Chain—Piece D			
Cut strips 2 1/2″ x width of fabric	5	14	18
Fabric 2, Inner Border			
Cut strips 2 1/2″ x width of fabric	5	7	9
Fabric 3, Outer Chain—Piece C			
Cut strips 2 1/2″ x width of fabric	9	25	32
Fabric 4, Outer Border			
Cut strips 5 1/2″ x width of fabric	6	8	10
Fabric 4, Binding			
Cut strips 2 1/4″ x width of fabric	6	8	10

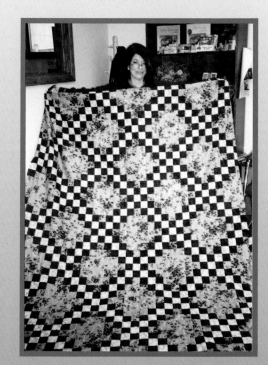

Stephanie Lemenowsky teamed up with her friend Natalie Beck to create this novice-duo's Double Irish Chain.

Piecing Directions

Press strips as you sew. Alternate direction of sewing as you add strips.

1 Using **Pieces D, C, A, C, D**, sew **Strip Set 1**. Make **1(3,4) strip sets**. Press.

D	↓
C	↓
A	↓
C	↓
D	

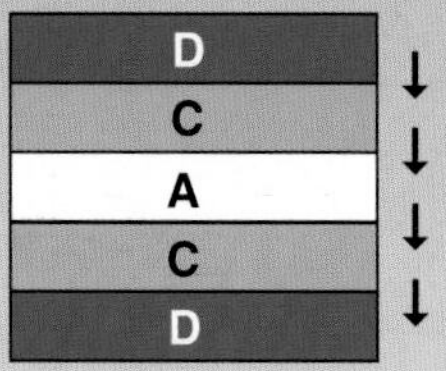

Strip Set 1

2 Crosscut into 2½" segments. Make **16(36,64)** segments.

| D |
| C |
| A |
| C |
| D |

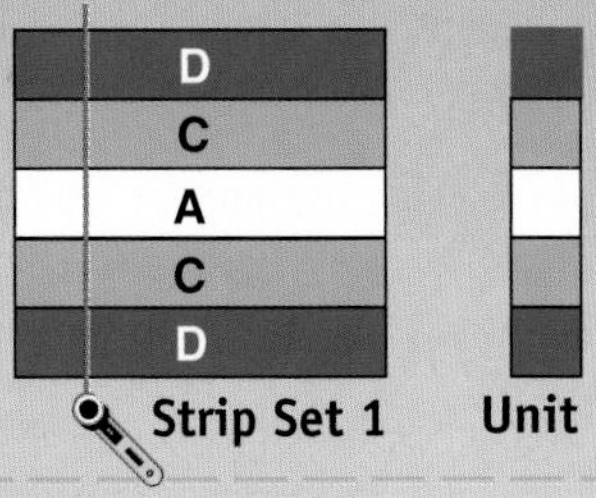

Strip Set 1   **Unit 1**

3 Using **Pieces C, D, C, D, C**, sew **Strip Set 2**. Make **1(3,4) strip sets**. Press.

C	↓
D	↓
C	↓
D	↓
C	

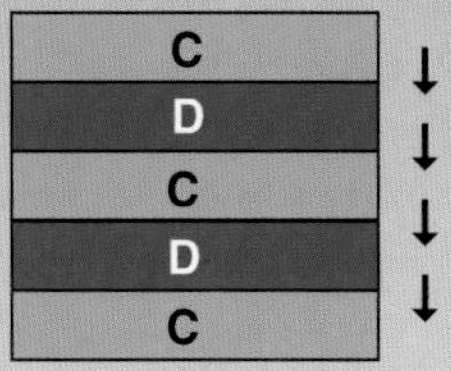

Strip Set 2

4 Crosscut into 2½" segments. Make **16(36,64)** segments.

| C |
| D |
| C |
| D |
| C |

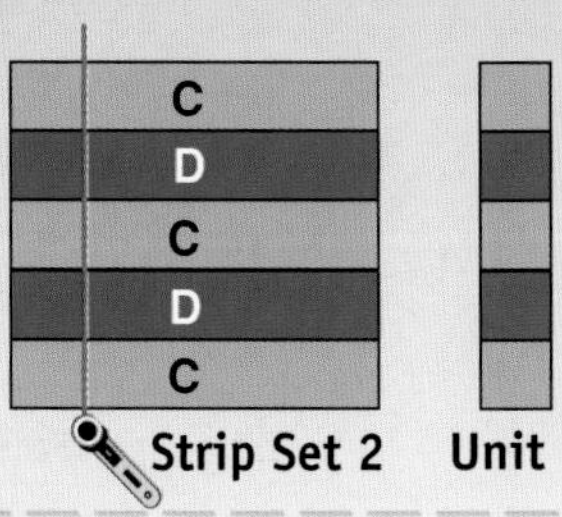

Strip Set 2   **Unit 2**

5 Using **Pieces A, C, D, C, A**, sew **Strip Set 3**. Make **1(2,2)**. Press.

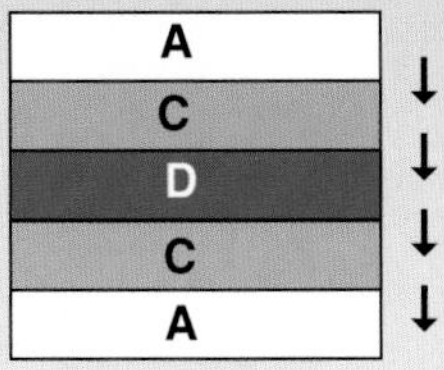

A	↓
C	↓
D	↓
C	↓
A	↓

Strip Set 3

6 Crosscut into 2½" segments. Make **8(18,32)** segments.

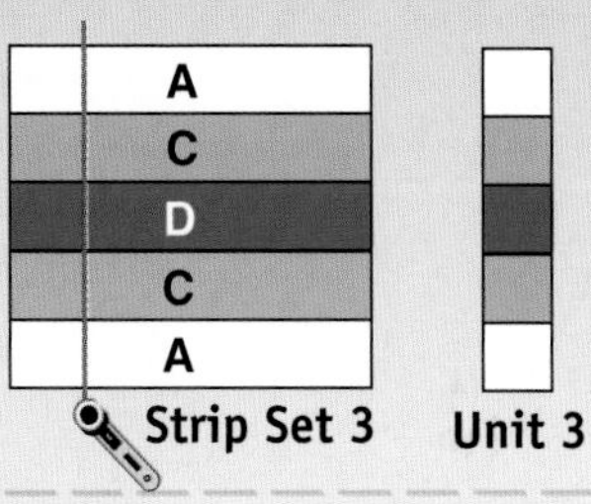

| A |
| C |
| D |
| C |
| A |

Strip Set 3   **Unit 3**

7 With seam allowances alternating, sew **Block A** using **Units 1, 2, 3, 2, 1**. Make **8(18,32)** blocks. Press.

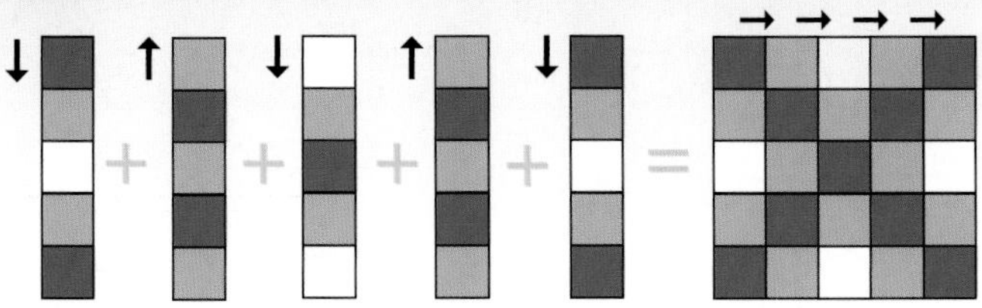

Unit 1   Unit 2   Unit 3   Unit 2   Unit 1   Block A

8 Using **Pieces A, B, A**, sew **Strip Set 4**. Make **2(3,6)** sets. Press.

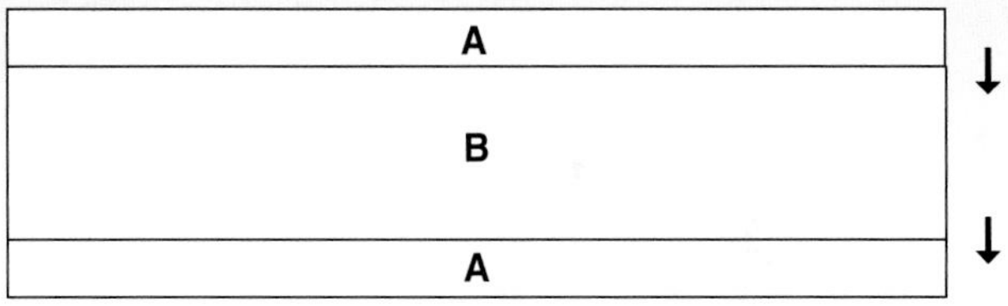

A	↓
B	
A	↓

Strip Set 4

9 Crosscut into 6½" segments. Make **7(17,31)** segments.

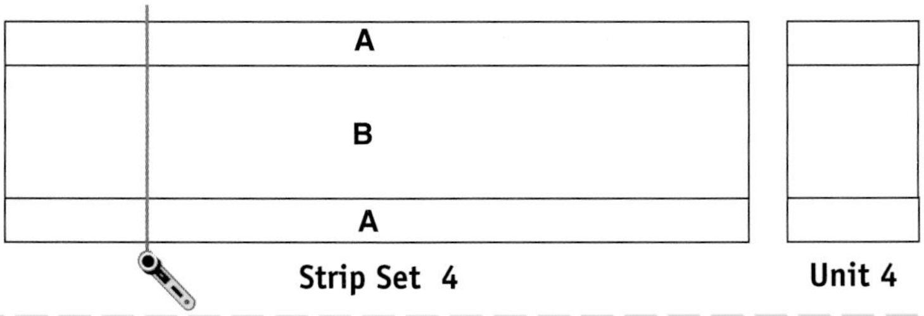

| A |
| B |
| A |

Strip Set 4   **Unit 4**

10 Using **Pieces C, B, C**, sew **Strip Set 5**. Make **1(3,4)** sets. Press.

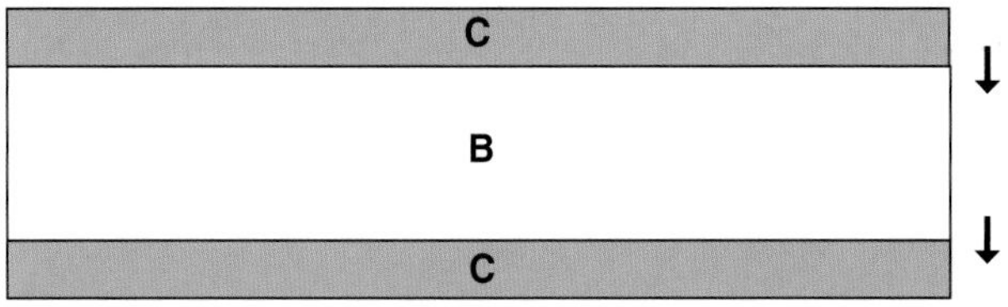

C	↓
B	
C	↓

Strip Set 5

11 Crosscut into 2½" segments. Make **14(34,62)** segments.

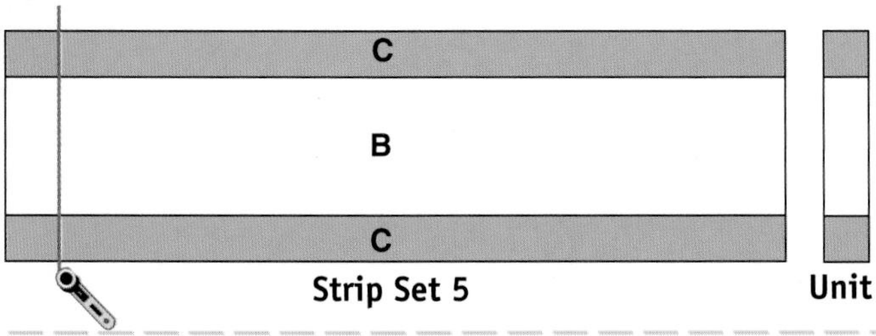

| C |
| B |
| C |

Strip Set 5   **Unit 5**

12 With seam allowances of **Unit 4** down and seam allowances of **Unit 5** up, sew block together as shown. Make **7(17,31)** blocks. Press.

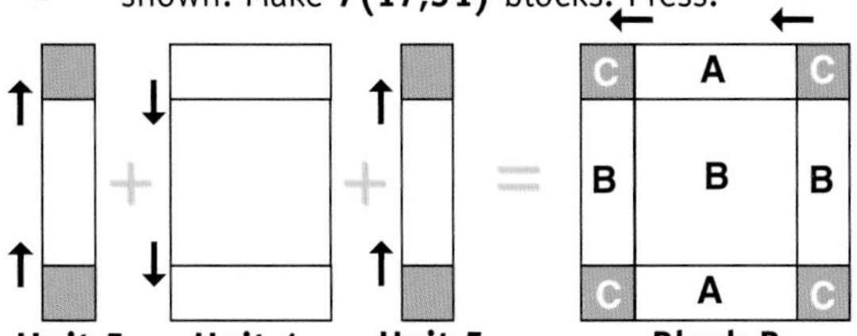

Unit 5   Unit 4   Unit 5   Block B

C	A	C
B	B	B
C	A	C

Quilt Assembly

◆ Lay out the blocks in rows, **3(5,7)** across and **5(7,9)** down, alternating **Block A** and **Block B**.

◆ Sew blocks and rows together following the instructions on pages 136–137.

◆ Press seams in odd rows to the left and press even rows to the right.

◆ Press seams between rows down.

◆ For optional border, follow instructions on page 138.

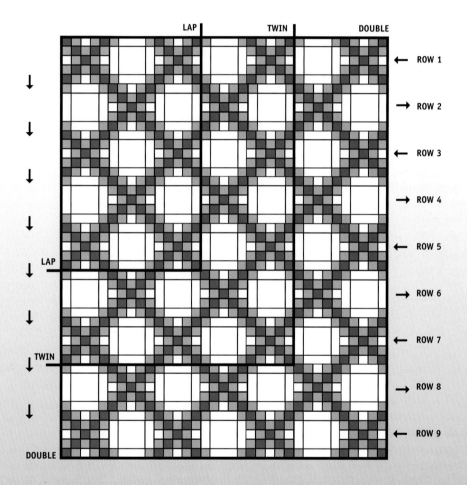

Finishing the Quilt

◆ Follow the instructions on pages 138–139 for making the quilt sandwich.

◆ Follow the instructions on page 139 for basting the quilt.

◆ Refer to page 138–139 for information on quilting.

◆ Follow the instructions on page 140 for binding the quilt.

Double Irish Chain

Waiting Room Blues, 45" x 60"
7" blocks (35), two plain borders
Carol Jean Brooks, Duluth, MN
quilted by Sue Munns, Duluth, MN

Carol Jean is a retired surgical technician who took up quilting when several coworkers brought their quilt blocks to hand-piece during breaks. Carol Jean makes only comfort quilts that she gives away to whoever needs some intensive TLC, in this case the mom of a newborn undergoing heart surgery.

Look for the pressing arrows in every diagram. If you press each unit as you go, in the directions noted, your seam allowances will interlock and match perfectly.

Barb McKeever stacks her strips in order before assembling and pressing strip sets. After Barb crosscuts the strip sets, she stacks each new strip and arranges the stacks in order for sewing the final block.

43

Trip Around the World

Wanderlust, 84" x 97"
1,073 squares, two mitered borders

Joanne Larsen Line, Duluth, MN
quilted by Carolyn & Charles Peters,
Woodbury, MN

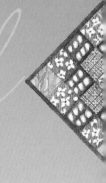

Trip Around the World

Brackman/BlockBase Number: 2286B
Earliest publication date: 1975
Alternate names: Squares Around the World, Postage Stamp, Sunshine and Shadow, Grandma's Dream, Sun and Shadow

Trip Around the World uses only one block—a square—to make an entire quilt top. "Postage stamp" or "checkerboard" one-patch-type patterns date back to the earliest days of quilting, but the version we know today as Trip Around the World was first published in 1975 under the name Squares Around the World.

This simplest of all patchwork quilts is made more complex by the choice of fabrics, their placement in concentric rounds of graduated value, and the strip-piecing technique used for assembling the final quilt. Beginners will have no difficulty if they follow the diagrams carefully and keep their strips in order. Make a reference chart using fabric scraps. Label the fabrics 1–10 and keep the chart handy so you can identify fabrics easily as you cut and stitch the strips.

Joanne is partial to purple. She donates several quilts each year to local charities for fund-raising auctions or raffles.

Artist's Secrets

Early in the book development process, Jeff and I decided that the king's generosity should extend beyond his own city and kingdom, so Trip Around the World was a natural choice. I enjoyed going through my mental stash of international fabrics to find examples from all continents to use in the final quilt illustration. I put the quilt at the end of the book, paired with the Around the Corner block and a Next Door Neighbor quilt, because those three patterns sum up the moral of this fable: our next door neighbors are just around the corner and all around the world.

Quiltmaker's Design Challenges

◆ Reverse the value placement of fabrics to create a dark center radiating out to light.

◆ Around the World quilts lend themselves to the colorwash technique, combining twelve or more florals in graduated values.

◆ Experiment with mixing two color families, placing fabrics in sequence by value only.

◆ If you are using many different fabrics in this quilt, wait until the top is finished before deciding on border fabrics and treatments. The overall impression of the quilt is often quite different from what you can imagine beforehand. You may want to make several narrow borders before adding a final border that is a totally different fabric from any included in your quilt.

◆ Consider framing your quilt with a narrow plain border and an Around the World outer border made of Unit 2s.

. . . the king slowly emptied his wagons, trading his treasures for smiles around the world.

Quilt Information (finished size measurements)

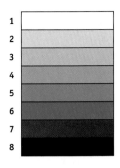

	DOUBLE/QUEEN
Quilt Size without Borders	77 1/2" x 92 1/2"
Quilt Size with Borders	89 1/2" x 104 1/2"
Backing Layout	

The **Quiltmaker** *says...*

Read all the instructions before you begin.

Always place right sides of fabric together for stitching.

Use scant 1/4" seam allowances.

Press seam allowances in the direction of arrows.

To make a crib size quilt, substitute 1 1/2" strips for 3" strips, and use a 3" outer border.

Fabric Requirements (42-45" wide, in yards)

	DOUBLE/QUEEN
Fabric 1, **Lightest**	1 1/8
Fabric 2, **Light**	1 1/8
Fabric 3, **Light Medium**	1 1/8
Fabric 4, **Medium Light**	1 1/8
Fabric 5, **Medium**	1 1/8
Fabric 6, **Medium Dark**	1 1/8
Fabric 7, **Dark**	1 1/8
Fabric 8, **Darkest**	1 1/8
Fabric 9, **Inner Border**	3/8
Fabric 10, **Outer Border & Binding**	2 1/2
Backing Fabric	7 3/4

Diane Nyman is a surgical nurse specializing in eye surgery. She tends to work in warm colors and is partial to the earth tones. Diane has never made a small quilt! Pam Stolan did free motion quilting, incorporating elements of patterns designed by Marcia Stevens and Keryn Emmerson in the border.

Cutting Instructions

	DOUBLE/QUEEN
Fabric 1, Lightest	
Cut strips 3" x width of fabric	11
Crosscut 3 of the 11 strips into thirds	9
Fabric 2, Light	
Cut strips 3" x width of fabric	11
Crosscut 3 of the 11 strips into thirds	9
Fabric 3, Light Medium	
Cut strips 3" x width of fabric	11
Crosscut 3 of the 11 strips into thirds	9
Fabric 4, Medium Light	
Cut strips 3" x width of fabric	11
Crosscut 3 of the 11 strips into thirds	9
Fabric 5, Medium	
Cut strips 3" x width of fabric	11
Crosscut 3 of the 11 strips into thirds	9
Fabric 6, Medium Dark	
Cut strips 3" x width of fabric	11
Crosscut 3 of the 11 strips into thirds	9
Fabric 7, Dark	
Cut strips 3" x width of fabric	11
Crosscut 3 of the 11 strips into thirds	9
Fabric 8, Darkest	
Cut strips 3" x width of fabric	11
Crosscut 3 of the 11 strips into thirds	9
Fabric 9, Inner Border	
Cut strips 1 1/2" x width of fabric	9
Fabric 10, Outer Border	
Cut strips 5 1/2" x width of fabric	10
Fabric 10, Binding	
Cut strips 2 1/4" x 40 strips	11

Trip Around the World

Trip Around the World at Summer's End, 96" x 109"
1147 blocks, two plain borders
Diane Nyman, Duluth, MN
quilted by Pam Stolan, Duluth, MN

Piecing Directions

Use scraps to make a numerical fabric indentification chart for ready reference.

This pattern is based on sewing 16 strip sets, crosscutting them into 3" segments and assembling the segments in a specific order. Blanche Young and Dalene Young Stone introduced this method of construction in their book *Tradition with a Twist* (C&T Publishing, 1996).

Follow the diagrams below for making **Strip Sets A–H** and **S–Z (Step 1)**. Work on one strip set at a time. As you crosscut strip sets into segments **(Step 2)**, place each set in a separate sealable, quart-size plastic bag. Label the bag with its strip set letter and the number of segments in the bag. Indicate which fabric should be in the top position. Move on to the next strip set and repeat the process.

To avoid curving strip sets, stitch the first two strips from right to left. Add the third strip and stitch from left to right. Continue reversing the sewing direction until you have the number of strips needed. By following this stitching plan, the final strip sets will lie flat and square to the seams.

1 Sew the following **Strip Sets. Press toward even numbered fabrics.**

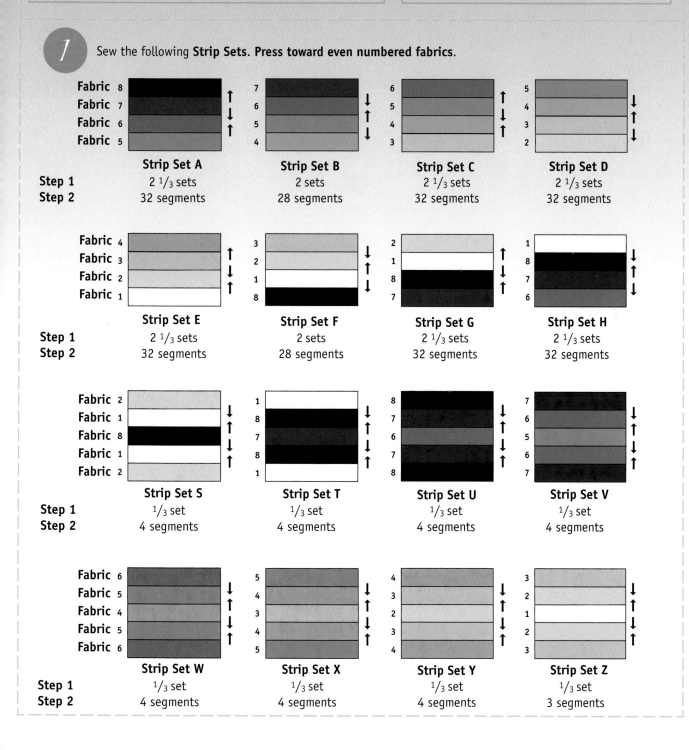

	Strip Set A	Strip Set B	Strip Set C	Strip Set D
Step 1	2 1/3 sets	2 sets	2 1/3 sets	2 1/3 sets
Step 2	32 segments	28 segments	32 segments	32 segments

	Strip Set E	Strip Set F	Strip Set G	Strip Set H
Step 1	2 1/3 sets	2 sets	2 1/3 sets	2 1/3 sets
Step 2	32 segments	28 segments	32 segments	32 segments

	Strip Set S	Strip Set T	Strip Set U	Strip Set V
Step 1	1/3 set	1/3 set	1/3 set	1/3 set
Step 2	4 segments	4 segments	4 segments	4 segments

	Strip Set W	Strip Set X	Strip Set Y	Strip Set Z
Step 1	1/3 set	1/3 set	1/3 set	1/3 set
Step 2	4 segments	4 segments	4 segments	3 segments

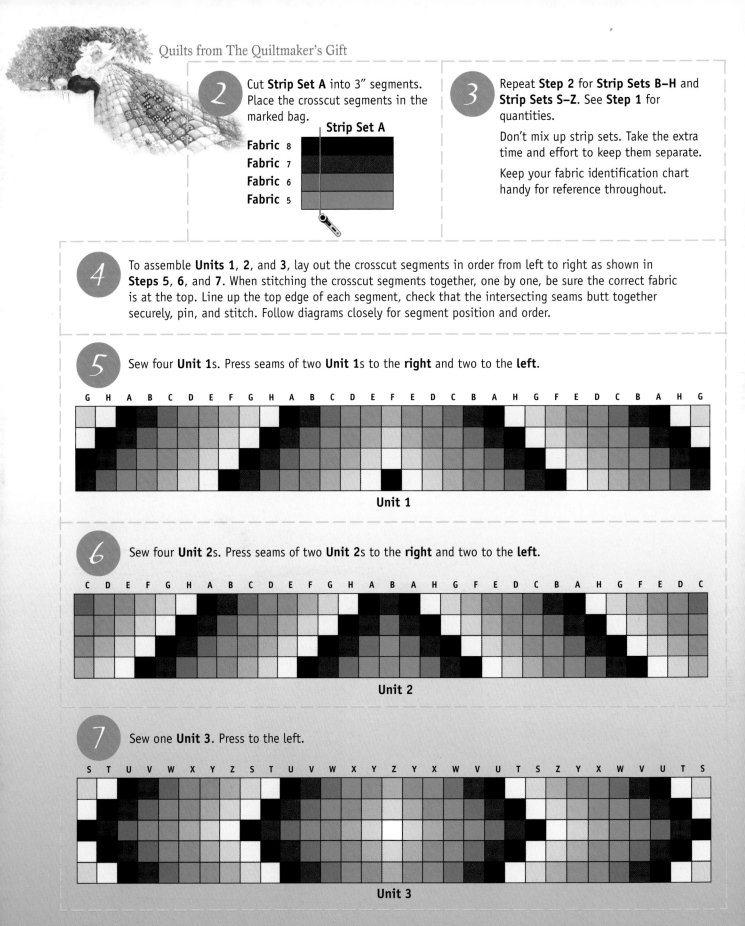

2 Cut **Strip Set A** into 3" segments. Place the crosscut segments in the marked bag.

Strip Set A

Fabric 8
Fabric 7
Fabric 6
Fabric 5

3 Repeat **Step 2** for **Strip Sets B–H** and **Strip Sets S–Z**. See **Step 1** for quantities.

Don't mix up strip sets. Take the extra time and effort to keep them separate.

Keep your fabric identification chart handy for reference throughout.

4 To assemble **Units 1**, **2**, and **3**, lay out the crosscut segments in order from left to right as shown in **Steps 5**, **6**, and **7**. When stitching the crosscut segments together, one by one, be sure the correct fabric is at the top. Line up the top edge of each segment, check that the intersecting seams butt together securely, pin, and stitch. Follow diagrams closely for segment position and order.

5 Sew four **Unit 1**s. Press seams of two **Unit 1**s to the **right** and two to the **left**.

G H A B C D E F G H A B C D E F E D C B A H G F E D C B A H G

Unit 1

6 Sew four **Unit 2**s. Press seams of two **Unit 2**s to the **right** and two to the **left**.

C D E F G H A B C D E F G H A B A H G F E D C B A H G F E D C

Unit 2

7 Sew one **Unit 3**. Press to the left.

S T U V W X Y Z S T U V W X Y Z Y X W V U T S Z Y X W V U T S

Unit 3

 When pressing a seam, set the stitches first by pressing the seam flat as sewn. Then press from the right side of the fabric, making sure the underlying seam goes in the direction of the pressing arrow in the diagram.

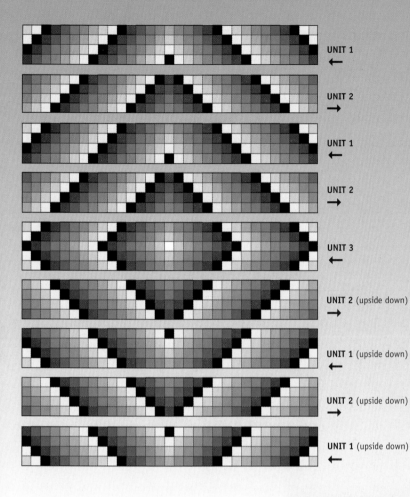

UNIT 1 ←

UNIT 2 →

UNIT 1 ←

UNIT 2 →

UNIT 3 ←

UNIT 2 (upside down) →

UNIT 1 (upside down) ←

UNIT 2 (upside down) →

UNIT 1 (upside down) ←

Quilt Assembly

◆ Lay out **Units 1, 2,** and **3** as shown at left. Watch direction of pressed seams.

◆ Make sure the seams of **Unit 1**s and **Unit 2**s butt together. Pin all intersections. Stitch rows together, alternating sewing directions.

◆ Follow the instructions on page 138 for adding borders.

Finishing the Quilt

◆ Follow the instructions on pages 138–139 for making the quilt sandwich.

◆ Follow the instructions on page 139 for basting the quilt.

◆ Refer to pages 138–139 for information on quilting.

◆ Follow the instructions on page 140 for binding the quilt.

Trip Around the World

Trip Around the World, 52" x 64"
567 blocks, two plain borders.
Barb Engelking, Superior, WI
quilted by Angela Haworth, Superior, WI

Barb owns Fabric Works in Superior, Wisconsin, a popular gathering place for quilters in Northern Wisconsin and Northeastern Minnesota. Her interest in quilting began with hand marbling fabrics and selling them at quilt shows.

Friendship Star

Friends with the Animals, 43" x 56"
9" blocks (12), one border with corner squares

Jessica & Spencer Torvinen, Duluth, MN
quilted by Claudia Clark Myers, Duluth, MN

Friendship Star

Artist's Secrets

Even though this pattern is more modern than I would have liked, it fit well with the concept of the king needing to learn about true friendship. It seems a wonderful idea that friendship just flies out the window and comes down wherever it happens to land—in this case to wrap some distant dog sledders several pages later. I live in chilly Minnesota and Latvia, so I know they appreciated the warmth and comfort of that quilt.

Brackman/BlockBase Number: none (1717, 1683A,B are similar)
Alternate names: Simplex Star, Pin Wheel, Lost Goslin', Eccentric Star

Although most patterns in this book date back to the late 1800s or early 1900s, the familiar Friendship Star has modern (post-1970) rather than traditional origins. The three-color Simplex Star (#1717), first published by Hearth and Home in the early 1900s has star points facing the opposite direction (as in Milky Way). The Eccentric Star (#1683B), attributed to Nancy Cabot in the 1930s, has half-square triangle units in the corners. The names and construction of these similar blocks are often confused—a common occurrence in the oral tradition of quiltmaking.

This easy, equal nine-patch block makes an excellent introduction to making half-square triangle units and stitching accurate seams when joining blocks for precise star points. Beginners should review diagrams inside the front cover and the piecing instructions on pages 134–135 before starting. Follow the construction diagrams carefully to discover the amazing disappearing and reappearing triangle points.

Quiltmaker's Design Challenges

◆ Make a real Friendship Star quilt for a special occasion or farewell. Have each person make a block from their stash, using a common background color/value. Sign the blocks.

◆ Use more than one fabric for each star, putting a large-scale pattern in the center square and coordinating small-scale patterns in the points.

◆ Solids, hand-dyes, or tone-on-tones in bold Amish colors would make a striking Friendship Star quilt.

◆ Divide the corner squares of the block into half-square triangles of differing values to create an interesting secondary design where the blocks meet.

◆ Try mixing several sizes (4", 6", 8", 12") of Friendship Stars in the same quilt. This takes some advance planning!

◆ For a simple but vibrant quilt, make stars with dark blue or black backgrounds and set them with an alternate plain block of the same dark fabric.

◆ Plan for a 6" border and make four 6" Friendship Star blocks to use as corner posts.

◆ Make a sawtooth inner border of half-square triangles with an outer plain border.

◆ Or use several narrow inner borders and an outside pieced border of Friendship Stars on point.

Spencer Torvinen, age 9, chose all the fabrics for his quilt, cut the pieces, and sewed the stars and blocks together, with a bit of help from his mom, Jessica Torvinen. Grandma Claudia Clark Myers did the machine quilting. Check out their rhinoceros quilt label.

... the king ordered his soldiers to seize the beautiful star quilt from the quiltmaker. But when they rushed upon her, she tossed the quilt out the window, and a great gust of wind carried it up, up and away.

Quilt Information (finished size measurements)

	LAP	TWIN	QUEEN
Quilt Size without Borders	45" x 63"	54" x 72"	72" x 90"
Quilt Size with Borders	56" x 74"	65" x 83"	83" x 101"
Block Size	9"	9"	9"
Number of Blocks	35	48	80
Block Layout	5 x 7	6 x 8	8 x 10
Backing Layout	← → ← →	↑ ↑	↑ ↑ ↑ ↑ ↑

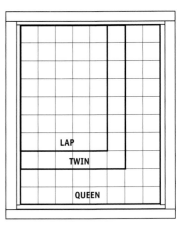

The Quiltmaker says . . .

Read all the instructions before you begin.

Always place right sides of fabric together for stitching.

Use scant $1/4$" seam allowances.

Press seam allowances in the direction of arrows.

Fabric Requirements (42-45"wide, in yards)

	LAP	TWIN	QUEEN
Fabric 1, **Background**—Piece A & C	$2\frac{1}{4}$	3	$4\frac{7}{8}$
Fabric 2, **Accent**—Piece B & Inner Border	$1\frac{1}{2}$	$1\frac{2}{3}$	$2\frac{1}{2}$
Fabric 3, **Focus**—Piece D, Outer Border & Binding	$2\frac{1}{8}$	$2\frac{3}{8}$	$3\frac{1}{8}$
Backing Fabric	$3\frac{1}{2}$	5	$7\frac{1}{2}$

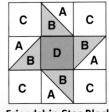

Friendship Star Block

To make stars in a variety of fabrics and colors, one-eighth of a yard will make the points for five stars. If you want the star center to be the same as the star points, you will be able to get four stars from an eighth of a yard of fabric.

Cutting Instructions

Trudie Hughes' "Big Mama" ruler, with its clear $7/8$" markings is great for cutting $3\frac{7}{8}$" strips and half-square triangles.

	LAP	TWIN	QUEEN
Fabric 1, Background—Piece C			
Cut strips $3\frac{1}{2}$" x width of fabric	13	18	30
☐ Crosscut into $3\frac{1}{2}$" squares	140	192	320
Fabric 1, Background—Piece A			
Cut strips $3\frac{7}{8}$" x width of fabric	7	10	16
☐ Crosscut into $3\frac{7}{8}$" squares	70	96	160
◪ Crosscut diagonally once into half-square triangles	140	192	320
Fabric 2, Accent Fabric—Piece B			
Cut strips $3\frac{7}{8}$" x width of fabric	7	10	16
☐ Crosscut into $3\frac{7}{8}$" squares	70	96	160
◪ Crosscut diagonally once into half-square triangles	140	192	320
Fabric 2, Accent Fabric, Inner Border			
Cut strips $1\frac{1}{2}$" x width of fabric	7	7	9
Fabric 3, Focus Fabric—Piece D			
Cut strips $3\frac{1}{2}$" x width of fabric	4	5	8
☐ Crosscut into $3\frac{1}{2}$" squares	35	48	80
Fabric 3, Focus Fabric, Outer Border			
Cut strips 5" x width of fabric	7	8	10
Fabric 3, Focus Fabric, Binding			
Cut strips $2\frac{1}{4}$" x width of fabric	7	8	10

Pattern tester Jennifer Isley shows her first ever quilt—Fiesta del Soul.

Piecing Directions — Be careful not to stretch bias seams when stitching and pressing triangle squares.

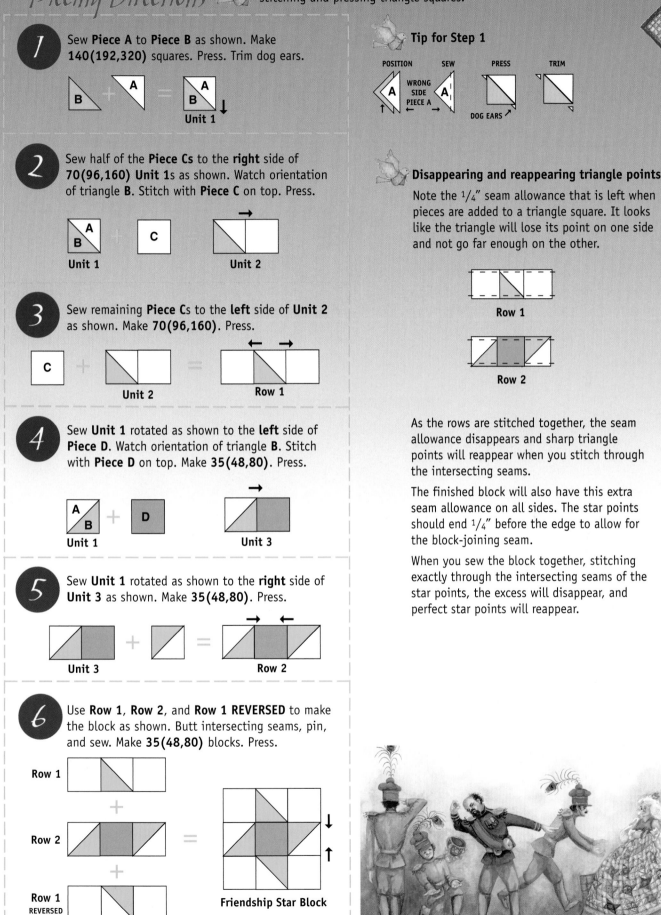

1 Sew **Piece A** to **Piece B** as shown. Make **140(192,320)** squares. Press. Trim dog ears.

B + A = A/B Unit 1

2 Sew half of the **Piece C**s to the **right** side of **70(96,160) Unit 1**s as shown. Watch orientation of triangle **B**. Stitch with **Piece C** on top. Press.

A/B Unit 1 + C = Unit 2

3 Sew remaining **Piece C**s to the **left** side of **Unit 2** as shown. Make **70(96,160)**. Press.

C + Unit 2 = Row 1

4 Sew **Unit 1** rotated as shown to the **left** side of **Piece D**. Watch orientation of triangle **B**. Stitch with **Piece D** on top. Make **35(48,80)**. Press.

A/B Unit 1 + D = Unit 3

5 Sew **Unit 1** rotated as shown to the **right** side of **Unit 3** as shown. Make **35(48,80)**. Press.

Unit 3 + = Row 2

6 Use **Row 1**, **Row 2**, and **Row 1 REVERSED** to make the block as shown. Butt intersecting seams, pin, and sew. Make **35(48,80)** blocks. Press.

Row 1
+
Row 2
+
Row 1 REVERSED
=
Friendship Star Block

Tip for Step 1

POSITION SEW PRESS TRIM
WRONG SIDE PIECE A A A DOG EARS

Disappearing and reappearing triangle points

Note the 1/4" seam allowance that is left when pieces are added to a triangle square. It looks like the triangle will lose its point on one side and not go far enough on the other.

Row 1

Row 2

As the rows are stitched together, the seam allowance disappears and sharp triangle points will reappear when you stitch through the intersecting seams.

The finished block will also have this extra seam allowance on all sides. The star points should end 1/4" before the edge to allow for the block-joining seam.

When you sew the block together, stitching exactly through the intersecting seams of the star points, the excess will disappear, and perfect star points will reappear.

Quilt Assembly

◆ Lay out the blocks **5(6,8)** across and **7(8,10)** down. Rotate blocks so pressed seams alternate directions and butt together nicely.

◆ Pin intersecting seams before sewing. Be especially careful to position star points accurately.

◆ Follow the instructions on pages 136–137 for sewing the blocks and rows together.

◆ Follow the instructions on page 138 for adding borders.

Finishing the Quilt

◆ Follow the instructions on pages 138–139 for making the quilt sandwich.

◆ Follow the instructions on page 139 for basting the quilt.

◆ Refer to pages 138–139 for information on quilting.

◆ Follow the instructions on page 140 for binding the quilt.

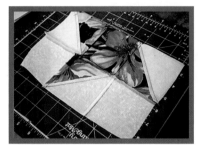

Pattern tester Bonnie Malterer shows how to pin and stitch for precise points and perfect intersections.

Friendship Star

Camp Miller Memories, 54" x 62"
9" blocks (30), two mitered borders
Ann Ketcham Palmer, Duluth, MN
quilted by Merry Ellestad & Rosemary Walsberg, Two Harbors, MN

Surgical nurse Ann Palmer used batiks of all colors as she tried to match the feeling of the Friendship Star quilt Gail painted for The Quiltmaker's Gift. Ann especially enjoys miniature quilts and specializes in paper piecing.

Spencer is a fourth-grade student at the Lowell music magnet school, where he plays violin and piano. He is a Cub Scout, plays ice hockey and golf, and enjoys swimming, dinosaurs, and bugs.

Spencer learned to quilt by osmosis from his mom, Jessica, and grandma, Claudia Clark Myers, who are both award-winning quiltmakers. Spencer's eye for color is evident in the Friendship Star quilt he designed, cut, and pieced—using scores of batiks from the family stash.

Betty Firth mixes and matches Friendship Stars from Lone Pine Needlers, Heart of the Woods, Going to Pieces, and North Country quilt guilds.

Quilters from four different guilds made Friendship Star quilts to go on tour with **The Quiltmaker's Gift**. A total of 97 quilters made over 300 blocks.

Members of Shirley Kirsch's Wednesday Soup Group tied all the quilts and added bindings.

Milky Way

Black and White and Red All Over, 63" x 75"
12" blocks (20), 2 mitered borders

Barbara McKeever, Duluth, MN
quilted by Deb Lussier Quinn, Superior, WI

Artist's Secrets

I made a Milky Way quilt even before drawing preliminary sketches for The Quiltmaker's Gift. I tried out several patterns that I thought the quiltmaker would have in the works as the story unfolds. Originally, I had conceived the quiltmaker as an old woman who sewed. As I searched for models and began to paint, the true nature of the quiltmaker was revealed—a timeless, magical person who created quilts out of the world around her, including the awesome night sky. Eventually I painted my practice quilt into the book.

Milky Way

Brackman/BlockBase Number: 1142B
Earliest publication date: 1920s (Ladies Art Company)
Alternate names: similar block (1142A) is called Friendly Hand, Indiana Puzzle, Monkey Wrench

The Milky Way block uses the same simple construction of the Friendship Star—squares and half-square triangle units—combined with easy four-patches in a 4 x 4 grid. The challenge comes in putting the pieces together in the correct orientation. Notice that the tips of the Milky Way Stars point in the opposite direction from the Friendship Star.

A three-color/value scheme distinguishes the Milky Way block from other blocks of the same construction (Brackman #1142A), which have a two-color/value scheme: the complete star and the light squares in the four-patches are of the same light value and the other (partial) star is of medium value, with dark squares in the four-patches.

The tessellating Milky Way block does not stand alone. For the full pattern of stars to be revealed, interlocking blocks need to be repeated without rotation across the rows.

Quiltmaker's Design Challenges

◆ Experiment with different color/value placements. Use a different light in the point of each star, with the same fabric in all the centers.

◆ Put a focus fabric in the center of every star or use the stars as photograph frames in a special occasion gift or remembrance quilt.

◆ Or make both the background and the medium stars scrappy.

◆ For dramatic effect, try a borderless, all-geometric-fabrics Milky Way.

◆ Plaid flannels, feedsack prints, novelties, Victorian reproductions, and florals could make intriguing interpretations of this block.

◆ Echo the Milky Way four-patches in your inner or outer border with a two-row checkerboard.

◆ Alternate a sawtooth border and a four-patch border before adding a plain outer border.

◆ Use the top three rows of the block to make a continuous star border. This border pattern would set off quilts made with other blocks constructed of half-square triangles or four-patches.

◆ Use Barb's design as inspiration for extending the star points into the borders.

"How can this be?" he cried. "How can I feel so happy about giving my things away?"

Barb McKeever, who usually works in purples and blues, really stretched her color comfort zone in creating this graphic Milky Way. The result seems appropriate for a charter member of the Ladies of the Evening quilt group.

Quilt Information (finished size measurements)

	LAP	DOUBLE	QUEEN
Quilt Size without Borders	36" x 48"	60" x 84"	72" x 96"
Quilt Size with Borders	48" x 60"	72" x 96"	84" x 108"
Block Size	12"	12"	12"
Number of Blocks	12	35	48
Block Layout	3 x 4	5 x 7	6 x 8
Backing Layout	↔ ↔	↑ ↑	↓ ↑ ↓ ↑ ↑ ↑

For crib quilt, use 8" blocks and follow instructions for lap size quilt.

Fabric Requirements (42–45" wide, in yards)

	LAP	DOUBLE	QUEEN
Fabric 1, **Light**—Pieces A, B & C	1 1/3	3 1/8	4 1/2
Fabric 2, **Dark**—Piece D, E & Outer Border	2	3 7/8	4 3/4
Fabric 3, **Medium**—Piece F, Inner Border & Binding	1 1/4	2	2 1/2
Backing Fabric	3	5 2/3	7 7/8

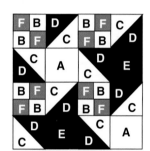

Milky Way Block #1142B

Cutting Instructions

	LAP	DOUBLE	QUEEN
Fabric 1, Light—Piece A			
Cut strips 3 1/2" x width of fabric	3	7	9
☐ Crosscut into 3 1/2" squares	24	70	96
Fabric 1, Light—Piece B			
Cut strips 2 x width of fabric	5	14	20
Fabric 1, Light—Piece C			
Cut strips 3 7/8" x width of fabric	5	14	20
☐ Crosscut into 3 7/8" squares	48	140	192
◹ Crosscut diagonally once into half-square triangles	96	280	384
Fabric 2, Dark—Piece D			
Cut strips 3 7/8" x width of fabric	5	14	20
☐ Crosscut into 3 7/8" squares	48	140	192
◹ Crosscut diagonally once into half-square triangles	96	280	384
Fabric 2, Dark—Piece E			
Cut strips 3 1/2" x width of fabric	3	7	9
☐ Crosscut into 3 1/2" squares	24	70	96
Fabric 2, Dark—Outer Border			
Cut strips 5" x width of fabric	6	9	10
Fabric 3, Medium—Piece F			
Cut strips 2" x width of fabric	5	14	20
Fabric 3, Medium—Inner Border			
Cut strips 2" x width of fabric	5	8	9
Fabric 3, Medium—Binding			
Cut strips 2 1/4" x width of fabric	6	9	10

The points of all stars in this quilt are made from the same **C/D** triangle square. Try using half-square triangle paper or Triangles-on-a-Roll to speed up the process.

When using these alternative methods, do not pre-cut 3 7/8" strips for **Pieces C** and **D**. Follow cutting and sewing instructions printed on the triangle square paper.

Piecing Directions

Follow pressing arrows carefully. Watch intersections for precise points.

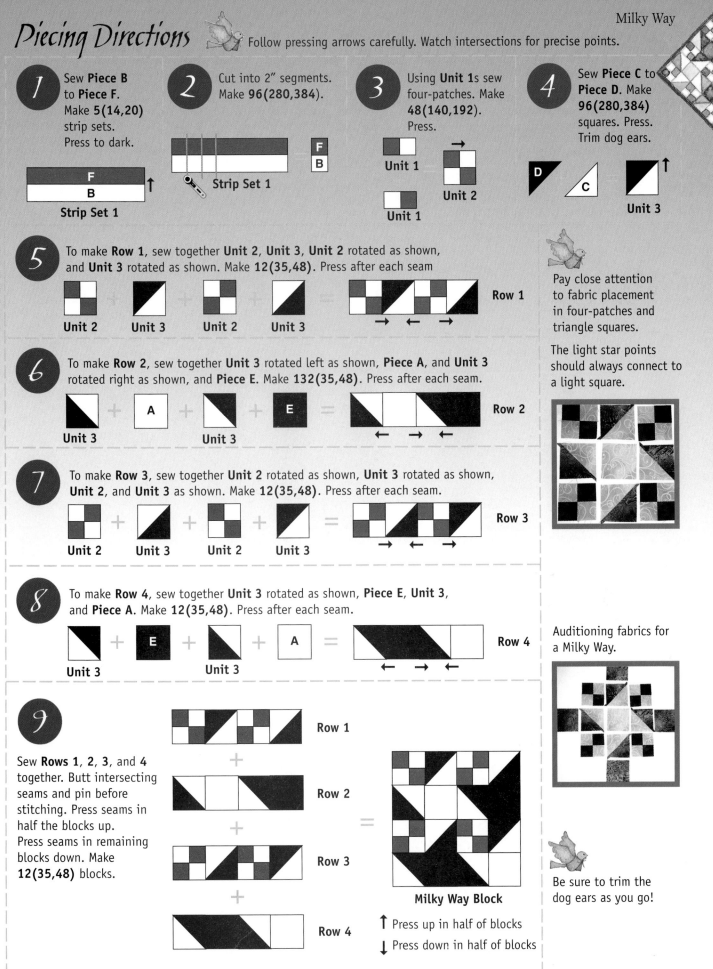

1 Sew **Piece B** to **Piece F**. Make **5(14,20)** strip sets. Press to dark.

F
B
Strip Set 1

2 Cut into 2" segments. Make **96(280,384)**.

Strip Set 1
F
B

3 Using **Unit 1**s sew four-patches. Make **48(140,192)**. Press.

Unit 1
Unit 2
Unit 1

4 Sew **Piece C** to **Piece D**. Make **96(280,384)** squares. Press. Trim dog ears.

D
C
Unit 3

5 To make **Row 1**, sew together **Unit 2**, **Unit 3**, **Unit 2** rotated as shown, and **Unit 3** rotated as shown. Make **12(35,48)**. Press after each seam

Unit 2 + Unit 3 + Unit 2 + Unit 3 = Row 1

Pay close attention to fabric placement in four-patches and triangle squares.

The light star points should always connect to a light square.

6 To make **Row 2**, sew together **Unit 3** rotated left as shown, **Piece A**, and **Unit 3** rotated right as shown, and **Piece E**. Make **132(35,48)**. Press after each seam.

Unit 3 + A + Unit 3 + E = Row 2

7 To make **Row 3**, sew together **Unit 2** rotated as shown, **Unit 3** rotated as shown, **Unit 2**, and **Unit 3** as shown. Make **12(35,48)**. Press after each seam.

Unit 2 + Unit 3 + Unit 2 + Unit 3 = Row 3

8 To make **Row 4**, sew together **Unit 3** rotated as shown, **Piece E**, **Unit 3**, and **Piece A**. Make **12(35,48)**. Press after each seam.

Unit 3 + E + Unit 3 + A = Row 4

Auditioning fabrics for a Milky Way.

9 Sew **Rows 1**, **2**, **3**, and **4** together. Butt intersecting seams and pin before stitching. Press seams in half the blocks up. Press seams in remaining blocks down. Make **12(35,48)** blocks.

Row 1
+
Row 2
+
Row 3
+
Row 4

= **Milky Way Block**

↑ Press up in half of blocks
↓ Press down in half of blocks

Be sure to trim the dog ears as you go!

Quilt Assembly

◆ Lay out the blocks **3(5,6)** across and **4(7,8)** down. In each row, alternate blocks with seams pressed up and down so intersecting seams butt nicely. Pin all intersections before sewing.

◆ Follow the instructions on pages 136–137 for sewing blocks and rows together

◆ Follow the instructions on page 138 for adding borders.

Finishing the Quilt

◆ Follow the instructions on pages 138–139 for making the quilt sandwich.

◆ Follow the instructions on page 139 for basting the quilt.

◆ Refer to pages 138–139 for information on quilting.

◆ Follow the instructions on page 140 for binding the quilt.

Jena demonstrates precision strip piecing to her mom, Barb Engelking.

Jena Engelking is a fifth grader at Superior Cathedral grade school. An enthusiastic piccolo player and Girl Scout, she plays goalie on the Superior Hurricanes ice hockey team, loves acting in community theater, and occasionally helps out at Fabric Works, her mom's quilt shop.

Jena's grandmother, LaVonne Horner, is a seasoned quilter and fabric artist who specializes in hand dying fabrics, garment construction, and surface embellishment. This is the first quilt they have made together.

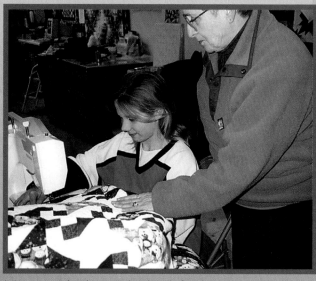

LaVonne coaches her grandaughter before hockey practice.

Milky Way

Milky Way, 63" x 83"
10" blocks (35), two borders
Jena Engelking & LaVonne Horner, Superior, WI
quilted by Carolyn & Charles Peters, Woodbury, MN

Jena, age 11, joined forces with her grandmother to make her second quilt—a Milky Way in cool colors, featuring a snowperson novelty print.

Rosebud

Anniversary Bouquet, 49" x 56"
7 1/2" blocks (24) on point
two side borders, four top borders
including checkerboard

Gail de Marcken, Ely, MN
quilted by Bonnie Jusczak, Duluth, MN

Rosebud

Brackman/BlockBase Number: 1273
Earliest publication date: 1898 (Ladies Art Company)
Alternate names: Hummingbird, Bright Star, Maple Leaf, Crow's Foot

This four-patch block is made up of four smaller diagonal blocks constructed from triangles and half-square triangle units. New challenges encountered in Rosebud involve:

◆ Sewing triangle square units together.

◆ Adding a half-square triangle to the left side of a square.

◆ Stitching a pieced strip of triangles to a larger half-square triangle.

◆ Keeping precise triangle points when making seams.

◆ Sewing a long bias seam without stretching.

For a simple-looking block, Rosebud requires deft piecing techniques. Beginners should review the piecing instructions on pages 134–135. Follow the diagrams carefully and pay special attention to keeping the background and foreground triangle points sharp and flush to the seam lines. This skill is essential for constructing all blocks with pieced triangles, including the rest of the patterns in this book.

Gail made this Rosebud as part of her warm-up for illustrating The Quiltmaker's Gift. A self-taught quilter, Gail brings her expert artist's eye to choosing colors and settings. In this quilt, she shows a contemporary interpretation of the Rosebud traditional colors—rose colored triangles on a green background—setting blocks on point and adding checkerboard borders at top and bottom.

"Once more the king asked her for a quilt, and once more she refused."

Artist's Secrets

This is another example of the quiltmaker using the abundant resources of her environment to create beautiful and useful quilts. She certainly grew roses around her cabin. And rosebuds are a good pattern for a new baby— especially for a baby with a young mother who is also so poor.

Quilter's Design Challenges

◆ This quilt would work well with a scrappy floral look. Use a different large or medium floral for each of the medium-sized triangles and a coordinating small floral for the rosebud points. Use a variety of greens for the backgrounds and large triangles.

◆ Use a black background with wild florals, primaries, or jewel tones for focus fabrics.

◆ Try setting Rosebud blocks on point like Gail did (see page 67). Alternate with plain blocks to show off exquisite quilting.

◆ Make a pieced outer border using half-size Rosebud blocks in a zigzag arrangement.

◆ Expand the traditional two-color scheme to four or more colors, while retaining two values. Light or dark "background" large triangles will form a secondary pattern of pinwheels.

◆ Echo the triangle buds with a sawtooth border.

◆ Create an entire border of Rosebud blocks to frame your quilt. Calculate border lengths based on full block repetitions. Then adjust the quilt top size to match by adding an inner border.

Quilt Information (finished size measurements)

	CRIB	TWIN	QUEEN
Quilt Size without Borders	24" x 36"	48" x 72"	72" x 84"
Quilt Size with Borders	34" x 46"	58" x 82"	82" x 94"
Finished Block Size	12"	12"	12"
Number of Blocks	6	24	42
Block Layout	2 x 3	4 x 6	6 x 7
Backing Layout			

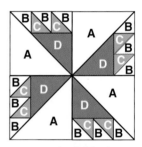

Fabric Requirements (42–45" wide, in yards)

	CRIB	TWIN	QUEEN
Fabric 1, **Background**—Pieces A & B	1 1/8	3 1/4	5 1/4
Fabric 2, **Accent 1**—Piece C	1/4	3/4	1 1/4
Fabric 3, **Focus**—Piece D, Outer Border & Binding	1 1/4	2 1/2	3 2/3
Fabric 4, **Accent 2**—Inner Border	1/4	3/8	1/2
Backing Fabric	2 1/4	5	7

Rosebud Block #1273

Rosebud

Half Price Bouquet, 62" x 74"
12" blocks (20), two plain borders
Barbara McKeever, Duluth, MN
quilted by Deb Lussier Quinn, Superior, WI

Barb recently retired from the University of Minnesota-Duluth and plans to finish the many quilts she has started over the years. An inveterate bargain hunter, she found all the fabrics for this quilt on the half-price SALE table at Fabric Works.

Cutting Instructions

	CRIB	TWIN	QUEEN
Fabric 1, Background—Piece A			
Cut strips 6 $7/8$" x width of fabric	3	10	17
☐ Crosscut into 6 $7/8$" squares	12	48	84
◪ Crosscut once diagonally into half-square triangles	24	96	168
Fabric 1, Background—Piece B			
Cut strips 2 $7/8$" x width of fabric	3	12	20
☐ Crosscut into 2 $7/8$" squares	36	144	252
◪ Crosscut once diagonally into half-square triangles	72	288	504
Fabric 2, Accent 1—Piece C			
Cut strips 2 $7/8$" x width of fabric	2	8	13
☐ Crosscut into 2 $7/8$" squares	24	96	168
◪ Crosscut once diagonally into half-square triangles	48	192	336
Fabric 3, Focus—Piece D			
Cut strips 4 $7/8$" x width of fabric	2	6	11
☐ Crosscut into 4 $7/8$" squares	12	48	84
◪ Crosscut once diagonally into half-square triangles	24	96	168
Fabric 3, Focus—Outer Border			
Cut strips 4 $1/2$" x width of fabric	4	7	9
Fabric 3, Focus—Binding			
Cut strips 2 $1/4$" x width of fabric	5	8	10
Fabric 4, Accent 2—Inner Border			
Cut strips 1 $1/2$" x width of fabric	4	7	8

Try using 2" half-square triangle paper to make **Unit 1**s. Do not cut strips for **Piece B** and **Piece C**. Follow the instructions on the triangle paper instead.

The "Big Mama" ruler by Trudie Hughes has clear markings for cutting 2 $7/8$" and 4 $7/8$" strips and squares.

Patty Lipe experiments with a diagonal (on-point) setting for her double dip blueberry Rosebud.

Pattern tester Marge Martin lays out her Rosebud block before final asssembly.

Piecing Directions

In this pattern, press all the seams toward the background fabric

The Quiltmaker says . . .

Read all the instructions before you begin.

Always place right sides of fabric together for stitching.

Use scant ¼" seam allowances.

Press seam allowances in the direction of arrows.

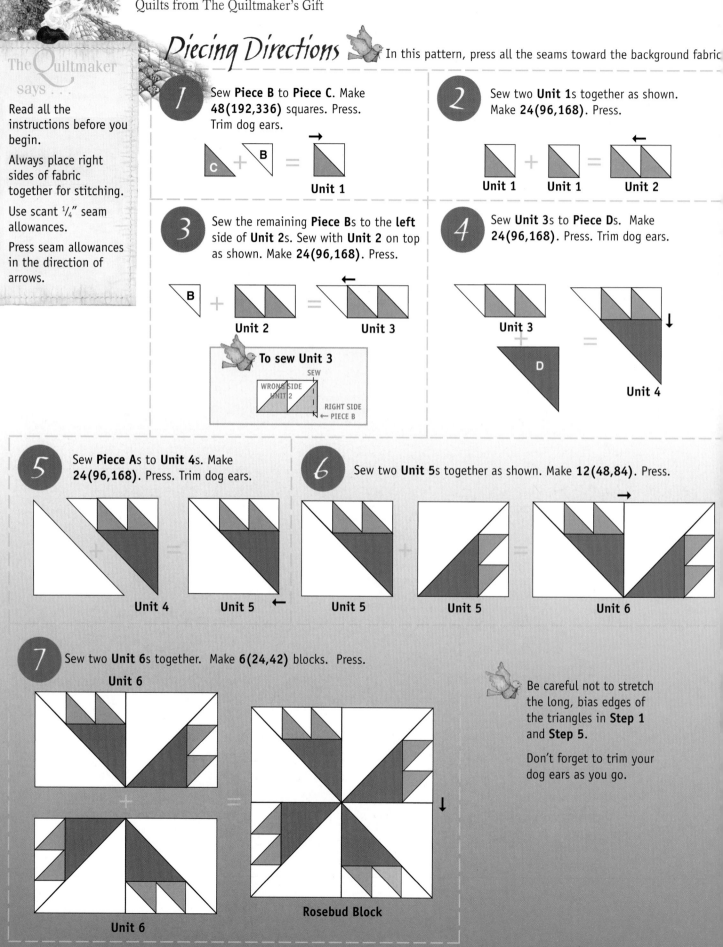

1 Sew **Piece B** to **Piece C**. Make **48(192,336)** squares. Press. Trim dog ears.

C + B = Unit 1

2 Sew two **Unit 1**s together as shown. Make **24(96,168)**. Press.

Unit 1 + Unit 1 = Unit 2

3 Sew the remaining **Piece B**s to the **left** side of **Unit 2**s. Sew with **Unit 2** on top as shown. Make **24(96,168)**. Press.

B + Unit 2 = Unit 3

To sew Unit 3

SEW
WRONG SIDE UNIT 2
RIGHT SIDE ← PIECE B

4 Sew **Unit 3**s to **Piece D**s. Make **24(96,168)**. Press. Trim dog ears.

Unit 3 + D = Unit 4

5 Sew **Piece A**s to **Unit 4**s. Make **24(96,168)**. Press. Trim dog ears.

Unit 4 + = Unit 5

6 Sew two **Unit 5**s together as shown. Make **12(48,84)**. Press.

Unit 5 + Unit 5 = Unit 6

7 Sew two **Unit 6**s together. Make **6(24,42)** blocks. Press.

Unit 6 + Unit 6 = Rosebud Block

Be careful not to stretch the long, bias edges of the triangles in **Step 1** and **Step 5**.

Don't forget to trim your dog ears as you go.

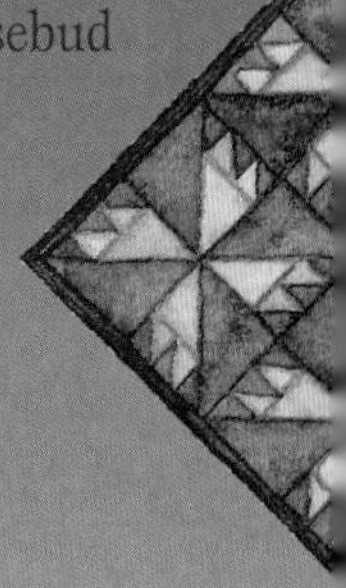

Quilt Assembly

◆ Lay out the blocks **2(4,6)** across and **3(6,7)** down. In each row, rotate adjacent blocks 180° so that pressed horizontal seams butt nicely. Pin all intersections before sewing.

◆ Follow the instructions on pages 136–137 for sewing the blocks and rows together. Be very careful of Rosebud points while sewing blocks together. Review the piecing instructions on pages 134-135 for pointers. Use pins to mark the hidden intersecting seams on the bottom block.

◆ Follow the instructions on page 138 for adding borders.

Finishing the Quilt

◆ Follow the instructions on pages 138–139 for making the quilt sandwich.

◆ Follow the instructions on page 139 for basting the quilt.

◆ Refer to pages 138–139 for information on quilting.

◆ Follow the instructions on page 140 for binding the quilt.

Diagonal Settings for Rosebud Blocks

When blocks are rotated diagonally (on point), the quilt needs to be filled out with triangles of fabric to create a straight, stable edge and square corners. If a diagonal arrangement is desirable, adjust fabric requirements and cutting directions to accommodate the reduced number of Rosebud blocks required and the increased amount of background fabric needed to make the setting and corner triangles.

Setting (side) triangles are cut as quarter-square triangles from a large square, so that the long side is on the straight grain of fabric for minimum stretch on the quilt edge. Corner half-square triangles are cut with the straight grain on the short sides for no-stretch edges at the corners.

The size of these triangles is determined by the BLOCK size, not the quilt size. For a 12" block like Rosebud, the corner triangles are cut from 9 3/8" squares as shown in the diagram. Setting triangles are cut from 18 1/4" squares. These triangles will be a bit larger than needed to allow for slight block size variation.

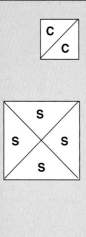

To make CORNER triangles (Piece C)
Cut TWO 9 3/8" squares diagonally ONCE to make 4 half-square triangles, Piece C.

To make SETTING triangles (Piece S)
Cut ONE 18 1/4" square diagonally TWICE to make 4 quarter-square triangles, Piece S.

Make as many as needed for the chosen quilt size.
Twin size will yield two leftover Piece S triangles.

Before measuring for borders, trim excess fabric on all sides of the quilt, leaving a 1/4" seam allowance at triangle points. Diagonally set quilts usually have mitered borders. For more information about on-point settings, see pages 136–137.

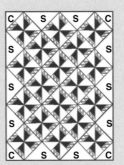

CRIB QUILT

(finished size of quilt 44" x 44")
Make FIVE 12" Rosebud blocks
Cut TWO 9 3/8" squares ONCE into 4 CORNER triangles (Piece C).
Cut ONE 18 1/4" square into 4 SETTING triangles (Piece S).

TWIN QUILT

(finished size of quilt 60" x 78")
Make EIGHTEEN 12" Rosebud blocks
Cut TWO 9 3/8" squares ONCE into 4 CORNER triangles (Piece C).
Cut THREE 18 1/4" squares into 10 SETTING triangles (Piece S).

QUEEN QUILT

(finished size of quilt 94" x 94")
Make FORTY-ONE 12" Rosebud blocks
Cut TWO 9 3/8" squares ONCE into 4 CORNER triangles (Piece C).
Cut FOUR 18 1/4" squares into 16 SETTING triangles (Piece S).

Bear's Paw

Double Paws, 36" x 47"
10 1/2" blocks (6), sashing and cornerstones,
2 plain borders
Carol Jean Brooks, Duluth, MN
quilted by Susan Brooks Wiitanen, Duluth, MN

Bear's Paw

Brackman/BlockBase Number: 1879
Earliest publication date: 1906 (Ladies Art Company #351)
Alternate names: Bear's Foot, Hand of Friendship, Tea Leaf,
Best Friend, Cat's Paw, Illinois Turkey Track

The Bear's Paw block is an unequal nine-patch with an underlying 7 x 7 grid—the width of the inner sashing (central square and rectangles) is the same as the paws. These instructions provide for an additional lattice and cornerstone sashing between the blocks, as pictured in the accompanying quilts.

Bear's Paw provides an opportunity to practice nearly all the construction techniques presented in earlier blocks: nine-patches, internal and external sashings, and half-square triangle units. Unless you are making a scrappy quilt, the triangle paper method for making large quantities of half-square triangles may be more efficient.

Although there are many pieces to this block, beginners will have no problem if they follow the diagrams carefully. Make a test block for reference—and to check your technique before you assemble the rest. For each step, stack the pieces you are joining and place them side by side in the correct orientation before sewing them together. Be sure to press each unit as you go, following the pressing arrows in the assembly diagrams. Don't forget to trim your dog ears (see page 53).

Carol Jean showcases bear paw fabric in this Double Paws quilt, made for the big brother of a preemie in the neonatal intensive care unit. Her sister, Susan Wiitanen, collaborated on the meandering part of the quilting while Carol Jean stitched in the ditch.

Artist's Secrets

I knew from the first that the bear would play a major role in my illustrations for The Quiltmaker's Gift, *so the Bear's Paw block was an obvious pairing. After all, I live in the summer on Bear Island Lake. Since Jeff had never specified what berries the bear was going to share for breakfast, of course I painted blueberries. Blueberry Festival is the highlight of August in Ely, Minnesota!*

Quiltmaker's Design Challenges

◆ The Bear's Paw pattern adapts well to nearly any fabric style. Flannel plaids, batiks, solids, juveniles, geometrics, botanicals, or hand dyes will make stunning quilts.

◆ Choose novelty or representational fabrics to match one of the many names for this block.

◆ To form secondary patterns, try different color and value placements for paws in adjacent blocks.

◆ Consider using flannel as backing for this or any quilt. It makes a cozy comforter.

◆ A Bear's Paw in Christmas colors instantly transforms the pattern.

◆ Experiment with secondary designs which are possible when you change the color and value placement of both the inner and outer sashing.

◆ Use the Bear's Paw block for a group block or fabric exchange. The internal sashing is a great place for signatures.

◆ The Amish often created spectacular two-color "floating" Bear's Paw quilts, setting the blocks on point (without extra sashing) and using alternate blocks of the background (internal sashing) fabric.

◆ Or use a white background with red or blue Bear's Paws on point for a delicate, antique look.

◆ Make four extra paws and use them as corners in a 4" outer border.

◆ Try a single, double, or triple sawtooth inner or outer border, reversing directions of the points at the center of each side. This is a great way to use up extra half-square triangle units.

"It's no wonder you're so grouchy," the quiltmaker said. "You've nothing but rocks on which to rest your head at night. Bring me an armful of needles and with my shawl, I'll make you a great big pillow."

Quilt Information (finished size measurements)

	CRIB	LAP	QUEEN
Quilt Size without borders	27" x 39½"	39½" x 52"	77" x 89½"
Quilt Size with borders	37" x 49½"	49½" x 62"	87" x 99½"
Block Size	10½"	10½"	10½"
Number of Blocks	6	12	42
Block Layout	2 x 3	3 x 4	6 x 7
Backing Layout			

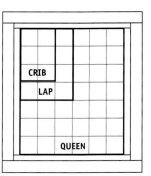

Fabric Requirements (42-45" wide, in yards)

	CRIB	LAP	QUEEN
Fabric 1, **Background**–Pieces A, B & C	¾	1 ¼	3 ⅓
Fabric 2, **Accent 1**—Piece D & Binding	¾	1 ¼	2 ⅓
Fabric 3, **Focus**—Pieces E, F, Outer Border	1 ¼	1 ⅝	3 ¼
Fabric 4, **Accent 2**—Piece G	⅝	1	2 ½
Fabric 5, **Accent 3**—Piece H & Inner Border	⅓	½	¾
Backing Fabric	2 ½	3 ⅛	7 ½

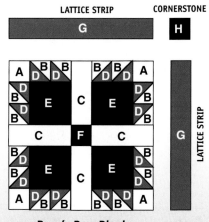

LATTICE STRIP — G
CORNERSTONE — H
LATTICE STRIP — G

Bear's Paw Block
#1879

Bear's Paw

Time to Hibernate, 52" x 66"
10 ½" blocks (12), sashing &
cornerstones, 3 mitered borders
Joanne Larsen Line, Duluth, MN
quilted by Sue Munns, Duluth, MN

Joanne lives in the big city of Duluth where every autumn, bears searching for food venture into her backyard. She chose warm contemporary fabrics here to give the impression of coziness for a long hibernation.

Cutting Instructions

	CRIB	LAP	QUEEN
Fabric 1, Background—Piece A			
Cut strips 2″ x width of fabric	2	3	9
☐ Crosscut into 2″ squares	24	48	168
Fabric 1, Background—Piece B			
Cut strips $2\frac{3}{8}$″ x width of fabric	3	6	21
☐ Crosscut into $2\frac{3}{8}$″ squares	48	96	336
◺ Crosscut diagonally once into half-square triangles	96	192	672
Fabric 1, Background—Piece C			
Cut strips 2″ x width of fabric	3	6	21
▭ Crosscut into 2″ x 5″ rectangles	24	48	168
Fabric 2, Accent Fabric 1—Piece D			
Cut strips $2\frac{3}{8}$″ x width of fabric	3	6	21
☐ Crosscut into $2\frac{3}{8}$″ squares	48	96	336
◺ Crosscut diagonally once into half-square triangles	96	192	672
Fabric 2, Binding			
Cut strips $2\frac{1}{4}$″ x width of fabric	5	6	10
Fabric 3, Focus Fabric—Piece E			
Cut strips $3\frac{1}{2}$″ x width of fabric	3	5	16
☐ Crosscut into $3\frac{1}{2}$″ squares	24	48	168
Fabric 3, Focus Fabric—Piece F			
Cut strips 2″ x width of fabric	1	1	3
☐ Crosscut into 2″ squares	6	12	42
Fabric 3, Focus Fabric—Outer Border			
Cut strips $4\frac{1}{2}$″ x width of fabric	5	6	10
Fabric 4, Accent Fabric 2—Piece G (Lattice Strip)			
Cut strips $2\frac{1}{2}$″ x width of fabric	6	11	33
▭ Crosscut into $2\frac{1}{2}$″ x 11″ rectangles	17	31	97
Fabric 5, Accent Fabric 3—Piece H (Cornerstone)			
Cut strips $2\frac{1}{2}$″ x width of fabric	1	2	4
☐ Crosscut into $2\frac{1}{2}$″ squares	12	20	56
Fabric 5, Accent Fabric 3—Inner Border			
Cut strips $1\frac{1}{2}$″ x width of fabric	4	5	9

Since the bear's toes in this block are all pieced from the same **B/D** triangle square, you may want to try a more efficient construction technique: triangle square paper, double squares, or bias-strip pieced methods all work well.

Do not cut **Pieces B** and **D** until you decide on the method. Then follow the instructions for that technique. Fabric requirements should be about the same, no matter what method you choose.

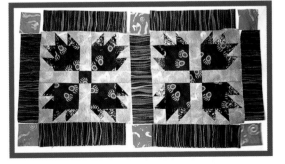

Carol Jean assembles her Bear's Paw.

Watch the placement of light and dark triangles carefully.

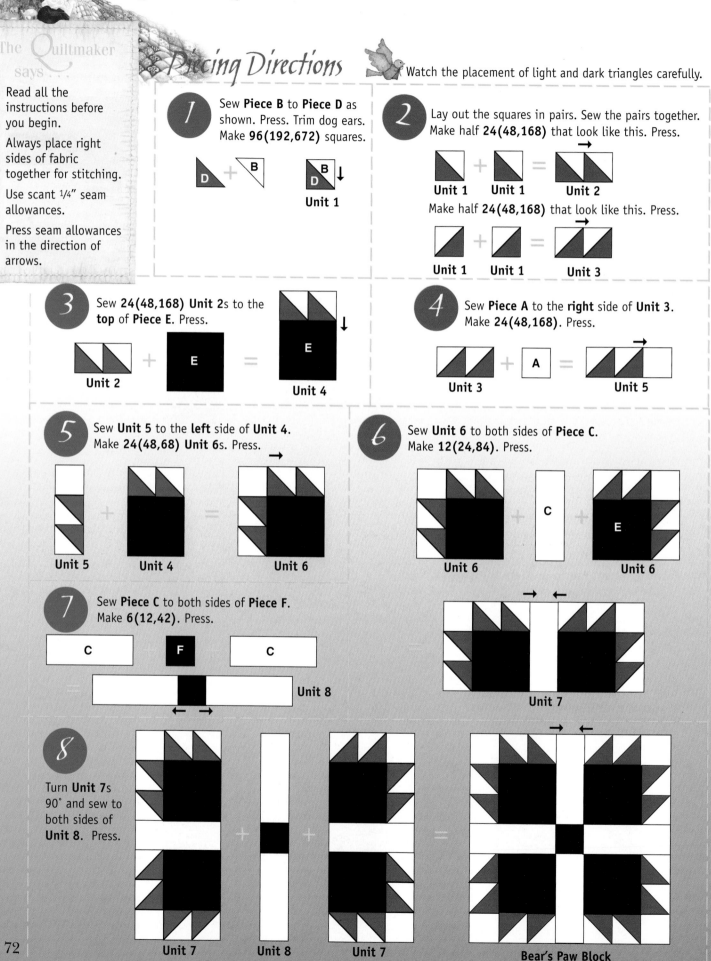

The Quiltmaker says . . .

Read all the instructions before you begin.

Always place right sides of fabric together for stitching.

Use scant 1/4" seam allowances.

Press seam allowances in the direction of arrows.

1 Sew **Piece B** to **Piece D** as shown. Press. Trim dog ears. Make **96(192,672)** squares.

D + B B D ↓

Unit 1

2 Lay out the squares in pairs. Sew the pairs together. Make half **24(48,168)** that look like this. Press.

Unit 1 + **Unit 1** = **Unit 2**

Make half **24(48,168)** that look like this. Press.

Unit 1 + **Unit 1** = **Unit 3**

3 Sew **24(48,168) Unit 2**s to the **top** of **Piece E**. Press.

Unit 2 + **E** = **E** **Unit 4**

4 Sew **Piece A** to the **right** side of **Unit 3**. Make **24(48,168)**. Press.

Unit 3 + **A** = **Unit 5**

5 Sew **Unit 5** to the **left** side of **Unit 4**. Make **24(48,68) Unit 6**s. Press.

Unit 5 + **Unit 4** = **Unit 6**

6 Sew **Unit 6** to both sides of **Piece C**. Make **12(24,84)**. Press.

Unit 6 + **C** + **E** **Unit 6**

Unit 7

7 Sew **Piece C** to both sides of **Piece F**. Make **6(12,42)**. Press.

C + **F** + **C**

Unit 8

8 Turn **Unit 7**s 90° and sew to both sides of **Unit 8**. Press.

Unit 7 + **Unit 8** + **Unit 7** = **Bear's Paw Block**

72

9 For the horizontal **Lattice Row**s, sew **Piece G** (lattice strips) and **Piece H** (cornerstones) together as shown. Each **Lattice Row** should have 2(3,6) **Piece G**s and 3(4,7) **Piece H**s. Make 4(5,8) rows. Press.

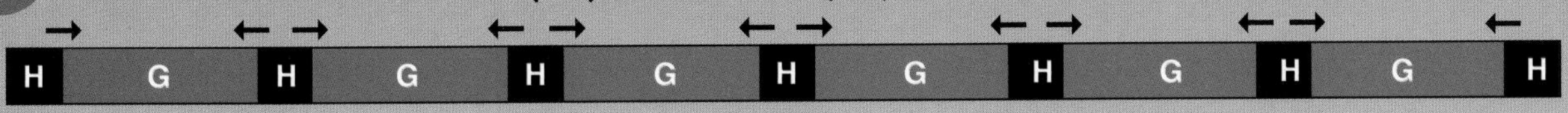

| H | G | H | G | H | G | H | G | H | G | H | G | H |

Lattice Row

10 To make **Block Row**s, use 2(3,6) **Bear Paw Block**s and 3(4,7) **Piece G**s. Sew the row together as shown. Make 3(4,7) rows. Press.

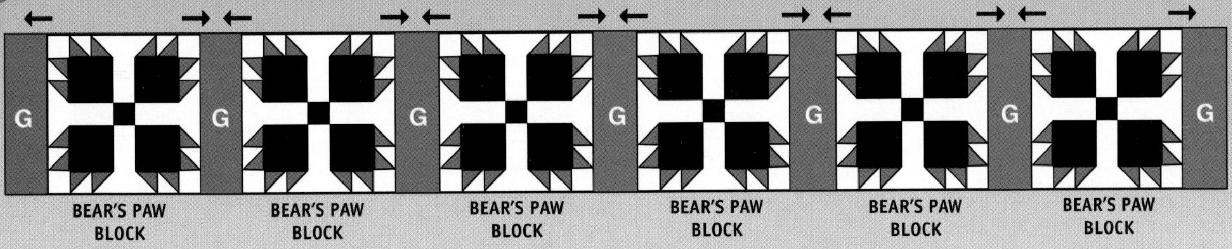

| G | BEAR'S PAW BLOCK | G | BEAR'S PAW BLOCK | G | BEAR'S PAW BLOCK | G | BEAR'S PAW BLOCK | G | BEAR'S PAW BLOCK | G | BEAR'S PAW BLOCK | G |

Block Row

Quilt Assembly

◆ For precision intersections, butt and pin all seams before sewing.

◆ Sew the rows together alternating **Lattice Row**s and **Block Row**s. Press.

◆ Reverse sewing direction row by row to prevent distortion.

◆ Follow the instructions on page 138 for adding borders.

Finishing the Quilt

◆ Follow the instructions on pages 138–139 for making the quilt sandwich.

◆ Follow the instructions on page 139 for basting the quilt.

◆ Refer to pages 138–139 for information on quilting.

◆ Follow the instructions on page 140 for binding the quilt.

Bear's Paw

Blueberries at Bear Island Lake, 64" x 64"
10 1/2" blocks (25), sashing & cornerstones
Gail de Marcken, Ely, MN
quilted by Merry Ellestad &
Rosemary Walsberg, Two Harbors, MN

During the summer, illustrator Gail de Marcken lives on Bear Island Lake near Ely. This wilderness area abounds with bears and their favorite food—blueberries. Gail made this thematic quilt as a warm-up to get in the mood before painting the bear sequences.

73

Hen & Chicks

HEleN and Chicks at Rose Hill Farm, 54" x 64"
10" blocks (20), three mitered borders

Nancy Loving Tubesing, Duluth, MN
quilted by Karen McTavish, Duluth, MN

Artist's Secrets

Of course the quiltmaker raises chickens! And chickens or eggs make perfect gifts because, with care, they keep multiplying. The woman who was forced to give a chicken to the king for his birthday party gratefully receives it back again, along with a silver basket. She, in turn, gives away eggs that mature into hens that lay more eggs to be given away. I have always found poor people to be most generous.

Hen and Chicks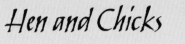

Brackman/BlockBase Number: 1859A, 1859B
Earliest publication date: 1928
Alternate names: Wild Goose Chase, Fox and Geese,
Duck and Ducklings, Corn and Beans, Handy Andy, Shoo-Fly

This two-color block belongs to the Shoo-Fly family of nine-patches with triangles in the corner. Hen and Chicks is based on a 5 x 5 grid that results in an uneven nine-patch.

The rectangles and square in the center of the block make a built-in sashing that creates an optical illusion. When the blocks are sewn together, they split in fourths and make new diamond-in-a-square blocks with the adjacent Hen and Chicks. This illusion is particularly evident in Gail's quilt.

The construction of this block introduces two new techniques that may be challenging to less experienced quilters:

◆ Adding triangles to the left and right side of a square unit (the process is different left and right);

◆ Sewing a plain triangle to a pieced triangle unit, stitching through the X made by intersecting seams.

Even beginners can have perfect points on the wings of their final hens and chicks if they follow the diagrams and instructions carefully.

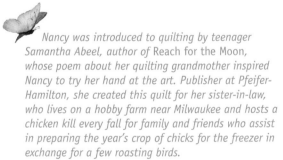

Nancy was introduced to quilting by teenager Samantha Abeel, author of Reach for the Moon, *whose poem about her quilting grandmother inspired Nancy to try her hand at the art. Publisher at Pfeifer-Hamilton, she created this quilt for her sister-in-law, who lives on a hobby farm near Milwaukee and hosts a chicken kill every fall for family and friends who assist in preparing the year's crop of chicks for the freezer in exchange for a few roasting birds.*

Quiltmaker's Design Challenges

◆ Add lattice strips between blocks like Judy did (page 79). Geometric sashing fabrics (stripes, plaids, checks) can make a stunning frame for nearly any focus fabric style.

◆ Choose a color family and make a planned scrappy version. Be open to intriguing fabric combinations that occur by accident. Use a design wall to play with block placement before sewing rows together.

◆ Set blocks on point to make your quilt jump and jive. The strong diagonal made by the central sashing really stands out and makes the block look quite different.

◆ For an Amish look, try a high-contrast two-color quilt, setting blocks on point with alternate plain blocks.

◆ Take advantage of the secondary design of the inner sashing. Adjust your pattern and color schemes within each block to highlight the secondary pattern that forms among adjacent blocks.

◆ Make a pieced outer border repeating the corner block from the Hen and Chicks pattern all around the edge of your quilt.

So the king kept on giving and giving.

Quilt Information (finished size measurements)

	LAP	DOUBLE	QUEEN
Quilt Size without Borders	40" x 50"	60" x 70"	80" x 90"
Quilt Size with Borders	54" x 64"	74" x 84"	94" x 104"
Block Size	10"	10"	10"
Number of Blocks	20	42	72
Block Layout	4 x 5	6 x 7	8 x 9
Backing Layout	← ←	↓ ↓ ↓	↑ ↓ ↑ ↓

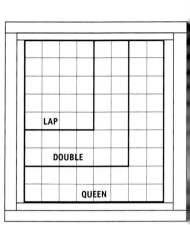

Fabric Requirements (42-45" wide, in yards)

	LAP	DOUBLE	QUEEN
Fabric 1, **Light**—Pieces A & B	1 3/4	3 1/2	3 3/4
Fabric 2, **Focus**—Pieces C, D & E	1 1/2	2 5/8	3 1/4
Fabric 3, **Accent**—Inner Border	1/2	3/4	7/8
Fabric 4, **Focus/Accent**—Outer Border & Binding	1 5/8	2 1/8	2 1/2
Backing Fabric	3 3/8	5	7 2/3

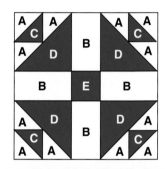

**Hen and Chicks Block
#1859B**

Hen & Chicks

A Chicken in Every Pot, 52" x 62"
10" blocks (20), two plain borders
Gail de Marcken, Ely, MN
quilted by Angela Haworth, Superior, WI

*Watercolor artist and fabric lover Gail
draws on her international vision and
experiences for nearly every quilt she makes.
Here she interprets the original Hen and
Chicks pattern (1859A) in the subtle moods
of Japanese fabrics. This is another in a
series of quilts Gail stitched as models and
creative warm-ups before embarking on
The Quiltmaker's Gift.*

Cutting Instructions

	LAP	DOUBLE	QUEEN
Fabric 1, Background—Piece A			
Cut strips 2 7/8" x width of fabric	10	20	34
☐ Crosscut into 2 7/8" squares	120	252	432
◩ Crosscut diagonally once into half-square triangles	240	504	864
Fabric 1, Background—Piece B			
Cut strips 2 1/2" x width of fabric	10	21	36
▭ Crosscut into 2 1/2" x 4 1/2" rectangles	80	168	288
Fabric 2, Focus—Piece C			
Cut strips 2 7/8" x width of fabric	4	7	12
☐ Crosscut into 2 7/8" squares	40	84	144
◩ Crosscut diagonally once into half-square triangles	80	168	288
Fabric 2, Focus—Piece D			
Cut strips 4 7/8" x width of fabric	5	11	18
☐ Crosscut into 4 7/8" squares	40	84	144
◩ Crosscut diagonally once into half-square triangles	80	168	288
Fabric 2, Focus—Piece E			
Cut strips 2 1/2" x width of fabric	2	3	5
☐ Crosscut into 2 1/2" squares	20	42	72
Fabric 3, Accent—Inner Border			
Cut strips 2 1/2" x width of fabric	5	7	9
Fabric 4, Focus/Accent—Outer Border			
Cut strips 5 1/2" x width of fabric	6	8	10
Fabric 4, Focus/Accent—Binding			
Cut strips 2 1/4" x width of fabric	7	9	11

If you want to use assorted fabrics for hens, chicks, or backgrounds, a generous eighth yard of fabric (5") will make pieces for four blocks.

**Hen and Chicks Block
Alternate Coloring
#1859A**

Piecing Directions

Be careful not to stretch the long bias edges of triangles while stitching.

The **Quiltmaker** says . . .

Read all the instructions before you begin.

Always place right sides of fabric together.

Use scant ¼″ seam allowances.

Press seam allowances in the direction of arrows.

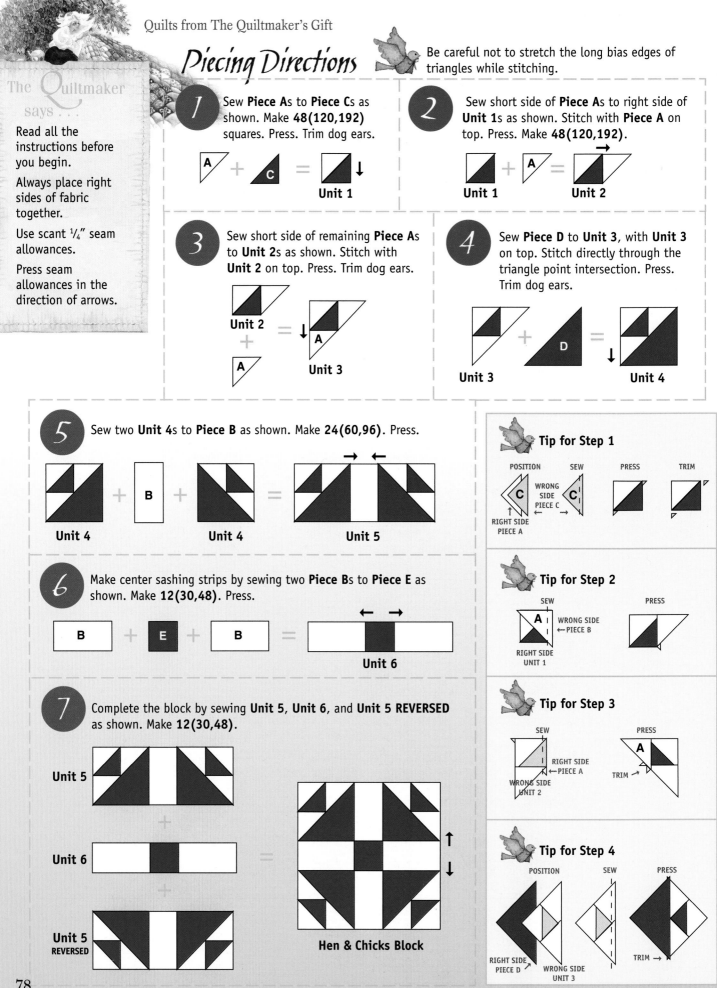

1 Sew **Piece A**s to **Piece C**s as shown. Make **48(120,192)** squares. Press. Trim dog ears.

A + C = Unit 1

2 Sew short side of **Piece A**s to right side of **Unit 1**s as shown. Stitch with **Piece A** on top. Press. Make **48(120,192)**.

Unit 1 + A = Unit 2

3 Sew short side of remaining **Piece A**s to **Unit 2**s as shown. Stitch with **Unit 2** on top. Press. Trim dog ears.

Unit 2 + A = Unit 3

4 Sew **Piece D** to **Unit 3**, with **Unit 3** on top. Stitch directly through the triangle point intersection. Press. Trim dog ears.

Unit 3 + D = Unit 4

5 Sew two **Unit 4**s to **Piece B** as shown. Make **24(60,96)**. Press.

Unit 4 + B + Unit 4 = Unit 5

6 Make center sashing strips by sewing two **Piece B**s to **Piece E** as shown. Make **12(30,48)**. Press.

B + E + B = Unit 6

7 Complete the block by sewing **Unit 5**, **Unit 6**, and **Unit 5 REVERSED** as shown. Make **12(30,48)**.

Unit 5
+
Unit 6
+
Unit 5 REVERSED
=
Hen & Chicks Block

Tip for Step 1

POSITION — SEW — PRESS — TRIM

WRONG SIDE PIECE C

RIGHT SIDE PIECE A

Tip for Step 2

SEW — PRESS

WRONG SIDE ← PIECE B

RIGHT SIDE UNIT 1

Tip for Step 3

SEW — PRESS

RIGHT SIDE ← PIECE A

WRONG SIDE UNIT 2

TRIM →

Tip for Step 4

POSITION — SEW — PRESS

RIGHT SIDE PIECE D — WRONG SIDE UNIT 3

TRIM →

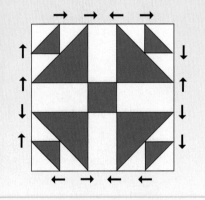

Quilt Assembly

◆ Lay out the blocks **4(6,8)** across and **5(7,9)** down. In each row, rotate adjacent blocks 90° so pressed seams of inner sashing butt nicely. The first block in each row alternates direction.

◆ If you use sashing and cornerstones between the Hen and Chicks blocks, press toward the sashing on every piece (blocks and cornerstones) and your intersections will always butt together perfectly.

◆ Follow the directions on pages 136–137 for sewing the blocks and rows together.

◆ Follow the directions on page 138 for adding borders.

Finishing the Quilt

◆ Follow the instructions on pages 138–139 for making the quilt sandwich.

◆ Follow the instructions on page 139 for basting the quilt.

◆ Refer to pages 138–139 for information on quilting.

◆ Follow the instructions on page 140 for binding the quilt.

This block represents a common pressing dilemma in quilting: press for perfectly nested opposing seams with minimal bulk, or press for easy view of intersections and precision points.

The pressing instructions here follow the easy-view/precision-points-within-the-block method.

More experienced quilters may want to use a circular pressing pattern to reduce bulk in seams between adjacent blocks.

Hen & Chicks

Down on the Farm, 46" x 58"
10" blocks (12), sashing & cornerstones
two mitered borders
Judy Pearson, Duluth, MN
quilted by Joan's Quilting, Clinton, MO

Judy is the textbook buyer at the University of Minnesota-Duluth bookstore. Sister of Joanne Line, in recent years Judy has made quilts for her eight grandchildren and is now starting the second time around. For a country look, Judy added another set of sashing and cornerstones between her Hen and Chicks blocks.

79

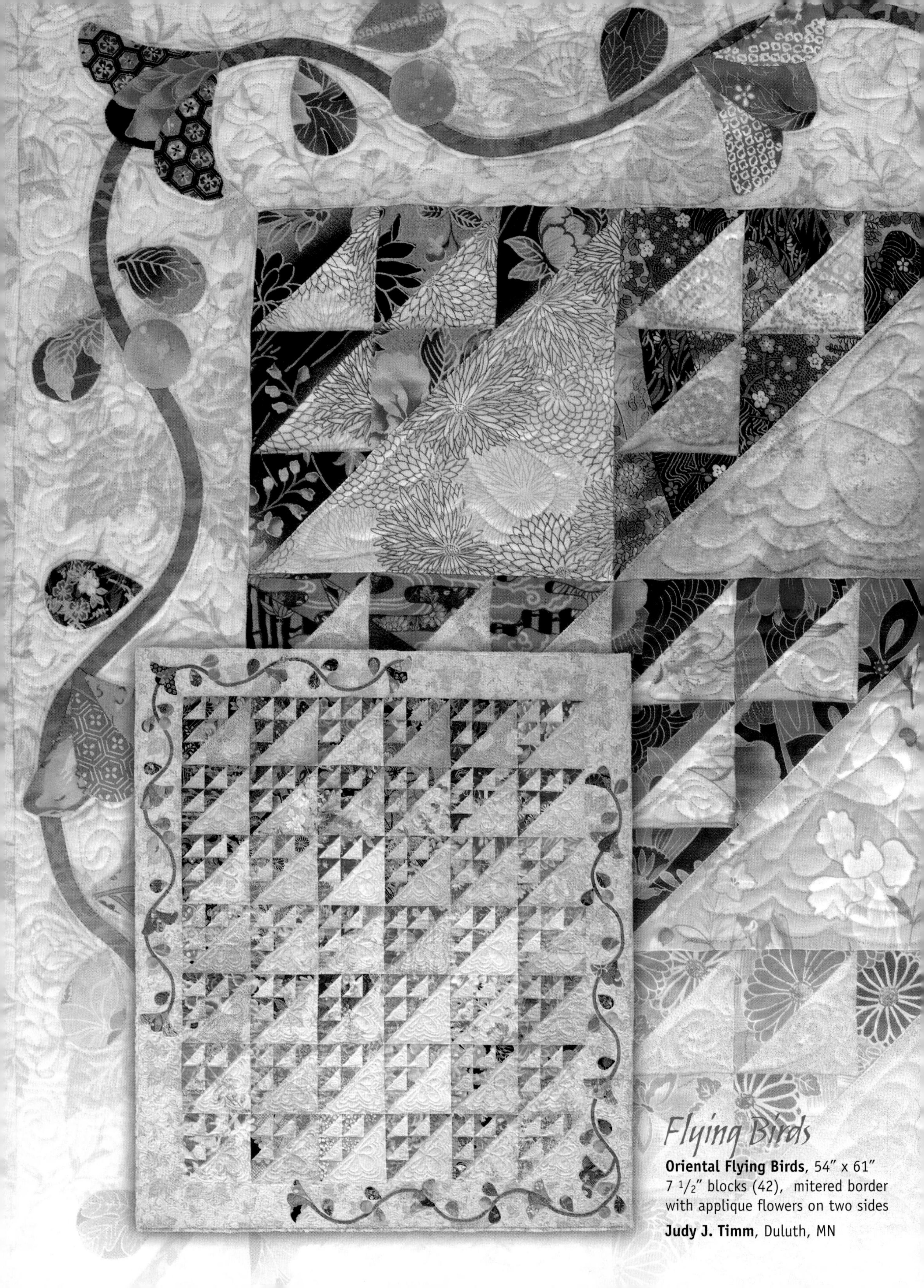

Flying Birds

Oriental Flying Birds, 54" x 61"
7 ½" blocks (42), mitered border
with applique flowers on two sides

Judy J. Timm, Duluth, MN

Flying Birds

Brackman/BlockBase Number: 3161 (single block)
Earliest publication date: 1929 (Finley)
Alternate names: Birds in the Air, Flock of Geese, Flight of Swallows, Flying Geese

This versatile block dates back to at least 1820 and was especially popular from 1840–1865. The Flying Birds pattern was particularly appealing in eras of frugality. When cloth was scarce, the abundant triangles were made entirely from scraps. Flying Birds offers lots of practice making precision triangle points. Beginners should review the piecing instructions on pages 134–135. Follow the diagrams carefully.

Like other diagonal blocks, Flying Birds can be set in any of the traditional Log Cabin block settings (see pages 33, 84, 91). Experiment with different block orientations until you find one that is pleasing with your particular fabric choices.

Artist's Secrets

This pattern is an obvious match for a book filled with birds who rescue and console and rejoice and act as king's messengers. I painted over a thousand birds in The Quiltmaker's Gift, including my favorite African Grey Parrots who pose as a chess set. When we lived in Zaire, my daughters were enchanted with the parrots who flew about wild and hung around our home.

Quiltmaker's Design Challenges

◆ In keeping with the mood of birds on the wing, use a blue color scheme: indigo birds flying in a sky made of shirting fabrics, Japanese yukata prints with white-on-whites, 19th century reproduction blues and neutrals.

◆ The design impact of this block depends on high light/dark contrast. Try mixing values in the large triangles. Then create an overall design, grouping blocks by value.

◆ Make the large triangle of a medium or dark value, then turn blocks on point to give the illusion of birds flying just above the horizon.

◆ Treat each row of small triangles with a different value/color to create an intriguing secondary pattern at block intersections.

◆ Consider adding sashing and cornerstones between the blocks.

◆ Use half-size Flying Birds blocks as the cornerposts in a 4 $1/2$" border.

◆ Make a pieced border using elements from the block. Try a whole border of pieced triangles (Unit 6) or alternate pieced triangles with plain ones (Piece C). Stabilize the long bias edge of each triangle with stay-stitching before assembling. Incorporate Flying Geese into your border design.

Judy Timm is a popular teacher at Fabric Works. An expert needle artist as well as quilter, Judy created an appliqué design for her Flying Birds border, inspired by the exquisite work of Kumiko Sudo (East Quilts West, Quilt Digest Press, 1992).

Soon the sky darkened as the air filled with a huge cloud of sparrows.

Quilt Information (finished size measurements)

	LAP	DOUBLE	QUEEN
Quilt Size without Borders	36" x 45"	63" x 81"	81" x 90"
Quilt Size with Borders	48" x 57"	75" x 93"	93" x 102"
Block Size	9"	9"	9"
No. of Blocks	20	63	90
Block Layout	4 x 5	7 x 9	9 x 10
Backing Layout			

The Quiltmaker says . . .

Read all the instructions before you begin.

Always place right sides of fabric together.

Use scant ¼" seam allowances.

Press seam allowances in the direction of arrows.

If you want to use assorted fabrics, one-eighth yard of fabric makes twenty half-square triangles.

Fabric Requirements (42-45" wide, in yards)

	LAP	DOUBLE	QUEEN
Fabric 1, **Assorted Lights**—Pieces A & C	1 1/2	3 5/8	5 1/2
Fabric 2, **Assorted Mediums to Darks**—Piece B	7/8	2 3/8	3 1/4
Fabric 3, **Light**—Border & Binding	1 1/2	2 3/8	3 1/4
Backing Fabric	3	5 1/2	7 1/2

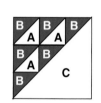

Flying Birds Block #3161

Cutting Instructions

The "Big Mama" ruler designed by Trudie Hughes is great for cutting 3 7/8" strips and squares.

	LAP	DOUBLE	QUEEN
Fabric 1, Assorted Lights—Piece A			
Cut strips 3 7/8" x width of fabric	3	10	14
☐ Crosscut into 3 7/8" squares	30	95	135
◹ Crosscut diagonally once into half-square triangles	60	190	270
Fabric 1, Assorted Lights—Piece C			
Cut strips 9 7/8" x width of fabric	3	8	12
☐ Crosscut into 9 7/8" squares	10	32	45
◹ Crosscut diagonally once into half-square triangles	20	64	90
Fabric 2, Assorted Mediums to Darks—Piece B			
Cut strips 3 7/8" x width of fabric	6	19	27
☐ Crosscut into 3 7/8" squares	60	189	270
◹ Crosscut diagonally once into half-square triangles	120	378	540
Fabric 3, Light—Outer Border			
Cut strips 6 1/2" x width of fabric	5	9	10
Fabric 3, Light—Binding			
Cut strips 2 1/4" x width of fabric	6	9	11

Piecing Directions Pay close attention to fabric placement in adjacent pieces.

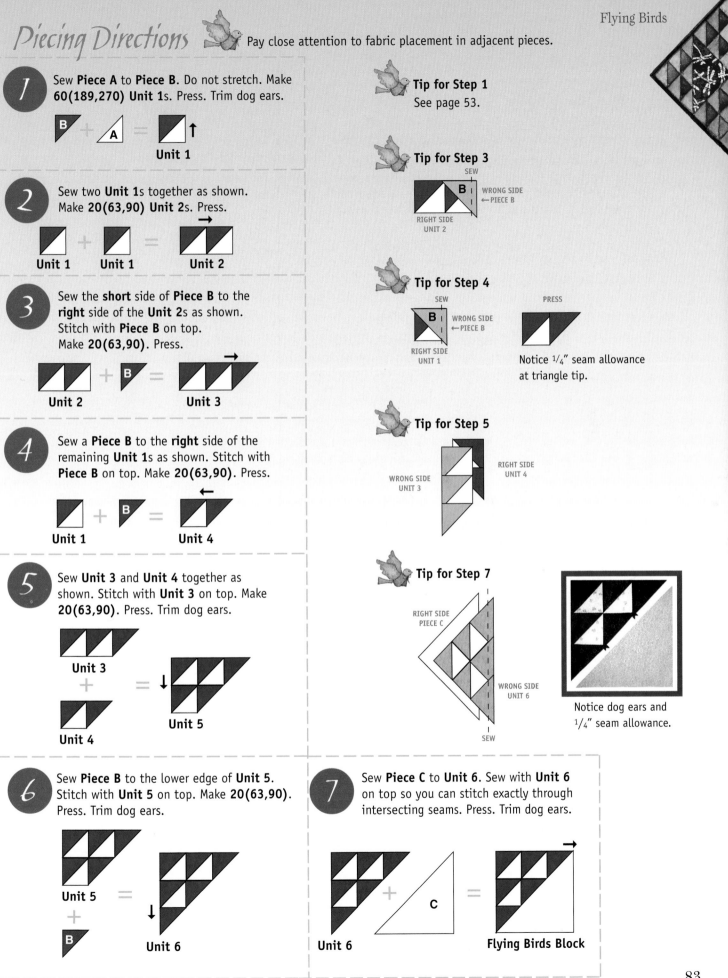

1 Sew **Piece A** to **Piece B**. Do not stretch. Make **60(189,270) Unit 1**s. Press. Trim dog ears.

B + A = ↑
Unit 1

2 Sew two **Unit 1**s together as shown. Make **20(63,90) Unit 2**s. Press.

Unit 1 + Unit 1 = → Unit 2

3 Sew the **short** side of **Piece B** to the **right** side of the **Unit 2**s as shown. Stitch with **Piece B** on top. Make **20(63,90)**. Press.

Unit 2 + B = → Unit 3

4 Sew a **Piece B** to the **right** side of the remaining **Unit 1**s as shown. Stitch with **Piece B** on top. Make **20(63,90)**. Press.

Unit 1 + B = ← Unit 4

5 Sew **Unit 3** and **Unit 4** together as shown. Stitch with **Unit 3** on top. Make **20(63,90)**. Press. Trim dog ears.

Unit 3 + Unit 4 = ↓ Unit 5

6 Sew **Piece B** to the lower edge of **Unit 5**. Stitch with **Unit 5** on top. Make **20(63,90)**. Press. Trim dog ears.

Unit 5 + B = ↓ Unit 6

7 Sew **Piece C** to **Unit 6**. Sew with **Unit 6** on top so you can stitch exactly through intersecting seams. Press. Trim dog ears.

Unit 6 + C = → Flying Birds Block

Tip for Step 1
See page 53.

Tip for Step 3

SEW
B WRONG SIDE ← PIECE B
RIGHT SIDE UNIT 2

Tip for Step 4

SEW
B WRONG SIDE ← PIECE B
RIGHT SIDE UNIT 1

PRESS

Notice $1/4''$ seam allowance at triangle tip.

Tip for Step 5

WRONG SIDE UNIT 3
RIGHT SIDE UNIT 4

Tip for Step 7

RIGHT SIDE PIECE C
WRONG SIDE UNIT 6
SEW

Notice dog ears and $1/4''$ seam allowance.

Quilt Assembly

◆ Lay out the quilt in rows of **4(7,9)** across and **5(9,10)** down.

◆ Experiment with different arrangements of the diagonally divided Flying Birds blocks before deciding on a final setting. The diagrams here and on pages 33 and 91 show a few models for block layout, but the possibilites are as boundless as your imagination.

◆ After choosing a setting design, follow the instructions on pages 136–137 for sewing the blocks and rows together. Press.

◆ Follow the instructions on page 138 for adding borders.

Finishing the Quilt

◆ Follow the instructions on pages 138–139 for making the quilt sandwich.

◆ Follow the instructions on page 139 for basting the quilt.

◆ See pages 138–139 for information on quilting.

◆ Follow the instructions on page 140 for binding the quilt.

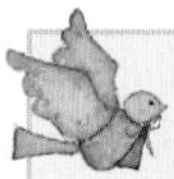

If you choose a setting where the small triangle units of adjacent blocks intersect, adjust the pressing plan so seams will butt nicely. Make a plan on paper first. Depending on your setting, a circular pattern within the block might work. (See Hen and Chicks, page 79.) Or you may need to press half the blocks as shown in the diagrams and half the opposite direction.

Myrna Giesbrecht's book *Press for Success* (That Patchwork Place, 1999) presents a thorough guide to pressing plans.

Broken Diamond Setting

Wild Goose Chase Setting

Asymmetrical Barn Raising Setting

Light Star Setting

Dark Star Setting

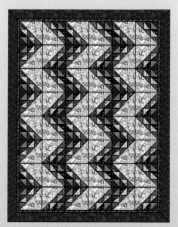

Streak of Lightning Setting

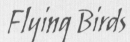

Flying Birds

God Gave Us Bluebirds for Happiness, 77" x 95"
9" blocks (63), two plain borders
Cindy Provencher, Duluth, MN

Cindy machine quilted each row of her flying birds before assembling the entire quilt. Cindy read The Quiltmaker's Gift *to first and second grade students at Laura MacArthur and Stowe elementary schools. They hope to follow the traveling exhibit of Quilts from* The Quiltmaker's Gift *via postcards returned to them from exhibition locations.*

Pattern tester Claudia Dodge lays out a trial Flying Birds block before assembly.

Northwind

Northwind, 33 ¹/₂" x 33 ¹/₂"
6" blocks (16), two inner borders,
piping strip, plain outer border

Barb Engelking, Superior, WI
quilted by Claudia Clark Myers,
Duluth, MN

Northwind

Brackman/BlockBase Number: 3162
Earliest publication date: Early 1900s (Hearth and Home)
Alternate names: Simple Design, Corn and Beans

Originally called Simple Design, this equal diagonal block is closely related to the traditional Corn and Beans block, page 118, which looks like a quartet of smaller Northwind blocks.

Although this block has more pieces than previous patterns, its construction uses the same principles. Beginners will get more practice piecing triangles and making sharp points. The challenging aspect of this pattern is design: choice and placement of fabrics within the block and arrangement of blocks within the quilt.

Traditionally a two-color block, modern quilters often interpret Northwind in multiple colors, while maintaining the light/dark value contrast. Barb McKeever's scrappy Northwind (page 88) is a good example. Barb Engelking experimented with less contrast, using a range of medium values in her version (opposite) to create a low contrast but lively Northwind interpretation. Yellow lemons provide a random "light" background and the neutral black and white stripe boldly frames and contains the forces of nature.

The traditional setting of Northwind turns the blocks so that all the dark triangles face in the same direction—to indicate the movement of the wind. But since Northwind is a diagonally divided block, you can use any of the setting options for Log Cabin and other diagonal light/dark blocks. See pages 33, 84, and 91 for ideas or make up a design of your own.

See pages 33, 84, and 91 for ideas

Artist's Secrets

The name of this block emphasizes the misery of sleeping outside, which the homeless do in all parts of the world and all sorts of climates. I didn't want kids to mistake sleeping on the cobblestones with camping out for the fun of it. No wonder the quiltmaker is so intent on giving her quilts to those who truly need shelter from the north wind.

Quiltmaker's Design Challenges

◆ To create a unified scrappy look, use several different darks for the Bs and several different lights for the As. Or use two color families.

◆ Gail chose a blue/purple Amish effect for her illustration block. How would you portray the north wind in fabric color and texture?

◆ Incorporate geometrics to jazz up your quilt.

◆ Stretch your color boundaries with an unusual (for you) color scheme: brick red and brown, olive and eggplant, pale mango and mint, black and red.

◆ Make up a creative setting of your own by experimenting with block placement and rotation on your design wall.

◆ Echo the block in a pieced border. Use a scrappy single or double strip of adjacent triangles, or create a 3-color border of diagonal triangle strips.

◆ Make miniature Northwind blocks and set them on point in an inner or outer border.

◆ For your quilting, consider an overall curved design (waves, scrolls) to simulate the wind.

◆ Make a computer quilt (page 91). Experiment with fabric color and placement within the Nortwind block. Then try out a whole host of setting options. When you find a design combination you love, print it out and take it with you fabric shopping—unless seeing it on screen is so satisfying you don't need to make it in cloth!

There she would wander the cobblestone streets until she came upon someone sleeping outside in the chill.

Barb Engelking owns Fabric Works, a quilt store specializing in contemporary fabrics, located in Superior, Wisconsin. On Thursday nights, area quilters gather in the shop to check out new fabrics for the week, show off their nearly-completed projects, consult with each other on new creative visions, and swap quilting experiences.

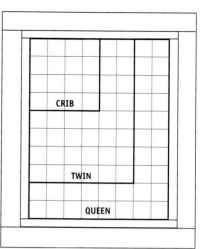

Quilt Information (finished size measurements)

	CRIB	TWIN	QUEEN
Quilt Size without Borders	36" x 36"	54" x 72"	72" x 90"
Quilt Size with Borders	48" x 48"	66" x 84"	84" x 102"
Block Size	9"	9"	9"
Number of Blocks	16	48	80
Block Layout	4 x 4	6 x 8	8 x 10
Backing Layout	← → ← →	↑ ↑ ↑	↑ ↓ ↑ ↑ ↑

Fabric Requirements (42-45" wide, in yards)

	CRIB	TWIN	QUEEN
Fabric 1, **Light**—Pieces A & C	1 1/8	2 5/8	4
Fabric 2, **Assorted Mediums**—Piece B	5/8	1 3/4	2 1/2
Fabric 3, **Medium**—Piece D	5/8	1 1/4	1 7/8
Fabric 4, **Accent**—Inner Border	3/8	1/2	5/8
Fabric 5, **Focus**—Outer Border & Binding	1 3/8	1 3/4	2 1/4
Backing Fabric	3	5	7 1/2

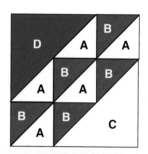

Northwind Block
#3162

Northwind

Southwest Up North, 51" x 63"
6" blocks (48), pinwheel setting
plain inner border, outer border with
four corner squares
Barbara McKeever, Duluth, MN
Deb Lussier Quinn, Superior, WI

Barb is one of the Thursday night regulars at Fabric Works. An enthusiastic square dancer, she uses quilting fabrics to create her dosey-do-ing outfits and donates quilts to the group to use as fund-raisers.

Cutting Instructions

	CRIB	TWIN	QUEEN
Fabric 1, Light—Piece A			
Cut strips 3 7/8" x width of fabric	4	12	20
☐ Crosscut into 3 7/8" squares	40	120	200
◩ Crosscut diagonally once into half-square triangles	80	240	400
Fabric 1, Light—Piece C			
Cut strips 6 7/8" x width of fabric	2	5	8
☐ Crosscut into 6 7/8" squares	8	24	40
◩ Crosscut diagonally once into half-square triangles	16	48	80
Fabric 2, Assorted Mediums—Piece B			
Cut strips 3 7/8" x width of fabric	4	12	20
☐ Crosscut into 3 7/8" squares	40	120	200
◩ Crosscut diagonally once into half-square triangles	80	240	400
Fabric 3, Medium—Piece D			
Cut strips 6 7/8" x width of fabric	2	5	8
☐ Crosscut into 6 7/8" squares	8	24	40
◩ Crosscut diagonally once into half-square triangles	16	48	80
Fabric 4, Accent—Inner Border			
Cut strips 1 1/2" x width of fabric	4	7	9
Fabric 5, Focus— Outer Border			
Cut strips 5 1/2" x width of fabric	5	7	9
Fabric 5, Focus— Binding			
Cut strips 2 1/4" x width of fabric	6	8	10

Barb auditions border fabrics for Jennifer's Friendship Star quilt.

Barb offers an adventurous fabric to a timid quilter.

Words of wisdom from the quilt shop

In her foolproof formula for choosing fabrics, Fabric Works owner and award-winning quiltmaker Barb Engelking recommends these steps to beginning quilters:

◆ Start with a focus fabric you really love—a floral, an abstract, a novelty print, an international fabric. Choose a fabric with many colors and shades in the design.

◆ Select several coordinating fabrics in colors that appear in the focus fabric. Don't overmatch the color! Variation is what gives the quilt its liveliness. Unless they are complements to the main colors in the focus fabric, do not use colors that appear in very small quantities.

◆ Use the color wheel to identify complementary accents.

◆ Include additional prints as well as fabrics that look like solids (tone-on-tones, batiks, hand-dyes).

◆ Pay attention to value contrast as well as color. Always add a very deep dark along with mediums and lights.

◆ Look for variety in scale and texture among your fabrics.

◆ Ask for help! Quilt shop workers and other customers love to give their opinions!

Barb's greatest delight as a quilt shop owner is helping customers pick out fabrics for their quilts. The next most fun for her is seeing works in progress or finished products when quilters bring their projects back. Take your finished top to your quilt shop and show it off!

Piecing Directions

Pin all intersections before stitching. For precision points, sew directly through the intersecting seams at triangle points.

1 Sew **Piece A** to **Piece B**. Make **48(144,240)**. Press. Trim dog ears. Set aside **16(48,80) Unit 1**s to be used in **Step 5**.

B + A = **Unit 1**

2 Sew **Piece A** to the dark side of **32(96,160) Unit 1**s as shown. Press. Trim dog ears. Set aside **16(48,80) Unit 2**s to be used in **Step 4**.

A + **Unit 1** = **Unit 2**

3 Sew **Piece B** to the light side of the remaining **16(48,80) Unit 2**s as shown. Press. Trim dog ears.

Unit 2 + B = **Unit 3**

4 Pin **Unit 2** to **Unit 3** with **Unit 2** on top, tips of triangles in each unit hanging over the edge at top and bottom. Stitch. Make **16(48,80)**. Press. Trim dog ears.

Unit 2 + **Unit 3** = **Unit 4**

To sew Unit 4
SEW
UNIT 3 RIGHT SIDE
UNIT 2 WRONG SIDE

5 Sew remaining **Piece B**s to the light side of remaining **Unit 1**s as shown. Make **16(48,80)**. Press. Trim dog ears.

Unit 1 + B = **Unit 5**

6 Pin **Unit 4** to **Unit 5** as shown with **Unit 4** on top, tips of triangles in each unit hanging over the edge at top and bottom. Stitch. Press. Trim dog ears.

To sew Unit 6
SEW
UNIT 5 RIGHT SIDE
UNIT 4 WRONG SIDE

Unit 4 + **Unit 5** = **Unit 6**

7 Pin **Piece C** to the dark edge of **Unit 6** with **Unit 6** on top so intersections of triangle points are visible. Tips of **Piece C** triangles hang over both ends. Stitch. Make **16(48,80)**. Press. Trim dog ears.

Unit 6 + C = **Unit 7**

8 Pin **Piece D** to the light edge of **Unit 7** with **Unit 7** on top so intersections are visible. Tips of **Piece D** hang over edges. Stitch. Make **16(48,80)**. Press. Trim dog ears.

D + **Unit 7** = **Northwind Block**

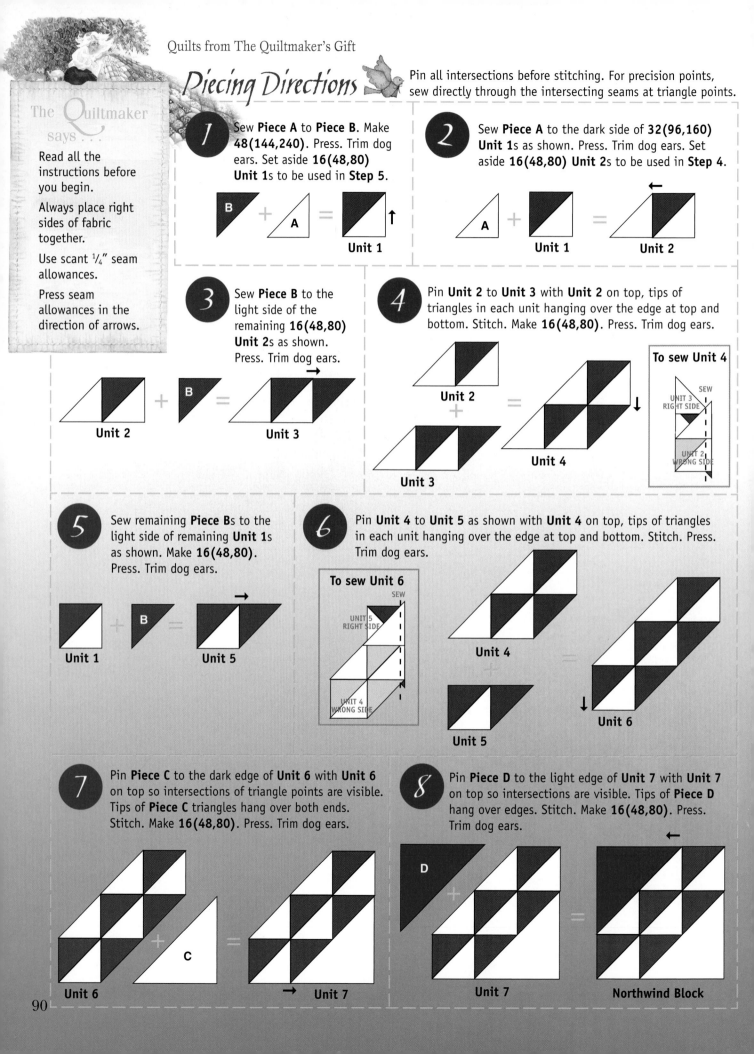

Quilt Assembly

◆ Since this is a diagonal block, there are many intriguing setting options. Study the examples shown here and on pages 33 and 84 for design ideas.

◆ Lay out the blocks in rows **4(6,8)** across and **4(8,10)** down. Rotate the blocks as needed, experimenting with different designs until you are satisfied. If possible, use a design wall as described on page 131.

◆ Sew the blocks and rows together following the instructions on pages 136–137. Press.

◆ Follow the instructions on page 138 for adding borders.

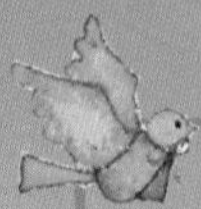

Finishing the Quilt

◆ Follow the instructions on pages 138–139 for making the quilt sandwich.

◆ Follow the instructions on page 139 for basting the quilt.

◆ Refer to pages 138–139 for information on quilting.

◆ Follow the instructions on page 140 for binding the quilt.

Computer programs such as Electric Quilt, QuiltPro, and PCQuilt let you play around with block settings to your heart's content. Try out all the traditional settings or experiment with random and/or orderly block rotation and placement to create your own unique version.

Kids love this magical approach to individualized quilt design.

The Northwind settings on this page were created in less than an hour with Electric Quilt.

Medallion Setting

Pinwheel Setting

Crossroads Setting

Follow the Leader

I'd Rather Lead, 49" x 58"
10" blocks (20), two mitered borders

Joanne Larsen Line, Duluth, MN
Karen McTavish, Duluth, MN

When I first imagined the king with his thousand soldiers, I pictured a much more fearsome monarch. The sheer difficulty of creating the effect of a thousand soldiers changed the image to a demanding king whose soldiers followed in single file. They do what the king orders, but with a bit of an, "Oh, no! Here we go again!" attitude. So Follow the Leader was a perfect block to represent that bit of the story.

Follow the Leader

Brackman/BlockBase Number: 1856
Earliest publication date: 1929 (Finley)
Alternate names: Crazy Ann, Twist & Turn

This old block with a decidedly contemporary flair is another member of the Shoo Fly family: an uneven nine-patch with an underlying 5 x 5 grid. Construction is similar to Hen and Chicks (page 77), but the internal sashing-strip rectangles are divided into triangles that create a whole new design where they connect with the corner blocks. Follow the Leader introduces an easy technique for making half-rectangle triangles that is similar to the corner triangle method described in True Lover's Knot (page 37).

Traditionally, this quilt used a light background and several fabrics of the same value for the other pieces, resulting in a scrappy two-color pinwheel look. The instructions here call for three values to add depth to the half-rectangle triangle blades.

The challenges of this block are in choosing fabrics to create the illusion of movement and in keeping the orientation of pieces correct during assembly. Even beginners will be successful if they follow the diagrams closely. Make a sample block first for reference and to test color/value combinations.

Quiltmaker's Design Challenges

◆ This snappy block begs for jazzy fabrics—bold colors, abstracts, geometrics, novelties.

◆ Experiment with fabric choice (value, color, texture, scale) and placement to maximize the feeling of movement within each block and between adjacent blocks. How can you represent fabrics following the leader around the block or around the quilt?

◆ Create a Follow the Leader pattern over the whole quilt top by graduating values/colors in some overall pattern or working around the color wheel in adjacent blocks.

◆ Repeat one of the elements from the block in a pieced border: rotate corner blocks around the quilt or piece divided rectangles end to end in a pleasing pattern.

For her border, Joanne used a vibrant piece of fabric designed by Diana Leone and made most of the blocks from a multi-color pointillist fabric. Notice the touch of purple. Karen incorporated neon rayon, variegated Sulky, and cotton threads in her stippling, free motion, and stitch-in-the-ditch quilting.

"Bring me a horse and a thousand soldiers." And they set off in search of the quiltmaker.

Quilt Information (finished size measurements)

	CRIB	TWIN	QUEEN
Quilt Size without Borders	30" x 40"	60" x 80"	80" x 100"
Quilt Size with Borders	42" x 52"	72" x 92"	92" x 112"
Block Size	10"	10"	10"
Number of Blocks	12	48	80
Block Layout	3 x 4	6 x 8	8 x 10
Backing Layout			

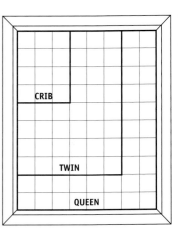

Fabric Requirements (42-45" wide, in yards)

	CRIB	TWIN	QUEEN
Fabric 1, **Light**—Pieces A & B	1	3 1/8	5 1/8
Fabric 2, **Medium**—Piece C & Inner Border	3/4	1 5/8	2 3/8
Fabric 3, **Medium**—Piece D	5/8	1 7/8	3
Fabric 4, **Focus**—Piece E, Outer Border & Binding	1 3/4	4	5 1/2
Backing Fabric	2 2/3	5 1/2	8 1/4

Follow the Leader Block #1856

Cutting Instructions

	CRIB	TWIN	QUEEN
Fabric 1, Light—Piece A			
Cut strips 2 7/8" x width of fabric	4	15	25
☐ Crosscut into 2 7/8" squares	48	192	320
◩ Crosscut diagonally once into half-square triangles	96	384	640
Fabric 1, Light—Piece B			
Cut strips 2 1/2" x width of fabric	6	24	40
☐ Crosscut into 2 1/2" x 4 1/2" rectangles	48	192	320
Fabric 2, Medium—Piece C			
Cut strips 2 1/2" x width of fabric	4	15	25
☐ Crosscut into 2 1/2" squares	60	240	400
Fabric 2, Medium—Inner Border			
Cut strips 1 1/2" x width of fabric	4	8	10
Fabric 3, Medium—Piece D			
Cut strips 4 7/8" x width of fabric	3	12	20
☐ Crosscut into 4 7/8" squares	24	96	160
◩ Crosscut diagonally once into half-square triangles	48	192	320
Fabric 4, Focus—Piece E			
Cut strips 2 1/2" x width of fabric	6	24	40
☐ Crosscut into 2 1/2" x 4 1/2" rectangles	48	192	320
Fabric 4, Focus—Outer Border			
Cut strips 5 1/2" x width of fabric	5	9	11
Fabric 4, Focus—Binding			
Cut strips 2 1/4" x width of fabric	6	9	11

Follow the Leader

Marching to the Beat of My Own Drummer, 87" x 100"
10" blocks (50) on point, sashing & cornerstones
plain inner border, pieced outer border
Jessica Torvinen, Duluth, MN

Piecing Directions

Placement of pieces in this block is tricky. Lay out pieces and check diagrams carefully before sewing.

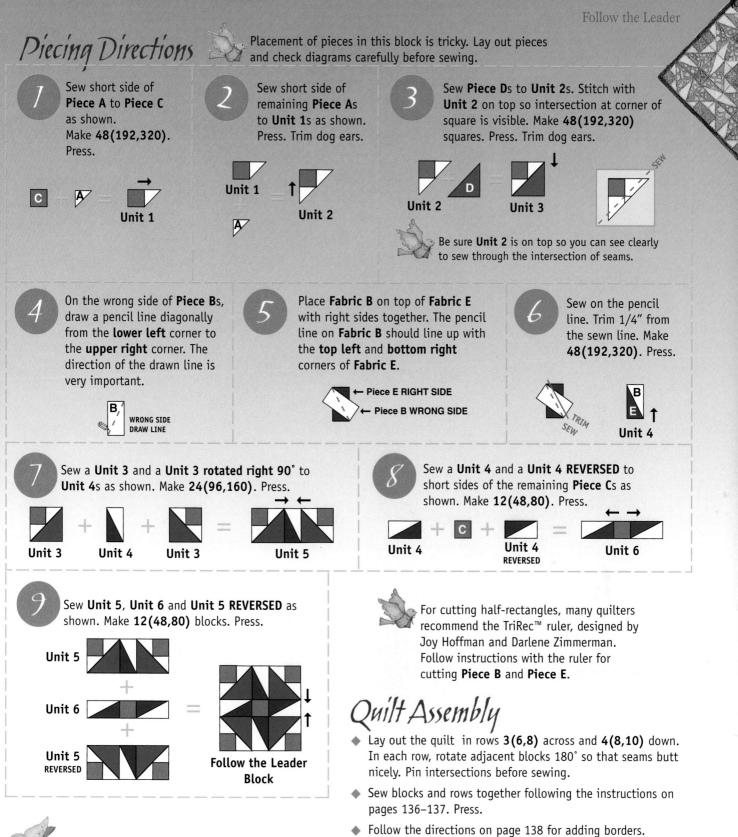

1 Sew short side of **Piece A** to **Piece C** as shown. Make **48(192,320)**. Press.

C + A = Unit 1

2 Sew short side of remaining **Piece A**s to **Unit 1**s as shown. Press. Trim dog ears.

Unit 1   Unit 2

3 Sew **Piece D**s to **Unit 2**s. Stitch with **Unit 2** on top so intersection at corner of square is visible. Make **48(192,320)** squares. Press. Trim dog ears.

Unit 2 + D   Unit 3   SEW

Be sure **Unit 2** is on top so you can see clearly to sew through the intersection of seams.

4 On the wrong side of **Piece B**s, draw a pencil line diagonally from the **lower left** corner to the **upper right** corner. The direction of the drawn line is very important.

B   WRONG SIDE DRAW LINE

5 Place **Fabric B** on top of **Fabric E** with right sides together. The pencil line on **Fabric B** should line up with the **top left** and **bottom right** corners of **Fabric E**.

← Piece E RIGHT SIDE
← Piece B WRONG SIDE

6 Sew on the pencil line. Trim 1/4" from the sewn line. Make **48(192,320)**. Press.

TRIM SEW   B E   Unit 4

7 Sew a **Unit 3** and a **Unit 3 rotated right 90°** to **Unit 4**s as shown. Make **24(96,160)**. Press.

Unit 3 + Unit 4 + Unit 3 = Unit 5

8 Sew a **Unit 4** and a **Unit 4 REVERSED** to short sides of the remaining **Piece C**s as shown. Make **12(48,80)**. Press.

Unit 4 + C + Unit 4 REVERSED = Unit 6

9 Sew **Unit 5**, **Unit 6** and **Unit 5 REVERSED** as shown. Make **12(48,80)** blocks. Press.

Unit 5
+
Unit 6
+
Unit 5 REVERSED
=
Follow the Leader Block

For cutting half-rectangles, many quilters recommend the TriRec™ ruler, designed by Joy Hoffman and Darlene Zimmerman. Follow instructions with the ruler for cutting **Piece B** and **Piece E**.

Quilt Assembly

- Lay out the quilt in rows **3(6,8)** across and **4(8,10)** down. In each row, rotate adjacent blocks 180° so that seams butt nicely. Pin intersections before sewing.

- Sew blocks and rows together following the instructions on pages 136–137. Press.

- Follow the directions on page 138 for adding borders.

- To recreate the effect of Jessica's queen size quilt (opposite), see instructions for setting blocks on point, pages 136–137.

Finishing the Quilt

- Follow the instructions on pages 138-140 for making and basting the quilt sandwich, hand or machine quilting, and binding.

Jessica set her Follow the Leader blocks on point, with sashing strips and cornerstones between the blocks. She machine quilted the interior of the quilt on her regular sewing machine but used her mother's long arm industrial machine to quilt the border. Daughter of an award-winning quilter and an expert seamstress in her own right (she won prizes for two quilts the first time she entered the Minnesota Quilt Show), Jessica is passing on the tradition to her son Spencer (see pages 50–55).

Snail's Trail

Global Globetrotters, 59" x 69"
7 ¹/₂" blocks (30), sashing & cornerstones
two plain borders

Gail de Marcken, Ely, MN
quilted by Carolyn & Charles Peters, Woodbury, MN

Snail's Trail

Brackman/BlockBase Number: 2398
Earliest publication date: 1928 (Ladies Art Company #504)
Alternate names: Journey to California, Whirlagig, Ocean Wave

The meandering Snail's Trail is often confused with Monkey Wrench and Indiana Puzzle blocks (Brackman #2397), which have one less "turn" in the block. Their center four-patches are on point. All versions were traditionally set with alternate light and dark plain blocks, continuing the spiraling value trail.

The Snail's Trail block uses square-in-a-square construction, beginning with a four-patch and adding triangles on opposite sides to make a new outer square on each round. In the process, an illusion of curves is created from a series of straight lines.

The success of square-in-a-square blocks depends on sewing absolutely accurate scant $1/4$" seams. See page 131 for seam-testing instructions. This block introduces three new techniques:

◆ Cutting and piecing quarter-square triangles.

◆ Squaring up the block to a specific size at each round.

◆ Preserving sharp corners of squares when adding triangle frames.

Construction of Snail's Trail can be confusing. Watch color placement carefully. Make a color key for your fabrics before you start and keep it near your machine for easy reference. Use a design wall to play with the block rotations and interactions before deciding on a final setting.

Gail used sashings to separate her blocks, but the colors are so vibrant they seem to jump across the sashing and connect. Her imaginative contemporary interpretation of Snail's Trail has inspired more than one quilter to give this old favorite another try.

*Here and there and wherever the sun
warmed the earth, it was said she
made the prettiest quilts anyone
had ever seen.*

Artist's Secrets

I painted this pattern into the book because I had made a Snail's Trail quilt and loved the block and its color and design possibilities. After trying to grow flowers and vegetables in Latvia, I no longer feel so friendly towards snails and their garden manners.

Quiltmaker's Design Challenges

◆ Incorporate theme-related fabrics into the Snail's Trail: nautical motifs, flora and fauna, water prints.

◆ Feedsack prints and depression-era reproduction fabrics give an antique look to this quilt. In each block, make alternate trails of plain muslin and scrappy prints.

◆ How would you interpret Snail's Trail for a country look?

◆ Try the traditional alternate plain block setting. Choose fabrics that will hold their appeal in a unpieced 12" square. What pieced 12" blocks would complement Snail's Trail in an alternate block setting?

◆ Since this block begins with a four-patch, try an inner or outer border of four-patch blocks.

◆ A miniature Snail's Trail block would make a nice cornerpost for the outer border.

◆ Replicate the block pattern in miniature or larger scale in your quilting.

Quilt Information (finished size measurements)

	LAP	TWIN	DOUBLE/QUEEN
Quilt Size without Borders	36" x 48"	48" x 72"	72" x 96"
Quilt Size with Borders	48" x 60"	60" x 84"	84" x 108"
Finished Block Size	12"	12"	12"
Number of Blocks	12	24	48
Block Layout	3 x 4	4 x 6	6 x 8
Backing Layout			

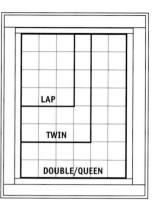

Fabric Requirements (42–45" wide, in yards)

	LAP	TWIN	DOUBLE/QUEEN
Fabric 1, **Light**—Pieces A, B, C, D & E	1 3/4	2 1/2	4 1/2
Fabric 2, **Dark**—Pieces F, G, H, I & J	1 3/4	2 1/2	4 1/2
Fabric 3, **Inner Border**	1/2	5/8	3/4
Fabric 4, **Outer Border & Binding**	1 1/2	1 7/8	2 1/4
Backing Fabric	3 1/8	5 1/8	8

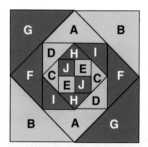

Snail's Trail Block
#2398

Snail's Trail

Autumn Stroll, 39" x 51"
12" blocks (12), two plain borders
Ann Degen, Hayward, WI
quilted by Rolinda Langham, Stone Lake, WI

Ann once owned a quilt shop in the Minneapolis/St. Paul area. Retired to northern Wisconsin, she now teaches quilting in the two-state area and indulges her love of country fabrics.

Cutting Instructions

	LAP	TWIN	DOUBLE/QUEEN
Fabric 1, Light, Piece A			
Cut strips 7 1/4" x width of fabric	2	3	5
☐ Crosscut into 7 1/4" squares	6	12	24
☒ Crosscut diagonally twice into quarter-square triangles	24	48	96
Fabric 1, Light, Piece B			
Cut strips 6 7/8" x width of fabric	3	5	10
☐ Crosscut into 6 7/8" squares	12	24	48
◩ Crosscut diagonally once into half-square triangles	24	48	96
Fabric 1, Light, Piece C			
Cut strips 4 1/4" x width of fabric	1	2	3
☐ Crosscut into 4 1/4" squares	6	12	24
☒ Crosscut diagonally twice into quarter-square triangles	24	48	96
Fabric 1, Light, Piece D			
Cut strips 3 7/8" x width of fabric	2	3	5
☐ Crosscut into 3 7/8" squares	12	24	48
◩ Crosscut diagonally once into half-square triangles	24	48	96
Fabric 1, Light, Piece E			
Cut strips 2" x width of fabric	2	3	5
Fabric 2, Dark, Piece F			
Cut strips 7 1/4" x width of fabric	2	3	5
☐ Crosscut into 7 1/4" squares	6	12	24
☒ Crosscut diagonally twice into quarter-square triangles	24	48	96
Fabric 2, Dark, Piece G			
Cut strips 6 7/8" x width of fabric	3	5	10
☐ Crosscut into 6 7/8" squares	12	24	48
◩ Crosscut diagonally once into half-square triangles	24	48	96
Fabric 2, Dark, Piece H			
Cut strips 4 1/4" x width of fabric	1	2	3
☐ Crosscut into 4 1/4" squares	6	12	24
☒ Crosscut diagonally twice into quarter-square triangles	24	48	96
Fabric 2, Dark, Piece I			
Cut strips 3 7/8" x width of fabric	2	3	5
☐ Crosscut into 3 7/8" squares	12	24	48
◩ Crosscut diagonally once into half-square triangles	24	48	96
Fabric 2, Dark, Piece J			
Cut strips 2" x width of fabric	2	3	5
Fabric 3, Inner Border			
Cut strips 2 1/2" x width of fabric	5	7	9
Fabric 4, Outer Border			
Cut strips 5" x width of fabric	6	8	10
Fabric 4, Binding			
Cut strips 2 1/4" x width of fabric	6	8	10

When measuring to cut **Piece F**, 7 1/4" squares for quarter-square triangles, use a 12" ruler or two narrower rulers side by side.

Piecing Directions

Accurate $1/4$" seams are essential. Be sure to measure and square up the block each round.

1 Sew **Piece E** to **Piece J**. Make **2(3,5)** strip sets. Press.

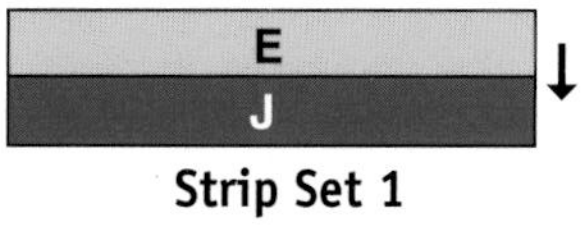

E
J
Strip Set 1

2 Crosscut **Strip Set 1** into 2" segments. Make **24(48,96)**. Press.

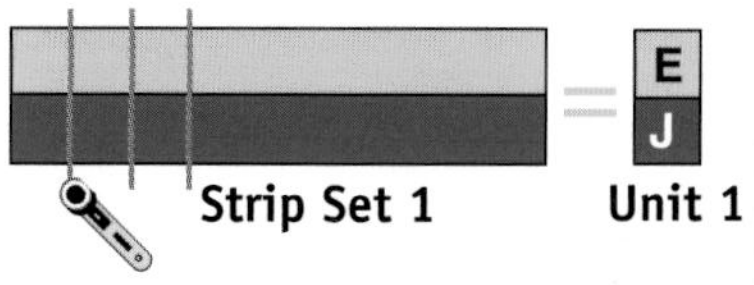

Strip Set 1   E J = **Unit 1**

3 Sew four-patches using **Unit 1**s. Make **12(24,48)**. Press.

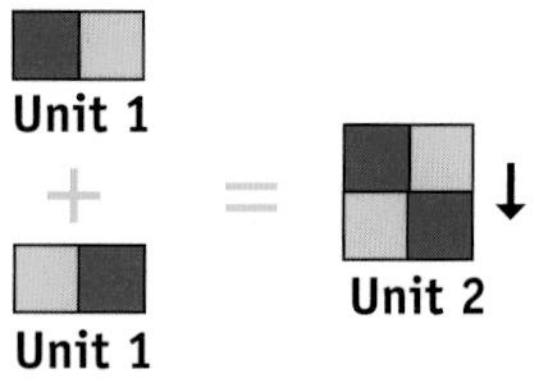

Unit 1
+
Unit 1
=
Unit 2

4 Sew **Piece H**s to top and bottom of **Unit 2** as shown. Make **12(24,48)**. Press. Do not trim dog ears.

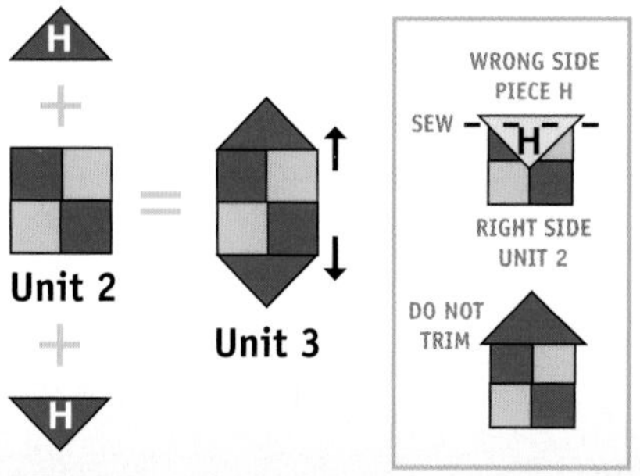

H
+
Unit 2
=
Unit 3
+
H

WRONG SIDE PIECE H
SEW — H
RIGHT SIDE UNIT 2
DO NOT TRIM

Watch fabric placement carefully so each Snail's Trail spirals outward.

5 Sew **Piece C**s to sides of **Unit 3** as shown. Press outward. Trim block to 4 $3/4$". Preserve seam allowance at center point of each edge.

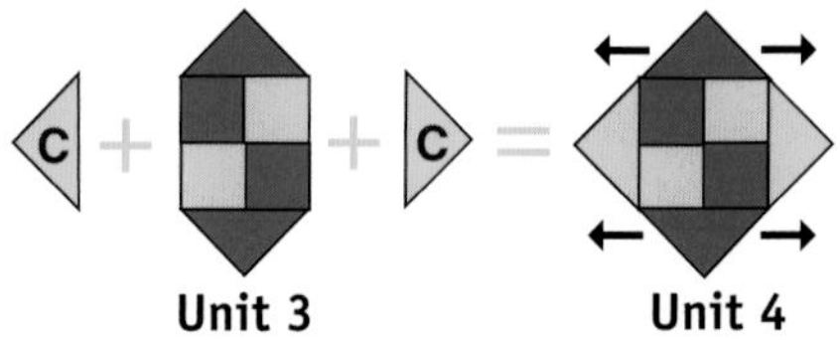

C + **Unit 3** + C = **Unit 4**

In **Steps 5–11**, place the triangle you are adding on the bottom, so intersecting seams of the previous round are visible on top. Stitch precisely through the intersection.

6 Sew **Piece I**s to top and bottom of **Unit 4** as shown. Stitch with **Unit 4** on top to view intersection. Press outward. Trim block to 6 $1/2$".

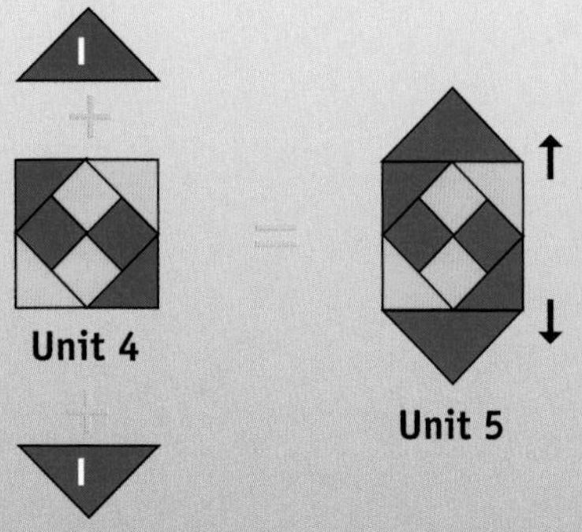

I
+
Unit 4
=
Unit 5
+
I

7 Sew **Piece D**s to sides of **Unit 5** as shown. Stitch with **Unit 5** on top to view intersection. Press. Preserve seam allowance at center point on each edge.

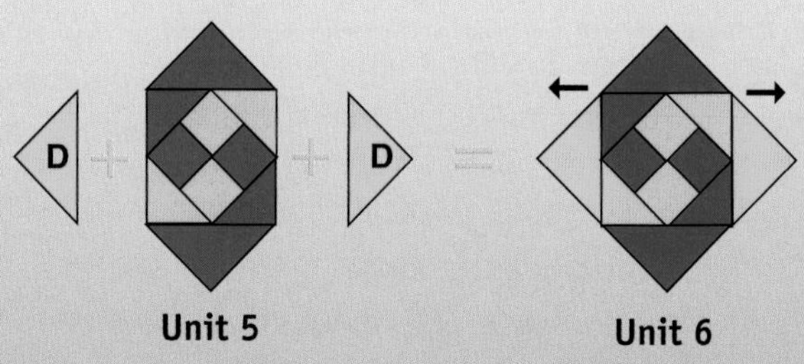

D + **Unit 5** + D = **Unit 6**

8 Sew **Piece F**s to top and bottom of **Unit 6** as shown. Press. Do not trim.

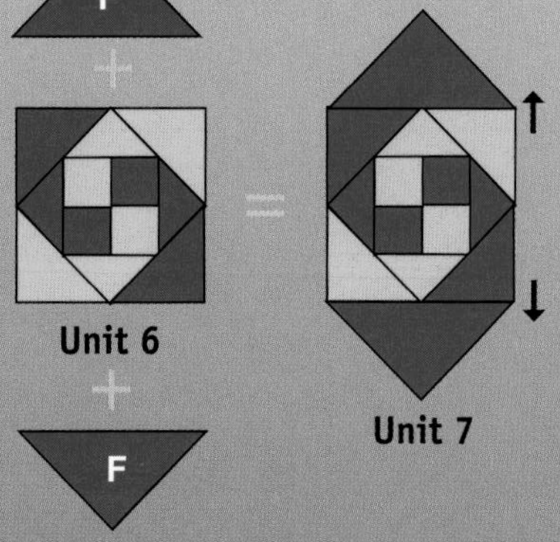

F
+
Unit 6
=
Unit 7
+
F

9 Sew **Piece A**s to sides of **Unit 7** as shown. Stitch with **Unit 7** on top. Press. Trim square to 9". Preserve seam allowances.

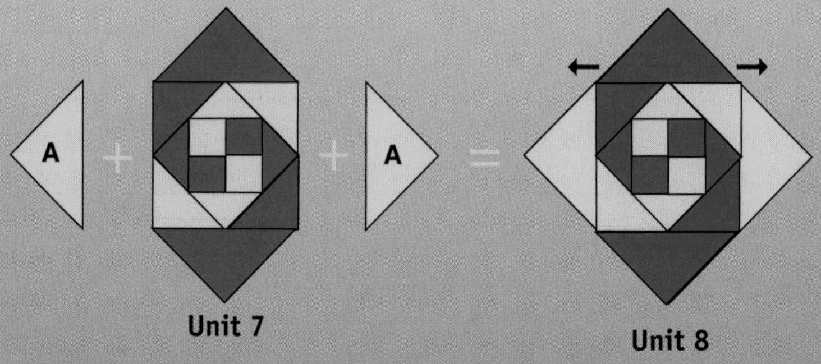

A + **Unit 7** + A = **Unit 8**

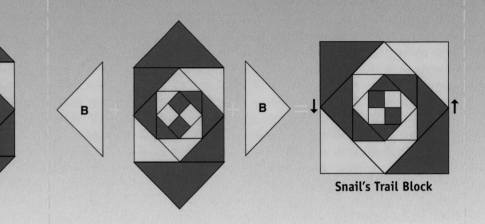

10 Sew **Piece G**s to top and bottom of **Unit 8** as shown. Press. Do not trim.

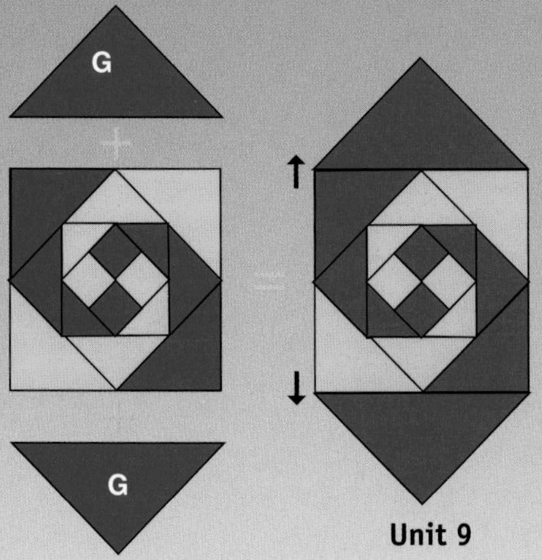

11 Sew **Piece B**s to sides of **Unit 9** as shown. Stitch with **Unit 9** on top. Press. Trim block to 12 ¹/₂" square, preserving seam allowances. Make **12(24,48)** blocks.

Unit 9

Snail's Trail Block

Quilt Assembly

◆ Lay out the blocks **3(4,6)** across and **4(6,8)** down, rotating blocks so Snail's Trails of the same fabric/value connect at their widest points.

◆ To add lattice strips and cornerstones between blocks, see pages 136–137.

◆ Follow the instructions on pages 136–137 for sewing the blocks and rows together.

◆ Follow the instructions on page 138 for adding borders.

Finishing the Quilt

◆ Follow the instructions on pages 138–139 for making the quilt sandwich.

◆ Follow the instructions on page 139 for basting the quilt.

◆ Refer to pages 138–139 for information on quilting.

◆ Follow the instructions on page 140 for binding the quilt.

Julie Ford uses extreme measures to cut giant quarter-square triangles for a jumbo Snail's Trail.

Geese Over Africa, 78" x 100"
6"x 3" blocks (180), sashings
two mitered borders

Toni Gotelaere, Superior, WI
quilted by Helen Smith Prekker,
Duluth, MN

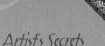

Living in the mystical mountains, a quiltmaker would surely know and love the geese flying over her cabin. I resisted the overpowering temptation to have the quiltmaker cut pieces out of the geese, not just the sky. My environmental biologist daughter never would have approved. There is another subtle message in the placement of this pattern. As the king embarks on his Wild Goose Chase for happiness, the quiltmaker is already tying her Spider Web quilt of generosity to capture his heart.

Wild Goose Chase

Brackman/BlockBase Number: 480
Earliest publication date: 1898 (Ladies Art Company #94)
Earliest examples: 1775-1800
Alternate names: Birds in Flight, Wild Geese Flying, Geese in Flight

The rectangular Flying Geese unit is one of the basic components used in more complicated quilt blocks such as Toad in the Puddle, Robbing Peter to Pay Paul, and Corn and Beans. One of many versions of Wild Goose Chase, this historic pattern makes a strip quilt, combining long strips of pieced Flying Geese units with alternate plain strips. The original pattern used an equilateral triangle for the goose rather than the easier isosceles triangle version described here.

Flying Geese are easy to make using the same stitch and fold corner triangle used in True Lover's Knot (page 37). The challenge comes in sewing the units together. For perfect points, keep the piece with the center point on top as you stitch so you can see clearly to sew through the intersection of the two background seams. Sewing through this intersection is more important than maintaining a perfect $1/4$" seam. Also, be sure the center points of your geese line up straight as you assemble the strips.

Quiltmaker's Design Challenges

◆ Try using a border print divided lengthwise for sashing and borders. Choose your Flying Geese colors from the colors in your sashing. Don't forget to include a few of the darkest color! Adding a few complementary color accent geese will give your quilt a bit of zing.

◆ Consider making a pieced border of geese flying sideways at the top and bottom of your quilt.

◆ Flying Geese make an excellent frame for the central motif in a medallion quilt. Arrange units so they follow each other around the medallion in clockwise or counterclockwise direction.

◆ Make a historically accurate version of this quilt with equilateral triangle Flying Geese.

Toni made this dynamic quilt from fabric collected by Nancy Loving Tubesing during a trip to South Africa. Toni is famous for incorporating vibrant colors in nearly all of her quilts. An enthusiastic cheerleader for quilters of all skill levels, Toni is unofficial show-and-tell photographer. She always orders double prints and gives a copy to the quiltmaker.

"Somewhere there must be one beautiful thing that will finally make me happy,"
he was often heard to say.

Quilt Information (finished size measurements)

	LAP	TWIN	QUEEN
Quilt Size without Borders	42" x 54"	54" x 72"	66" x 90"
Quilt Size with Borders	56" x 68"	68" x 86"	80" x 104"
Block Size	6" x 3"	6" x 3"	6" x 3"
Number of Blocks	72	120	180
Block Layout	4 x 18 plus lattice	5 x 24 plus lattice	6 x 30 plus lattice
Backing Layout			

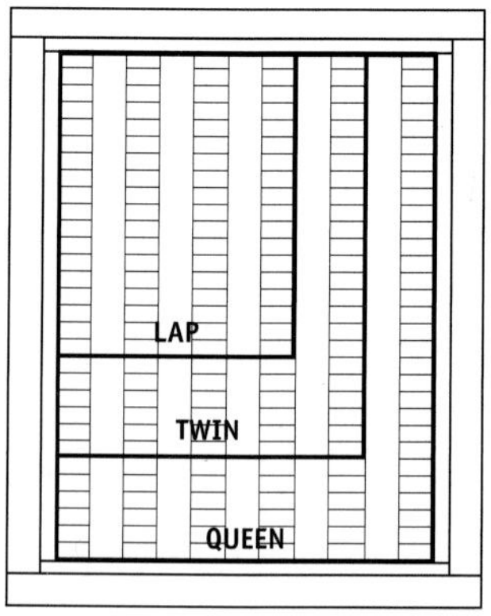

The Quiltmaker says . . .

Read all the instructions before you begin.

Always place right sides of fabric together for stitching.

Use scant ¼" seam allowances.

Press seam allowances in the direction of arrows.

There are many techniques for constructing Flying Geese blocks. The method outlined here is usually the easiest for beginners, but you may want to experiment with Geese-on-a-Grid paper piecing or with templates.

Fabric Requirements (42–45" wide, in yards)

	LAP	TWIN	QUEEN
Fabric 1, **Background**—Piece A	1 ½	2 ⅜	4 ¼
Fabric 2, **Assorted Mediums & Darks**—Piece B	1 ½	2 ¼	4 ⅛
Fabric 3, **Accent**—Inner Border	⅜	½	½
Fabric 4, **Focus**—Lattice, Outer Border & Binding	2 ¾	3 ⅜	6 ½
Backing Fabric	3 ½	5 ⅛	7 ¾

Flying Geese Unit #480

Cutting Instructions

	LAP	TWIN	QUEEN
Fabric 1, Background—Piece A			
Cut strips 3 ½" x width of fabric	13	22	33
☐ Crosscut into 3 ½" squares	144	240	360
Fabric 2, Geese—Piece B			
Cut strips 3 ½" x width of fabric	12	20	30
▭ Crosscut into 3 ½" x 6 ½" rectangles	72	120	180
Fabric 3, Accent—Inner Border			
Cut 1 ½" x width of fabric	6	7	9
Fabric 4, Binding			
Cut 2 ¼" x width of fabric	7	8	10
Cut these strips LENGTHWISE AFTER sewing and measuring Flying Geese Strips (Step 5)			
Fabric 4, Focus—Lattice Strips (cut fabric lengthwise)			
Cut strips 3 ½" x length of remaining fabric	3	4	5
Fabric 4, Focus—Top & Bottom Border Strips (cut fabric lengthwise)			
Cut strips 6 ½" x length of fabric	2	2	2
Fabric 4, Focus—Side Border Strips (cut fabric lengthwise)			
Cut strips 6 ½" x length of fabric	2	2	3

Toni Gotelaere's daughter Jan Peterson, a novice quilter, sewed the binding on her mom's Wild Goose Chase. Notice the surprisingly effective plaid backing.

Piecing Directions

For precision center and side points, always position pieces so intersections are visible when stitching.

1 Draw a pencil line corner to corner on the wrong side of **Piece A**.

2 Place **Piece A** on the left side of **Piece B** and sew on the line. Trim 1/4" from the line. Make **72(120,180)**. Press.

DISCARD
TRIM
SEW

A = B

← **Unit 1**

3 Place remaining **Piece A**s on the right side of **Unit 1** as shown. Sew on the pencil line. Trim 1/4" from the line. Make **72(120,180)** Flying Geese **Unit 2**s. Press. Trim dog ears.

B + A = A / DISCARD TRIM SEW =

Unit 1   **Unit 2**   **Unit 2** →

4 Sew **18(24,30) Unit 2**s in a strip. Stitch with center triangle intersection on top for precise points. Make **4(5,6)** strips. Press as you go.

CONTINUE TO 18(24,32)

Flying Geese Strip

5 Measure the completed **Flying Geese Strips**. The strips should measure approximately **54¹/₂"(72¹/₂",90¹/₂")**. Cut lattice strips to match the average length.

Quilt Assembly

◆ Lay out the **4(5,6) Flying Geese Strips**, alternated with the **3(4,5) Lattice Strips**, as shown on page 104.

◆ Pin and sew strips together with **Flying Geese Strips** on top, so triangle point intersections are visible. Stitch straight through the intersections for perfect side points.

◆ Reverse direction of sewing with each strip to prevent distortion. Ease in fullness as necessary.

◆ Follow the instructions on page 138 for adding borders. Adjust border measurements to match actual size of quilt top. Cut inner and outer borders to size. Assemble.

Finishing the Quilt

◆ Follow the instructions on pages 138–140 for making and basting the quilt sandwich, hand or machine quilting, and binding.

Wild Goose Chase

Gaggle of Jewels, 60" x 92"
6" x 3" blocks (130), four border-print sashings mitered border-print border
Carol Jean Brooks, Duluth, MN
quilted by Carolyn & Charles Peters, Woodbury, MN

Carol Jean chose a Jinny Beyer border print for sashings and borders, then raided her stash for a variety of coordinating fabrics in the teals and purples. Notice her color placement that represents various flocks of geese flying in V-formation.

Toad in a Puddle

Camouflage, 47" x 58"
12" blocks (12), plain inner border
outer border with square-in-a-square corners

Joanne Larsen Line, Duluth, MN
quilted by Angela Haworth, Superior, WI

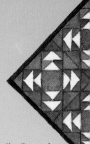

Toad in a Puddle

Brackman/BlockBase Number: 2797
Earliest publication date: 1898 (Ladies Art Company)
Alternate name: Rambler

Traditionally pieced as a two-color quilt, this block with a funky name begs for funky fabrics and a contemporary interpretation. The construction uses a variation of square-in-a-square technique—Flying Geese radiate out from the center square in a diagonal X.

The quilts shown here are adaptations of the historical Toad in a Puddle coloring. Gail's painted block reverses the traditional color scheme, creating an Amish-style dark two-tone. Joanne's quilt complicates the coloring to make intriguing secondary designs at the block intersections. Marcia (page 108) substituted a vibrant print with a partly-light background for the traditionally light center square. The pattern as outlined follows Joanne's innovative interpretation and adaptation.

In this adaptation of Toad in a Puddle, Joanne ventures around the tertiary color triad, including her usual purple! Angie quilted the border with her antique treadle sewing machine.

Artist's Secrets

I just loved the name of this pattern and tried to incorporate images of animals (and soldiers!) splashing in the water throughout the book. In painting the quilt block, I reversed the historical light and dark values for more visual impact. I guess that's what quiltmakers have always done—admire, imitate, adapt, and re-create. Before researching pattern history and names for The Quiltmaker's Gift, I never knew there was a RIGHT way to make a quilt block. Maybe there isn't!

Quiltmaker's Design Challenges

◆ Try a two-color quilt in some of the lovely reproduction fabrics.

◆ The central square/diamond of this block makes a perfect place to show off novelty prints.

◆ The use of black and white in a quilt dramatically changes the perspective and focal points. How could you use these neutrals effectively with the Toad in a Puddle block?

◆ How would an Amish quiltmaker interpret this pattern?

◆ Take an ugly fabric from your stash and create a Toad in a Puddle block that shows it off to advantage.

◆ The Flying Geese units create a secondary pattern over the entire quilt top. How could you use this quality to create more visual interest?

◆ Try using the Flying Geese element in your borders. An inner border of Flying Geese will set off both the quilt and a luscious outer border.

◆ How could you incorporate the square-in-a-square element of Toad in a Puddle in your borders?

. . . the king decided to go out into the world and find others who might be in need of his gifts.

107

Quilt Information (finished size measurements)

	CRIB	LAP	DOUBLE
Quilt Size without Borders	24" x 36"	36" x 48"	60" x 72"
Quilt Size with Borders	38" x 50"	50" x 62"	74" x 86"
Block Size	12"	12"	12"
Number of Blocks	6	12	30
Block Layout	2 x 3	3 x 4	5 x 6
Backing Layout	← → ← →	← → ← →	↓ ↓

Fabric Requirements (42-45" wide, in yards)

	CRIB	LAP	DOUBLE
Fabric 1, **Light**—Piece A	7/8	1 1/4	2 3/4
Fabric 2, **Medium**—Piece B	1/2	2/3	1 1/3
Fabric 3, **Medium**—Piece C	1/2	2/3	1 1/3
Fabric 4, **Focus**—Piece D	3/8	1/2	3/4
Fabric 5, **Light Accent**—Piece E	5/8	7/8	1 1/2
Fabric 6, **Medium Accent**—Piece F	1/2	5/8	7/8
Fabric 7, **Accent**—Inner Border	1/2	5/8	3/4
Fabric 8, **Focus**—Outer Border & Binding	1 1/8	1 3/4	2
Backing Fabric	2 1/2	3 1/8	5 1/8

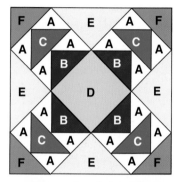

Toad in the Puddle Block
#2797

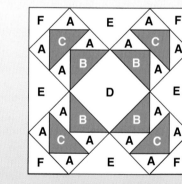

Toad in the Puddle Block
Historical Coloring

Toad in a Puddle

Frog and Toad Are Friends, 36" x 49"
12" blocks (6), sashing, one plain border
Marcia Bowker, Duluth, MN

An occupational therapist and ergonomics consultant to business and industry, Marcia does all her own machine quilting. Some of her favorite stretch prescriptions are described on pages 126–129. In her spare time, Marcia runs a small specialized garment business where she dyes silk scarves and creates custom quilted garments sold from her studio and at craft fairs.

Cutting Instructions

	CRIB	LAP	DOUBLE
Fabric 1, Light—Piece A			
Cut strips 2 $5/8$" x width of fabric	7	13	32
☐ Crosscut into 2 $5/8$" squares	96	192	480
Fabric 2, Medium—Piece B			
Cut strips 2 $5/8$" x width of fabric	3	6	15
▭ Crosscut into 2 $5/8$" x 4 $3/4$" rectangles	24	48	120
Fabric 3, Medium—Piece C			
Cut strips 2 $5/8$" x width of fabric	3	6	15
▭ Crosscut into 2 $5/8$" x 4 $3/4$" rectangles	24	48	120
Fabric 4, Focus—Piece D			
Cut strips 4 $3/4$" x width of fabric	1	2	4
☐ Crosscut into 4 $3/4$" squares	6	12	30
Fabric 5, Light Accent—Piece E			
Cut strips 7 $1/2$" x width of fabric	2	3	6
☐ Crosscut into 7 $1/2$" squares	5	12	30
⊠ Crosscut diagonally twice into quarter-square triangles	24	48	120
Fabric 6, Medium Accent—Piece F			
Cut strips 3 $7/8$" x width of fabric	2	3	6
☐ Crosscut into 3 $7/8$" squares	12	24	60
◿ Crosscut diagonally once into half-square triangles	24	48	120
Fabric 7, Accent—Inner Border			
Cut strips 2 $1/2$" x width of fabric	4	5	7
Fabric 8, Focus—Outer Border			
Cut strips 5 $1/2$" x width of fabric	4	7	8
Fabric 8, Focus—Binding			
Cut strips 2 $1/4$" x width of fabric	4	6	9

 When measuring to cut 7 $1/4$" squares for **Piece E**, use a 12" square ruler or two narrower rulers side by side.

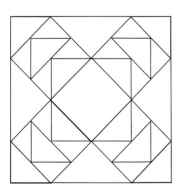

Design your own color scheme.

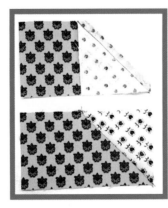

Stitch and fold triangle corners up close.

Flying Geese unit construction, Steps 1–5.

Piecing Directions

For sharp points at the head and wings of the Flying Geese unit, stitch exactly through the intersecting seams.

The Quiltmaker says...

Read all the instructions before you begin.

Always place right sides of fabric together for stitching.

Use scant ¼" seam allowances.

Press seam allowances in the direction of arrows.

1 Draw a pencil line corner to corner on the wrong side of all **Piece A**s.

2 Place **Piece A** on the left side of **Piece B**. Sew on the pencil line. Trim seam allowance to ¼" as shown. Make **24(48,120)**. Press.

TRIM SEW DISCARD | **A** = **B** **Unit 1**

3 Place another **Piece A** on the right side of **Unit 1** as shown. Sew on the pencil line. Trim 1/4" from the line. Make **24(48,120)** Flying Geese **Unit 2**s. Press. Trim dog ears.

B **Unit 1** + **A** = **A** **Unit 2** DISCARD TRIM SEW = **Unit 2**

4 To make **Unit 4**, repeat **Steps 1–3**, using **Piece C** and remaining **Piece A**s.

A. Place **Piece A** on the left corner of **Piece C** as shown. Sew on the pencil line. Trim seam allowance to ¼". Make **24(48,120)**. Press.

TRIM SEW DISCARD | **C** = **C** **Unit 3**

B. Place **Piece A** on the right corner of **Unit 3** as shown. Sew on the pencil line. Trim seam allowance to ¼". Press. Makes **24(48,120)**. Trim dog ears.

Unit 3 + **A** DISCARD TRIM SEW = **Unit 3** = **Unit 4**

5 Sew **Unit 2** and **Unit 4** together as shown. Stitch with triangle intersection on top for easy visibility. Make **24(48,120)** units. Press.

Unit 4 + **Unit 2** = **Unit 5**

6 Sew **Piece E**s to opposite sides of half the **Unit 5**s as shown. Stitch with **Unit 5** on top and tip of **Piece E** triangle extending beyond the edge. Stitch precisely through intersections. Make **12(24,60)**. Press. Trim dog ears.

E + **Unit 5** + **E** = ← **Unit 6** →

7 Sew **Piece F** to the top of **Unit 6** as shown. Stitch with **Unit 6** on top, both triangle tips of **Piece F** extending beyond the edges. Make **12(24,60)**. Press. Trim dog ears.

F + **Unit 6** = **Unit 7**

8 Sew remaining **Piece F**s to the top of remaining **Unit 5**s as shown. Make **12(24,60)**. Press.

F + **Unit 5** = **Unit 8**

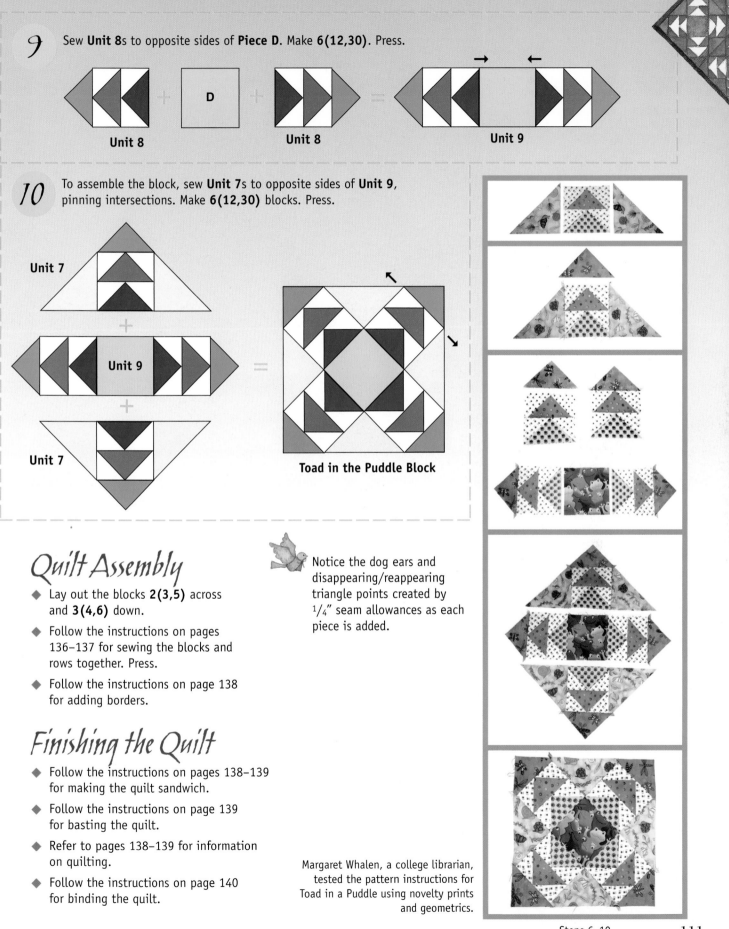

9 Sew **Unit 8**s to opposite sides of **Piece D**. Make **6(12,30)**. Press.

Unit 8   D   Unit 8   Unit 9

10 To assemble the block, sew **Unit 7**s to opposite sides of **Unit 9**, pinning intersections. Make **6(12,30)** blocks. Press.

Unit 7

Unit 9

Unit 7

Toad in the Puddle Block

Quilt Assembly

◆ Lay out the blocks **2(3,5)** across and **3(4,6)** down.

◆ Follow the instructions on pages 136–137 for sewing the blocks and rows together. Press.

◆ Follow the instructions on page 138 for adding borders.

Finishing the Quilt

◆ Follow the instructions on pages 138–139 for making the quilt sandwich.

◆ Follow the instructions on page 139 for basting the quilt.

◆ Refer to pages 138–139 for information on quilting.

◆ Follow the instructions on page 140 for binding the quilt.

Notice the dog ears and disappearing/reappearing triangle points created by $1/4$" seam allowances as each piece is added.

Margaret Whalen, a college librarian, tested the pattern instructions for Toad in a Puddle using novelty prints and geometrics.

Robbing Peter to Pay Paul

Rainbow Coalition, 61" x 71"
12" blocks (20), inner border, two pieced outer border

LaVonne Horner, Superior, WI
quilted by Bonnie Jusczak, Duluth, MN

Robbing Peter
to Pay Paul

Brackman/BlockBase Number: 1771
Earliest publication date: 1898 (Ladies Art Company #154)
Alternate names: Arizona

The Robbing Peter to Pay Paul block gets its name from the original two-color format where each square seems to "borrow" half of the adjacent square. When the blocks are set together, the pattern formed by four adjacent corners recreates the original central block in reverse coloring.

Most quilters are more familiar with the curving Drunkard's Path or Orange Peel pattern called Robbing Peter to Pay Paul. The equal nine-patch version Gail chose for *The Quiltmaker's Gift* is made from all the angular shapes used in this book—squares, rectangles, half-square triangles, and Flying Geese. Be sure to review the special instructions for cutting and assembling all these different units.

LaVonne, weaver-turned-quilter, is an accomplished fiber artist who specializes in fabric dying and fabric embellishment. She has written articles on this subject. LaVonne hand-dyed all the fabrics for this quilt. A meticulous piecer and color expert, LaVonne has won many prizes. Her one-of-a-kind creations are featured in several quilt books.

Artist's Secrets

I really like the symbolism of this block. The king was not at all pleased to have to "rob" himself to "pay" the poor. He had no idea about the wonderful benefit that the giver receives. The pattern has personal meaning as well. My husband and I are intimately familiar with the concept of Robbing Peter to Pay Paul—having finally put three kids through college!

Quiltmaker's Design Challenges

◆ Experiment with a variety of fabrics and placements to expand the visual potential of this block. Can you treat the four square corners in a way that creates a pleasing secondary pattern in the overall quilt?

◆ Use an Amish color scheme.

◆ If you set the blocks on point, will you get a more or less obvious diagonal?

◆ Center squares offer an opportunity to feature special fabric or photographs.

◆ Can you create a pieced border that incorporates all four elements of this block: square, rectangle, half-square triangle, and Flying Geese?

Eventually, he brought out a pile of velvet coats and went about the town, giving them to people dressed only in rags.

Quilt Information (finished size measurements)

	LAP	DOUBLE	KING
Quilt Size without Borders	36" x 48"	60" x 72"	84" x 96"
Quilt Size with Borders	52" x 64"	76" x 88"	100" x 112"
Block Size	12"	12"	12"
Number of Blocks	12	30	56
Block Layout	3 x 4	5 x 6	7 x 8
Backing Layout	←→ ←→	↓ ↓	↓ ↓ ↓ ↓

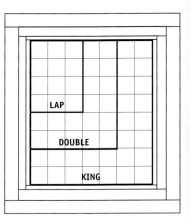

Fabric Requirements (42-45" wide, in yards)

	LAP	DOUBLE	KING
Fabric 1, **Light**—Pieces A, C, D, E & Middle Border	2 1/4	4 1/2	8 1/8
Fabric 2, **Medium or Dark**—Pieces B, F & G	1 1/2	3	5 3/8
Fabric 3, **Focus**—Inner Border, Outer Border & Binding	1 3/4	2 3/8	3 1/8
Backing Fabric	3 1/4	5 1/4	8 1/4

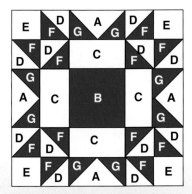

Robbing Peter to Pay Paul Block
#1771

Robbing Peter to Pay Paul

Poetic Justice, 48" x 61"
12" blocks (12), three plain borders
Toni Gotelaere, Superior, WI
quilted by Angela Haworth, Superior, WI

Toni is a night nurse in the post coronary care unit. Always an innovator, she replaces the center dark square in her Robbing Peter to Pay Paul quilt with a light one, giving a whole new look to the pattern. Angie has included spider webs, spiders, and dogwood flowers in her continuous line hand-guided machine quilting.

Cutting Instructions

	LAP	DOUBLE	KING
Fabric 1, Light—Piece A			
Cut strips 2 1/2" x width of fabric	6	15	28
▭ Crosscut into 2 1/2" x 4 1/2" rectangles	48	120	224
Fabric 1, Light—Piece C			
Cut strips 2 1/2" x width of fabric	6	15	28
▭ Crosscut into 2 1/2" x 4 1/2" rectangles	48	120	224
Fabric 1, Light—Piece D			
Cut strips 2 7/8" x width of fabric	6	14	26
□ Crosscut into 2 7/8" squares	72	180	336
◪ Crosscut once diagonally into half-square triangles	144	360	672
Fabric 1, Light—Piece E			
Cut strips 2 1/2" x width of fabric	3	8	14
□ Crosscut into 2 1/2" squares	48	120	224
Fabric 1, Light—Middle Border			
Cut strips 2 1/2" x width of fabric	5	7	10
Fabric 2, Medium or Dark—Piece B			
Cut strips 4 1/2" x width of fabric	2	4	7
□ Crosscut into 4 1/2" squares	12	30	56
Fabric 2, Medium or Dark—Piece F			
Cut strips 2 7/8" x width of fabric	6	14	26
□ Crosscut into 2 7/8" squares	72	180	336
◪ Crosscut once diagonally into half-square triangles	144	360	672
Fabric 2, Medium or Dark—Piece G			
Cut strips 2 1/2" x width of fabric	6	15	28
□ Crosscut into 2 1/2" squares	96	240	448
Fabric 3, Focus—Inner Border			
Cut strips 1 1/2" x width of fabric	5	7	10
Fabric 3, Focus—Outer Border			
Cut strips 5 1/2" x width of fabric	6	8	11
Fabric 3, Focus—Binding			
Cut strips 2 1/2" x width of fabric	7	9	11

If you are using only a few fabrics, consider making triangle squares from 2 1/2" (finished) half-square triangle paper.

Piecing Directions

Watch the orientation of half-square triangles as you assemble the units. It's easy to turn one in the wrong direction.

The Quiltmaker says . . .

Read all the instructions before you begin.

Always place right sides of fabric together for stitching.

Use scant ¼" seam allowances.

Press seam allowances in the direction of arrows.

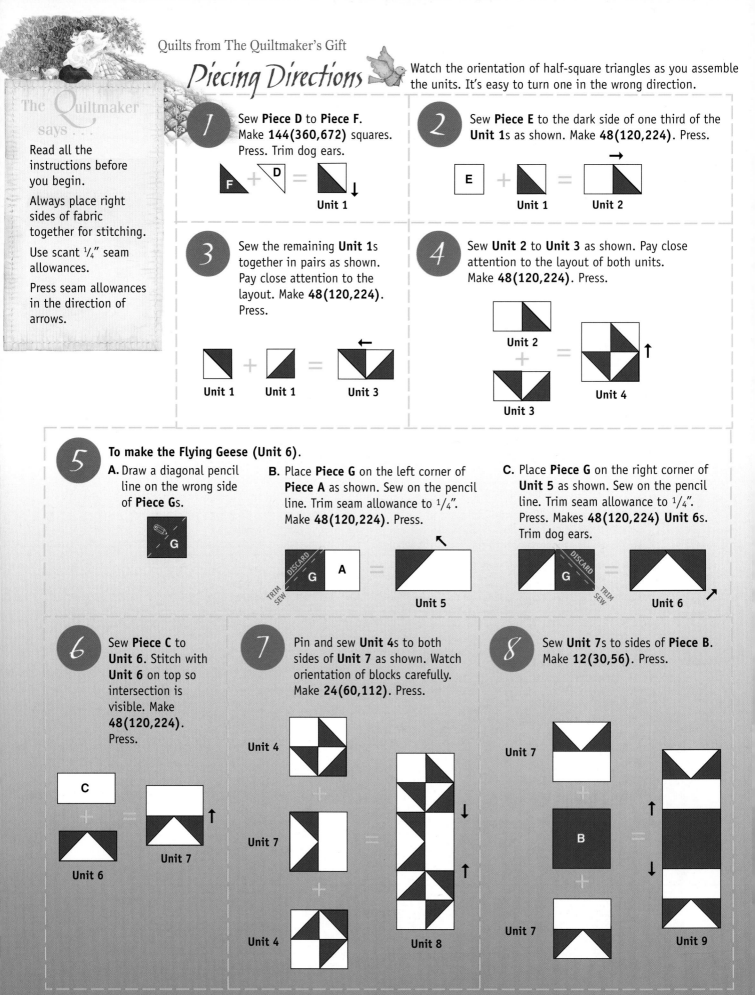

1 Sew **Piece D** to **Piece F**. Make **144(360,672)** squares. Press. Trim dog ears.

F + D = Unit 1

2 Sew **Piece E** to the dark side of one third of the **Unit 1**s as shown. Make **48(120,224)**. Press.

E + Unit 1 = Unit 2

3 Sew the remaining **Unit 1**s together in pairs as shown. Pay close attention to the layout. Make **48(120,224)**. Press.

Unit 1 + Unit 1 = Unit 3

4 Sew **Unit 2** to **Unit 3** as shown. Pay close attention to the layout of both units. Make **48(120,224)**. Press.

Unit 2 + Unit 3 = Unit 4

5 **To make the Flying Geese (Unit 6).**

A. Draw a diagonal pencil line on the wrong side of **Piece G**s.

G

B. Place **Piece G** on the left corner of **Piece A** as shown. Sew on the pencil line. Trim seam allowance to ¹/₄". Make **48(120,224)**. Press.

TRIM SEW DISCARD G A = Unit 5

C. Place **Piece G** on the right corner of **Unit 5** as shown. Sew on the pencil line. Trim seam allowance to ¹/₄". Press. Makes **48(120,224) Unit 6**s. Trim dog ears.

DISCARD G TRIM SEW = Unit 6

6 Sew **Piece C** to **Unit 6**. Stitch with **Unit 6** on top so intersection is visible. Make **48(120,224)**. Press.

C + Unit 6 = Unit 7

7 Pin and sew **Unit 4**s to both sides of **Unit 7** as shown. Watch orientation of blocks carefully. Make **24(60,112)**. Press.

Unit 4 + Unit 7 + Unit 4 = Unit 8

8 Sew **Unit 7**s to sides of **Piece B**. Make **12(30,56)**. Press.

Unit 7 + B + Unit 7 = Unit 9

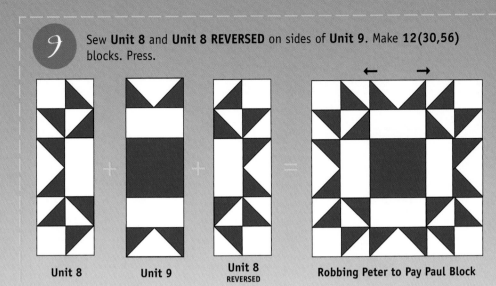

9 Sew **Unit 8** and **Unit 8 REVERSED** on sides of **Unit 9**. Make **12(30,56)** blocks. Press.

Unit 8   Unit 9   Unit 8 REVERSED   Robbing Peter to Pay Paul Block

Quilt Assembly

◆ Lay out the blocks **3(5,7)** across and **4(6,8)** down. Rotate blocks in each row so seams alternate and butt together nicely.

◆ Follow instructions on pages 136–137 for sewing blocks and rows together. Press.

◆ Follow the instructions on page 138 for adding borders.

Finishing the Quilt

◆ Follow the instructions on pages 138–139 for making the quilt sandwich.

◆ Follow the instructions on page 139 for basting the quilt.

◆ Refer to pages 138–139 for information on quilting.

◆ Follow the instructions on page 140 for binding the quilt.

Corn & Beans

Christmas Succotash, *46" x 57"*
12" blocks (12), two plain borders

Joanne Larsen Line, Duluth, MN
quilted by Karen McTavish, Duluth, MN

I chose the Corn and Beans block because I feel so strongly that generosity involves giving people what THEY want and need, not what WE want to get rid of. The hungry woman received the king's wonderful dog, but she also got a warm quilt and food.

Corn & Beans

Brackman/BlockBase Number: 1206A (two color);
2486 (three-color)
Earliest publication date: 1898 (Ladies Art Company #100)
Alternate names: Duck and Ducklings, Handy Andy,
Hen and Chicks, Shoo-Fly

This quilt block got its name from its traditional coloring of green and yellow with muslin background—but Stephanie's quilt (page 120) demonstrates that Corn and Beans doesn't have to look like succotash or a Green Bay Packers huddle! This block has had many different colorings historically, so feel free to adapt at will. The instructions here follow Joanne's interpretation. Notice that the block looks like four Northwind blocks sewn together, but the construction is slightly different.

Corn and Beans uses Flying Geese units as well as half-square triangles.

The complexity of the Corn and Beans block offers exciting design possibilities to novice and experienced quiltmakers alike. Take time to experiment with lots of fabric options before deciding on a final design scheme. Use colored pencils to test color combinations. Cut a few triangles from several fabrics and audition them in various configurations. If possible, try one of the computerized quilt design programs which make it easy to explore the impact of different values and colors within the block, and then translates the effect to the entire quilt top with the click of a mouse! But don't overlook the elegant simplicity of a stunning two-color quilt.

This block has LOTS of triangle points and intersections. Precise stitching is essential for sharp points.

Quiltmaker's Design Challenges

◆ This quilt works well with a scrappy look. Try placing different values in the inner and outer groups of triangles to create a secondary design.

◆ Hand-dyed fabrics across a colorway or across the spectrum would make a stunning interpretation.

◆ Incorporate theme-related fabrics into the block: vegetables, botanicals, landscapes.

◆ Try a Corn and Beans bouquet with a mixture of large-scale florals in the central triangles and small-scale florals in the small triangles.

◆ Consider a variety of color schemes. What about earth tones or sea and sky or harvest colors or autumn leaves or black and white or primaries?

◆ Experiment with many fabrics and values within each block. How could you make groups of small triangles stand out? What happens when all the large triangles are the same value?

◆ Substitute additional focus fabrics in the outer large triangles. What block does the secondary design resemble?

◆ Create a pieced border using one or more elements from the Corn and Beans block.

Joanne chose Christmas colors to create a flower-like appearance for her quilt. This may be her only quilt ever without purple!

"I give my quilts to those who are poor or homeless," she told all who knocked on her door. "They are not for the rich."

Quilt Information (finished size measurements)

	CRIB	LAP	QUEEN
Quilt Size without Borders	36" x 48"	48" x 60"	72" x 96"
Quilt Size with Borders	48" x 60"	60" x 72"	84" x 108"
Block Size	12"	12"	12"
Number of Blocks	12	20	48
Block Layout	3 x 4	4 x 5	6 x 8
Backing Layout			

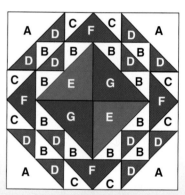

Fabric Requirements (42-45" wide, in yards)

	CRIB	LAP	QUEEN
Fabric 1, **Background**—Pieces A, B, & C	1 $5/8$	2 $5/8$	5 $1/2$
Fabric 2, **Accent 1**—Piece D	$3/4$	1 $1/8$	2 $1/8$
Fabric 3, **Focus**—Piece E & Outer Border	1 $5/8$	2	3 $3/4$
Fabric 4, **Accent 2**—Pieces F, G, Inner Border & Binding	1 $3/4$	2 $1/8$	4
Backing Fabric	3	4 $3/8$	8

**Corn and Beans Block
#1206A**

Corn & Beans

My Dad's John Deere, 60" x 72"
12" blocks (20), two plain borders
Stephanie Orlowski, Cloquet, MN
quilted by Pam Stolan, Duluth, MN

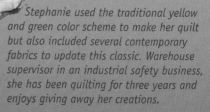
Stephanie used the traditional yellow and green color scheme to make her quilt but also included several contemporary fabrics to update this classic. Warehouse supervisor in an industrial safety business, she has been quilting for three years and enjoys giving away her creations.

120

Cutting Instructions

	CRIB	LAP	QUEEN
Fabric 1, Background—Piece A			
Cut strips 4 $7/8$" x width of fabric	3	5	12
☐ Crosscut into 4 $7/8$" squares	24	40	96
◩ Crosscut diagonally once into half square triangles	48	80	192
Fabric 1, Background—Piece B			
Cut strips 2 $7/8$" x width of fabric	6	10	23
☐ Crosscut into 2 $7/8$" squares	72	120	288
◩ Crosscut diagonally once into half-square triangles	144	240	576
Fabric 1, Background—Piece C			
Cut strips 2 $1/2$" x width of fabric	6	10	24
☐ Crosscut into 2 $1/2$" squares	96	160	384
Fabric 2, Accent 1—Piece D			
Cut strips 2 $7/8$" x width of fabric	6	10	23
☐ Crosscut into 2 $7/8$" squares	72	120	288
◩ Crosscut diagonally once into half-square triangles	144	240	576
Fabric 3, Focus—Piece E			
Cut strips 4 $7/8$" x width of fabric	2	3	6
☐ Crosscut into 4 $7/8$" squares	12	20	48
◩ Crosscut diagonally once into half-square triangles	24	40	96
Fabric 3, Focus—Outer Border			
Cut strips 5 $1/2$" x width of fabric	5	8	10
Fabric 4, Accent 2—Piece G			
Cut strips 4 $7/8$" x width of fabric	2	3	6
☐ Crosscut into 4 $7/8$" squares	12	20	48
◩ Crosscut diagonally once into half-square triangles	24	40	96
Fabric 4, Accent 2—Piece F			
Cut strips 2 $1/2$" x width of fabric	6	10	24
☐ Crosscut into 2 $1/2$" x 4 $1/2$" rectangles	48	80	192
Fabric 4, Accent 2—Inner Border			
Cut strips 1 $1/2$" x width of fabric	5	6	9
Fabric 4, Accent 2—Binding			
Cut strips 2 $1/4$" x width of fabric	6	7	10

The "Big Mama" ruler designed by Trudie Hughes is great for cutting 2 $7/8$" and 4 $7/8$" strips and squares.

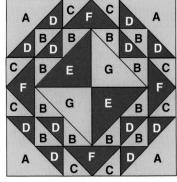

**Corn and Beans Block
Historical Coloring
#1206A**

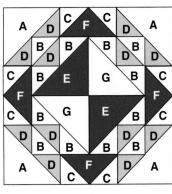

**Corn and Beans Block
Historical Coloring
#2486**

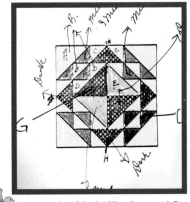

For complex blocks like Corn and Beans, make a color key and keep it handy for reference while cutting and piecing.

Piecing Directions

The **Quiltmaker** says . . .

Read all the instructions before you begin.

Always place right sides of fabric together for stitching.

Use scant ¼" seam allowances.

Press seam allowances in the direction of arrows.

1 Sew **Piece B** to one third of **Piece D**s. Make **48(80,192)** squares. Press. Trim dog ears.

B + D = B D ↓
Unit 1

2 Sew **Piece B** to right side of **Unit 1** as shown. Make **48(80,192)**. Press.

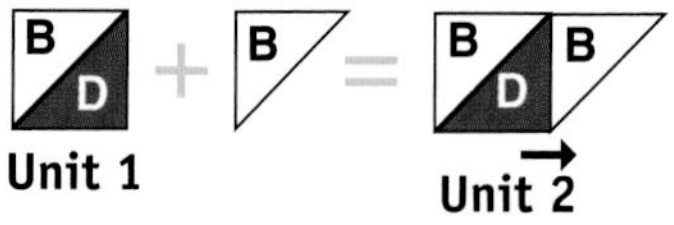

B D + B = B D B →
Unit 1   Unit 2

3 Sew **Piece B** to bottom of **Unit 2** as shown. Stitch with **Unit 1** on top. Make **48(80,192)**. Press. Trim dog ears.

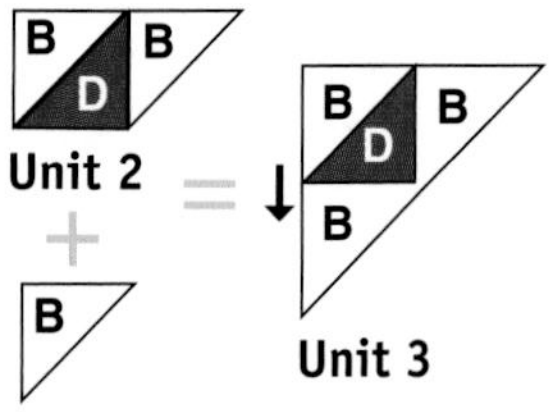

B B D + B = ↓ B D B / B
Unit 2   Unit 3

4 Sew **Piece E** to half of the **Unit 3**s as shown. Stitch with **Unit 3** on top. Make **24(40,96)**. Press. Trim dog ears.

Unit 3 + E = ↓ Unit 4

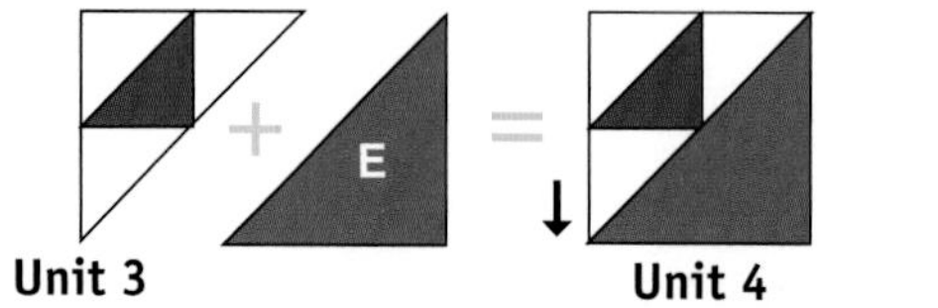

5 Sew **Piece G** to the remaining **Unit 3**s as shown. Stitch with **Unit 3** on top. Make **24(40,96)**. Press. Trim dog ears.

G + Unit 3 = ↑ Unit 5

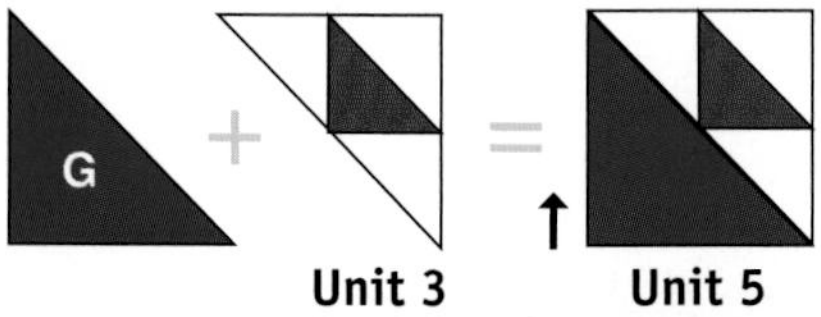

6 Pin and sew **Unit 3** and **Unit 4** together. Make **24(40,96)**. Press.

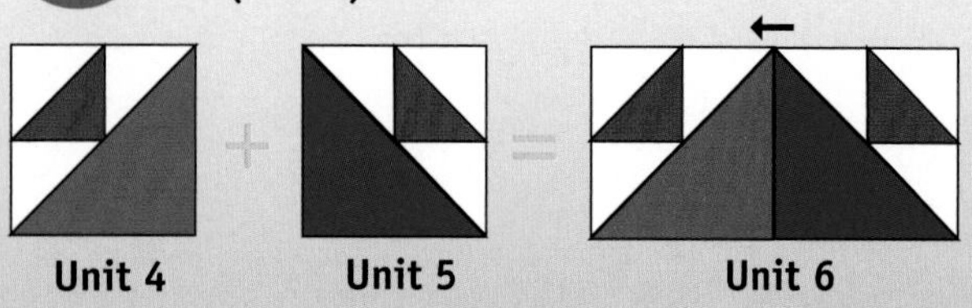

Unit 4 + Unit 5 = ← Unit 6

7 Pin and sew two **Unit 6**s together as shown. Sew **12(20,48)**. Press.

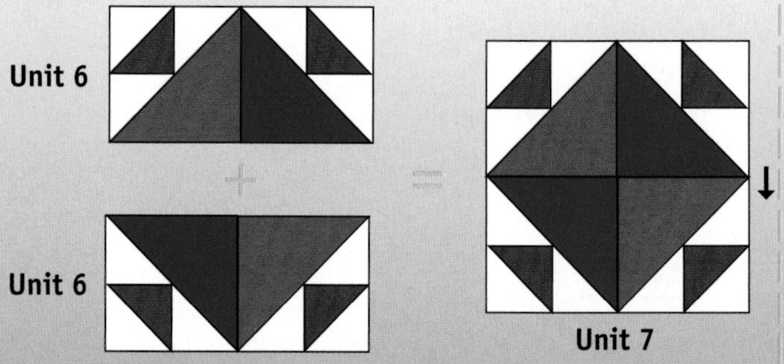

Unit 6 + Unit 6 = ↓ Unit 7

8 **To make Unit 9** (Flying Geese).

A. Draw a diagonal pencil line on the wrong side of **Piece C**s.

C

B. Place **Piece C** on the left corner of **Piece F** as shown. Sew on the pencil line. Trim seam allowance to ¹/₄". Make **48(80,192)**. Press.

TRIM SEW DISCARD C F = ↑ Unit 8

C. Place another **Piece C** on the right corner of **Unit 8** as shown. Sew on the pencil line. Trim seam allowance to ¹/₄". Press. Make **48(80,192)**. Trim dog ears.

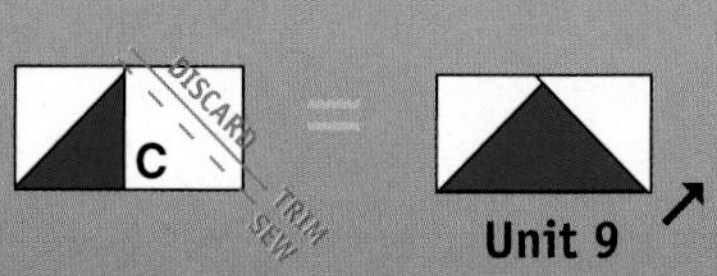

DISCARD C TRIM SEW = Unit 9 ↗

9 Sew **Piece D**s to the sides of **Unit 9**. Make **48(80,192)**. Press.

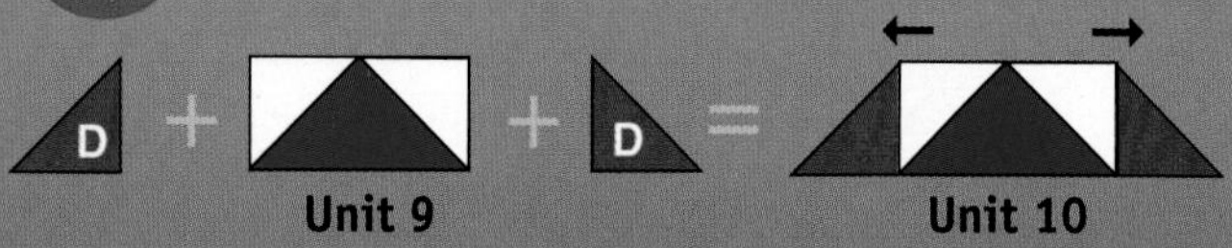

D + Unit 9 + D = ← → Unit 10

For precise points, always stitch directly through the intersecting seams of a triangle point, even if the seam allowance will not be exactly ¹/₄".

10 Pin and sew **Unit 10**s to top and bottom of **Unit 7**. Press toward **Unit 10**. Make **12(20,48)**. Do not trim.

Unit 10

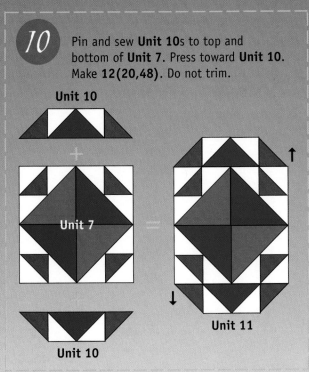

Unit 11

Unit 10

Quilt Assembly

◆ Lay out the blocks **3(4,6)** across and **4(5,8)** down.
◆ Follow the instructions on pages 136–137 for sewing the blocks and rows together.
◆ Follow the instruction on page 138 for adding borders.

Finishing the Quilt

◆ Follow the instructions on pages 138–139 for making the quilt sandwich.
◆ Follow the instructions on page 139 for basting the quilt.
◆ Refer to pages 138–139 for information on quilting.
◆ Follow the instructions on page 140 for binding the quilt.

11 Pin and sew **Unit 10**s to the sides of **Unit 11**. Press toward **Unit 10**. Press outward. Trim dog ears.

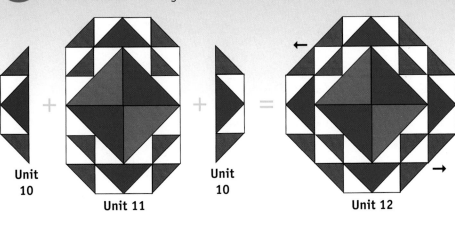

Unit 10   Unit 11   Unit 10   **Unit 12**

12 Sew **Piece A**s to the corners of **Unit 11**. Make **12(20,48)**. Press Toward **Piece A**. Trim dog ears.

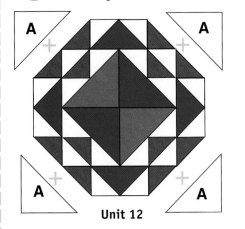

Unit 12

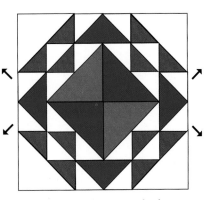

Corn and Beans Block

123

Sampler

Putting It All Together, 61" x 74"
multiple blocks in seven strips, two borders

LaVonne J. Horner, Superior, WI
quilted by Carolyn & Charles Peters,
Woodbury MN

Sampler

Quiltmaker's Design Challenge

Why not make a block of each pattern from this book and create your own sampler? Veteran quiltmaker LaVonne Horner took on the challenge and came up with the imaginative strip-setting sampler opposite. Her interpretation can serve as inspiration for you.

Since the size of blocks varies, consider one or more of these options in developing a design.

◆ Group blocks of the same size in rows and make a strip sampler.

◆ Combine 12" blocks with 6" and 9" blocks staggered.

◆ Adjust (reduce or enlarge) the size of some blocks before sewing so they match others in your design.

◆ Add narrow frames to smaller blocks so they fit with larger blocks.

◆ Set some blocks on point with corner triangles to make them larger.

◆ Create a center medallion with a large block or several odd-sized blocks. Surround the medallion with blocks of matched size. Try King's Highway in the center, framed by 10" and 12" blocks. Add smaller blocks, grouped in strips, to the top and bottom.

Finished sizes of blocks in this book:

2 1/2"	Trip Around the World
6" x 3"	Wild Goose Chase
7"	Children's Delight
9"	Log Cabin, Friendship Star, Flying Birds, Northwind
10"	Double Irish Chain (two blocks), Hen & Chicks, Follow the Leader
10 1/2"	Bear's Paw
12"	Puss in the Corner, True Lover's Knot, Milky Way, Rosebud, Toad in a Puddle, Snail's Trail, Robbing Peter to Pay Paul, Corn and Beans
19 1/2"	King's Highway

Meanwhile, the quiltmaker kept her word and started making a special quilt for the king. With each gift that he gave, she added another piece to his quilt.

Sampler

Before the advent of printed patterns in the late 1900s, quilters learned new quilt blocks by borrowing the designs from family, friends' and neighbors' quilts. They drew the pieces freehand on recycled paper or made a sample block in fabric to use for reference.

Today, many newcomers learn the art of quilting through sampler classes that teach all the basic construction techniques, one block at a time, much like this book. Experienced quilters often keep a sample block from each of their quilts. Since most quilters give their quilts away, such blocks are wonderful reminders of creative accomplishments!

LaVonne whipped up her sampler quilt one weekend to demonstrate how the blocks in this book could be combined into one quilt. LaVonne teaches an eight-week beginning quiltmaking class at Fabric Works three times a year. Most quilters in the area have her to thank for their enthusiasm and excellent techniques, as well as their unfinished—or completed—first sampler quilts.

Spectators might view quilting as a sedentary activity but quilters know better.

Quilting requires stamina and can be physically demanding. Hunching over the cutting table, standing at the ironing board for long periods, leaning over the sewing machine trying to keep your foot on the creeping accelerator, hand stitching in an uncomfortable setting, marathon quilting stints with a just-one-more-piece/block/row absorption—all of these quilting habits put substantial stress on the body. Repetitive activities may lead to serious neuromuscular problems. Unbalanced postures may cause chronic back trouble.

In fact, quilting can be downright unhealthy unless you intentionally practice some good health habits. Most quilters realize the physical demands and stress of quilting. Many are doing something about it so that quilting activities won't cause preventable injuries or disabilities.

Please read this section for your own well-being. Remember there are three keys to less-stress quilting: balanced posture, frequent movement, periodic muscle stretches. Set up your work space and quilting routines for wellness. Give yourself periodic breaks. Try some of the recommended stretches. And if you want to stay in top quilting condition, incorporate regular stretching into your quilting routine.

Ergonomics for Quilters

The principles of ergonomics for computer users translate well to the sewing room. To reduce muscle tension and strain on your joints, set up your work space to promote well-being rather than efficiency, to encourage frequent movement and balanced posture in every activity. An ironing board at your elbow is efficient, but discourages mobility. Force yourself to walk some distance from the cutting table to the sewing machine to the ironing board. The change in position and movement will decrease the accumulated strain of repetitive motions and prolonged standing or sitting.

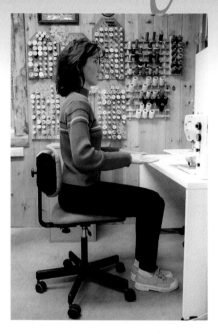

At the sewing machine

Pay attention to your body alignment while sitting. Adopt a less-stress posture.

Keep your ankle, knee, and elbow joints at ninety degree angles, or as close to that angle as is comfortable for you.

Make sure your work surface is low enough so you can keep your wrists in a neutral position (neither cocked nor bent) as you sew.

Support your lower back with a rolled towel, back cushion, or chair with an adjustable lumbar support.

As much as possible, do not lean forward. Keep your lower back in contact with its support.

An inclined foot rest may reduce pressure on the lower back and thighs.

At the cutting table

Whenever possible, raise your cutting surface to about counter height for rotary cutting.

Make sure the lighting is good so you can see the markings on rulers without hunching over.

Take periodic breaks to rebalance your posture. Try some gentle arching back stretches and torso turns.

At the ironing board

Concentrate on maintaining a balanced posture while pressing—shoulders, hips, and knees in a line above your ankles.

Make sure the lighting is good so you can see without leaning over.

A non-stick ironing board cover reduces the strain of moving larger pieces of fabric across the surface.

To ease strain on your lower back, try putting one foot up a few inches while pressing. A phone book works well. Alternate feet during a long session.

Quilters

Relaxing or Stressful Hobby?

Does the joy of quilting keep you glued to your chair for an hour or more? Time for a break!

The hobby you think of as so relaxing may at the same time be stressing you out!

Sitting for long periods is very stressful on the body—your muscles are busy holding in a steady position, but they are not doing the kind of work that promotes circulation. Forward bending at the waist (cutting, ironing, stitching) not only impedes circulation, it puts strain on all the muscles on the back side of your body. The sustained motion of grasping the fabric and pinching the needle in hand quilting or appliqué strains the hands, arms, wrists, and shoulders.

Quilting can take its toll. Many quilters eventually have a bout with carpal tunnel syndrome, tendonitis of the hand or wrist, upper or lower back pain, neck strain, or fatigue.

One potential antidote to the stress and strain of quilting is stretching—systematically releasing tension before it accumulates in unhealthy proportions.

Stretching Your Quilting Muscles

Occupational therapist and certified hand therapist Marcia Bowker suggests that recreational quilters take some coaching from recreational athletes. To enjoy your sport more fully and to protect yourself from possible injury, stretch out your muscles before you start, and again when you are finished with your play time. Stretching relieves tension and promotes circulation. Fresh blood brings a spurt of energizing oxygen to your quilting muscles and sweeps away the toxic wastes they give off. During a long quilting session, stretch several times for relaxation and revitalization.

Be kind to your body. Take a few minutes every day to move and stretch the muscles and joints that make your quilting activities possible. Stretching releases accumulated tension, enhances flexibility, improves circulation, and keeps you in top condition for quilting—and all your other activities.

Eye Stretches

Your eyes are essential tools for every quilting activity. The muscles that surround these busy body parts rarely get a break, but they certainly deserve one. Try one or both of these stretches several times during a quilting session

Shut and Open
Close eyelids tightly and hold five seconds.
Open eyelids wide and hold five seconds.
Repeat three to five times.

Roving Eyes
Keeping your head facing straight ahead, look to left as far as you can. Hold three seconds.
Look to the right and hold three seconds.
Look upward and hold three seconds.
Look downward and hold three seconds.
Repeat three times.

Safety Tips for Accident-Free Quilting

Be safety conscious

Keep your rotary cutter safely stowed when not in use.

Always cut going AWAY FROM your body.

Close the protective cover after EVERY stroke.

Never set down a rotary cutter with the blade open.

Check all electrical cords periodically for signs of wear.

Unplug the iron between quilting sessions.

Eliminate obstacles that might trip someone (including you!).

Mini-Curls Repeat the entire stretch sequence three times.

Finger and Wrist Stretches

Hold both arms out in front of you, with fingers pointing upward.

Curl your fingers just at the tips. Hold this position for a slow count of three to five seconds.

Curl your fingers at the first and second joints. Hold this position for a slow count of three to five seconds.

Guidelines for Stretching

Whenever you stretch, follow these guidelines.

Stretch only within your comfortable limits—never to the point of pain.

Stretch just to a point where you feel mild tension. Relax into the stretch as you hold it.

The feeling of tension in the stretch should subside slightly as you hold the stretch.

Do not overstretch—any sensation that grows in intensity or becomes painful to you is an overstretch.

Do not bounce.

While stretching, breathe slowly, deeply, and rhythmically.

Neck Stretches

Neckbends

Gently bend your neck to the right. Hold five seconds. Do not strain. Relax with the stretch.

Gently bend your neck to the left. Hold five seconds.

Repeat three to five times.

Gently bend your neck forward tucking your chin into your chest. Hold five seconds.

Repeat three to five times.

Head Turns

Turn your head slowly one-quarter turn to the right. Do not strain. Relax with the stretch. Hold five seconds.

Turn your head slowly to the left. Hold five seconds.

Repeat three to five times.

Shoulder Stretches

Alternating Lifts

Lift your right shoulder only, up toward your right ear. Hold five seconds.

Repeat three to five times.

Lift your left shoulder only up toward left ear. Hold five seconds.

Repeat three to five times.

Rotating Rolls

Roll both shoulders forward. Hold five seconds.

Repeat three times.

Roll shoulders back. Hold five seconds.

Repeat three times.

Roll shoulders forward in a circular motion.

Repeat five times.

Roll shoulders backward in a circular motion.

Repeat five times.

Curl your fingers all the way into your palm. Hold this position for a slow count of three to five seconds.

Reverse the process, uncurling your fingers slowly. Hold each position for three to five seconds.

Fists Repeat three times.

Make fists with both hands. Hold for five seconds.

Release and spread your fingers wide. Hold for five seconds.

At Rest

Put your hands in your lap. Relax.

Close your eyes.

Take three deep breaths.

Imagine the tension in your arms and hands draining out of your fingertips as you exhale.

Arm Stretches

Reach for Health

Reach upward with both arms and stretch toward the ceiling. Hold for five seconds.

Gently lower your arms and relax. Take three deep breaths.

Repeat three times.

Elbow Pull

With arms overhead, hold the elbow of one arm with the opposite hand.

Gently pull the elbow behind your head, creating an easy stretch. Do it slowly, without straining. Hold for fifteen seconds.

Relax and repeat.

Follow the same steps to stretch the other arm.

Upper Body Stretches

Torso Twist

Slowly twist your shoulders and whole upper body to the right. Do not strain. Hold five seconds. Return to centered posture. Take a deep breath.

Slowly twist to the left without straining. Hold five seconds. Return to centered posture. Take a deep breath.

Repeat three times in each direction.

Body Bend

Keeping your upper back straight, gently bend your upper body forward from the waist. Do not strain. Hold five seconds. Return to normal posture. Take a deep breath or two.

Gently bend your upper body backward by arching your back. Do not strain. Hold five seconds. Return to normal posture. Take a deep breath or two.

Repeat three times.

Wellness for Quilters Consultant

Quilter Marcia Bowker, OTR (occupational therapist), CHT (certified hand therapist), treats traumatic hand injuries and works as a consultant to business and industry. She supervises rehabilitation programs for employees who are recovering from repetitive task stress injuries and is frequently called on to teach ergonomics and preventive skills in the workplace.

Quilting requires having the right tools and equipment to complete a project. Here is a short list of the essential equipment you will need to successfully make one of the quilts in this book. Remember you can always add more tools and gadgets to your collection at a later time.

Iron

A hot steam iron and adjustable-height ironing board with cotton or Teflon cover.

Pins

Fine, sharp, glass head pins are best for most pinning and will not rust. For pin-basting the quilt layers, #2 safety pins work best.

Pin Cushion

A magnetic pin cushion keeps pins handy and helps locate strays.

Rotary Rulers

These clear, acrylic rulers are marked lengthwise, crosswise, and diagonally with easy to read lines and numbers. Buy two rulers to start, a 6" x 24" rectangle and a 6" or 12 $1/2$" square. Ask for sandpaper discs to put underneath to prevent slippage while cutting.

Keep a wish list of tools to jog your memory when asked what you want for your birthday.

Buy the best equipment, supplies, and materials you can afford. They will last longer and cost less in the long run.

Rotary Mat

Essential companion to the rotary cutter. Buy a self-healing mat that is at least 11" x 17". Both sides can be used for cutting. Beware—these magical mats will warp beyond salvation if left in direct sunlight, a hot car, or below zero temperatures.

Rotary Cutter

This is the tool that has revolutionized quilting. Buy a medium size (45 mm) straight or ergonomic cutter. Works for left or right-handers.

Scissors

A small, sharp scissors is needed for snipping threads and trimming dog ears.

Seam Ripper

Also known as the reverse sewing tool. Keep several sharp ones with fine points on hand for the inevitable undoing of seams.

Sewing Machine

A basic machine that stitches forward and backward will answer all your quilting needs. A special $1/4$" presser foot is well worth the investment. Keep your sewing machine clean and in good working order.

Sewing Machine Needles

A size 80/12 needle is an excellent choice for quilting. Change your needle every eight to ten hours or with each new project.

Thread

Use 100% cotton thread for machine piecing. A light to medium gray or tan thread will work on most projects.

Invest in the Essential Quilting Tool: An Accurate 1/4" Seam

Fabric Works owner Barb Engelking reports that inaccurate seam allowances account for 90% of the problems quilters have in following patterns.

The patterns in this book call for a scant 1/4" seam allowance (except when piecing quilt backings). Scant means just less than 1/4", to allow for the turn of fabric when the seam is pressed. Sewing a consistent, accurate 1/4" seam allowance is essential for precision piecing.

◆ Cut 3 pieces of scrap fabric 1 1/2" x 3 1/2".

◆ Sew these strips together along the lengthwise edge.

◆ Press the seams away from the center strip.

◆ Measure the sewn unit. It should measure EXACTLY 3 1/2" from edge to edge.

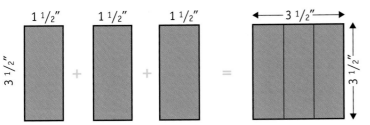

If the sewn unit is NARROWER than 3 1/2", your seam allowance is TOO WIDE.

If the sewn unit is WIDER than 3 1/2", your seam allowance is TOO NARROW.

Make the adjustments necessary to achieve an accurate 1/4" seam allowance every time.

Tips for Making an Accurate 1/4" Seam

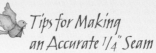

◆ Purchase a special 1/4" foot for your machine.

◆ Use a clear ruler to mark a 1/4" line from the throat plate all the way to the front edge of your machine.
Use a permanent marker, masking/duct tape, moleskin, or Post-it® notes to mark the line (see photo, page 54).

◆ The angle at which you feed the fabric under the presser foot helps determine the actual seam allowance. Try to keep fabric straight at 1/4" several inches in front of the needle.

◆ Practice until you can make consistent 1/4" seams.

Design Wall

Several quilts in this book lend themselves to a variety of artistic interpretations before and after the blocks are constructed. The best way to experiment with design options is to play with the pieces or finished blocks on a flat, vertical surface covered with fuzzy fabric (flannel, fleece, felt) that holds the blocks in place without pins, so you can rearrange and reconsider until you find a pleasing effect. Most quilters find a design wall essential to their creative process. We have suggested it in this book for experimenting with blocks like Log Cabin, Flying Birds, and Northwind.

A design wall doesn't have to be fancy. Five yards of white flannel or fleece will make a 90" x 94" portable wall you can pin up when needed and fold away easily for storage—with the quilt pieces still in place if you want! A flannel-back tablecloth also works fine. To make a more permanent installation, nail, tape, staple, or pin flannel to a foam insulation board or sheet of plywood—the bigger the better. Then step back and let your creative juices flow.

Helen Smith Prekker considers an unusual Log Cabin setting.

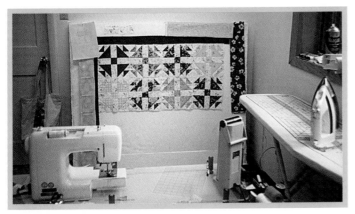

Auditioning borders for Hen & Chicks.

Planning a Trip Around the World.

Fabric

Cotton, Cotton, Cotton

Although quilts historically have been made from nearly every kind of fabric (including wools, silks, velvets, feedsacks, shirtings, muslin, sheetings, and recycled fabrics of all kinds), most quilters today prefer 100% cotton for its handling properties during construction and sturdiness after completion.

Stay away from polyester and polyester/cotton blends as they are difficult to work with and will not wear evenly with other fabrics in the quilt. Making a quilt requires repeated handling of the fabric, so buy the best quality you can afford.

Choices, Choices, Choices

Choosing fabric for a quilt can be exhilarating or intimidating. What color combination? How many fabrics? Country look or contemporary? Solids or patterns? Florals or calicoes? Brights or pastels?

If you feel unsure about colors or fabrics, try Joanne's recommended strategy below or ask at your local quilt shop. They need your support to stay in business and the staff will be delighted to help you find fabrics that fit YOUR tastes and your chosen quilt pattern.

Joanne's Fabric Selection Strategy

◆ Choose a fabric that makes your heart sing!

◆ Start with a multi-color focus fabric. Usually this will be a print with three or four color families in a harmonious combination and several variations within each color. See color wheel opposite for the twelve color families.

◆ You may not notice all the colors at first, but look closely to see the various families that are represented. For example, a floral usually has several shades of green and two or more colors of petals plus a background color and some accent color. Novelty prints may have every color under the rainbow.

◆ Select several coordinating fabrics. Don't hurry the process! Choose LOTS of possibilities first, then narrow down your options later.

◆ Start by choosing a light, medium, and dark value fabric from EACH of the color families in your focus fabric.

◆ Among these fabrics, mix and match different color intensity (bright to pastel, clear to grayed), type of pattern (geometric, floral, tone on tone, blender, abstract, pictorial), and scale (tiny, huge, and sizes in between).

◆ Assemble all your choices together on a counter where you can see them interact with the focus fabric and with each other. Step back and evaluate the collection.

◆ You do not need to use all the fabrics. Add and subtract fabrics until you find a combination that will work well in your quilt. Occasionally you may find that your original focus fabric is no longer needed.

◆ Start piecing! Don't be surprised if you find additional fabrics to add along the way. A quilt is a work in process until the final stitch is taken.

Fabric Preparation

Prewash all fabric in warm water with a mild soap to remove excess dye and chemicals. Always wash light and dark fabrics separately.

With dark colors and fabrics that may have unstable color (indigoes, batiks, hand-dyes, bargain fabrics), soak overnight in cold water. If the water discolors, the fabric will bleed. Wash until the water comes clear or do not use the fabric.

Damp dry the fabric on a warm cycle and press with a dry iron.

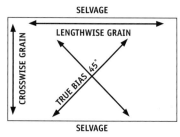 For extra body, use spray starch before cutting and piecing.

Grain Lines and Bias

Fabric is woven from perpendicular threads. The crosswise grain tends to stretch a little. The lengthwise grain stretches very little. These two grain lines are often referred to as straight of grain. The selvage (or self-edge), made where the thread turns back on itself at the edge, does not stretch at all and should be trimmed off before measuring and cutting quilt pieces.

When you cut diagonally across the straight of the grain, you create a bias edge. Bias edges stretch easily and must be handled, sewn, and pressed carefully.

SELVAGE / LENGTHWISE GRAIN / CROSSWISE GRAIN / TRUE BIAS 45° / SELVAGE

◆ Strips, squares, and rectangles are always cut on the straight of grain.

◆ Shapes such as triangles cannot have all edges cut on-grain. At least one side will be on the bias. To stabilize seams, most patterns try to sew the bias edge of a triangle to a straight edge of the adjacent piece.

◆ Be careful not to stretch bias edges. Do not press bias edges until after they are stitched.

Color Harmony

Color harmony refers to the pleasing choice, proportion, and arrangement of colors. Although our response to color is usually quite personal, there are several color harmonies that most people find pleasing and the basic principles are quite simple. Using the color wheel developed by Danish artist Johannes Itten, even beginners can choose color harmonies with confidence.

Experiment with the five basic color schemes and variations shown here. As you consider fabric choices, try to keep an open mind. Stretch your comfort zone following these principles.

◆ Every color is a good color, when used with harmonious companions.

◆ Each color around the color wheel actually represents a color *family* ranging from pale (light value) to very deep (dark value) and all the subtle variations in between.

◆ Contrast in value will give depth to your design and enrich whatever color harmony you choose.

Color Harmonies

Considering all the possible interpretations of each harmony in many color family combinations, you could make a lifetime of stunning quilts from following these five simple strategies. If you'd like to expand your color sense further, consult one of the excellent books listed in the resources, page 141.

Monochromatic

A monochromatic color scheme has only one color, usually in many shades or values, sometimes incorporating white or another neutral. Try any color around the wheel. ◆ To add liveliness to this soothing harmony, use equal amounts of light, medium, and dark values.

Analogous

Analogous means similar or related. Combine three colors that are side by side on the color wheel. Because the colors are close together, they will always blend in a pleasing way. Try yellow/yellow-green/green, blue-violet/violet/red-violet, or ANY adjacent colors. ◆ To spice up analogous color schemes, add an accent. Use one of the complements, across the color wheel from the analogous colors.

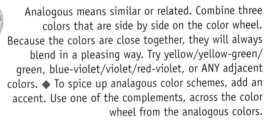

Complementary

Complementary colors are directly opposite each other on the color wheel. Every combination around the wheel will yield a rich, dynamic harmony in pastels or brights. Try yellow-orange/blue-violet or any other opposite pair. ◆ To add drama to this harmony, add a bit of an accent, two colors away from one of the complements.

Split Complementary

A split complementary scheme features a color and the colors on either side of its complement. Think of a Y with its tail at the main color and its arms reaching to the split complementary colors. This combination is a bit more adventurous. Try red-violet/yellow/green or any other Y-combinations around the wheel.

Triadic

A triadic harmony incorporates three colors that are equally distant on the color wheel (three colors between). Try red-orange/yellow-green/blue-violet, or other triangles around the wheel. ◆ These vibrant and exciting harmonies may need some black or white for respite.

Complements

red	green
red-orange	blue-green
orange	blue
yellow-orange	blue-violet
yellow	violet
yellow-green	red-violet

Split Complements

red	yellow-green	blue-green
red-orange	green	blue
orange	blue-green	blue-violet
yellow-orange	blue	violet
yellow	blue-violet	red-violet
yellow-green	violet	red
green	red-violet	red-orange
blue-green	red	orange
blue	red-orange	yellow-orange
blue-violet	orange	yellow
violet	yellow-orange	yellow-green
red-violet	yellow	green

Triads

Primary colors:	red	yellow	blue
Secondary colors:	orange	green	violet
Tertiary colors:	red-orange	yellow-green	blue-violet
	yellow-orange	blue-green	red-violet

Cutting Piecing

Rotary Cutting Basics

All the quilts in this book begin with cut strips of fabric. Cutting accurate and straight strips is the first secret to precision piecing in quiltmaking. See page 130 for essential tools.

Squaring Up the Fabric

Before cutting fabric, square up the uneven end so it is perpendicular to the fabric edge and all pieces will be cut on the straight grain.

1. Fold the fabric in half, selvage to selvage. Hold the fabric up to see if it hangs straight to the fold. If not, slide the layers a bit until the fabric hangs straight and selvages are together. It is important that the selvages are aligned and the folded edge is smooth.

2. Lay the fabric on the cutting mat with the folded edge closest to your body. Right-handed people should place the bulk of the fabric to their right. Left-handed people should place it to the left and reverse directions in the remaining instructions.

3. Fold the fabric in half again, bringing the fold up to meet the selvages. You will be cutting through four layers of fabric.

4. Line up your widest ruler precisely with the bottom fold, about 1/2" from the left edge of the fabric. Make sure all four layers of fabric extend beyond the left edge of the ruler.

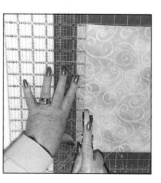

5. Line up a long ruler tight to the left edge of the wide ruler. Check that all four layers of fabric are under the long ruler.

6. Spread the fingertips of your left hand to apply even pressure on the long ruler. Remove the other ruler.

7. Using a rotary cutter, cut along the right edge of the long ruler, removing the uneven edge of all four layers of fabric with a single pass. Cut AWAY from your body.

Cutting Strips and Shapes

To cut strips for strip-piecing or crosscutting into shapes, always make sure the fabric is square to begin. Check it every three or four cuts. If necessary, square the fabric again.

1. Line up the required measurement on the ruler with the cut straight edge of the fabric.
Measure carefully!
A Post-it® note at the proper measurement on the ruler prevents errors.

2. Apply pressure with your fingertips on the ruler and make the cut with a single smooth pass of the rotary cutter. Cut AWAY from your body.

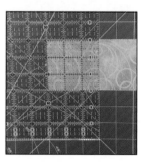

3. Crosscut the strips into squares or rectangles as called for in the pattern.

Make half-square triangles by cutting a square diagonally.

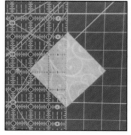

Make quarter-square triangles by cutting a square diagonally twice.

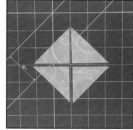

Stitching Basics

The quilts in this book use a scant 1/4" seam allowance. Sewing a scant 1/4" seam allowance is the second secret in precision piecing. Before you begin stitching your quilt top take a few minutes to check your scant 1/4" seam. See tips and test on page 131.

Set the stitch length to 12 stitches per inch. Use 100% cotton thread in a neutral color for light fabrics and a darker color for dark fabrics.

Focus on accuracy. Accuracy in cutting, accuracy in sewing, and accuracy in pressing.

Cutting Tips

◆ Always close the rotary cutter after EVERY stroke.

◆ Always cut AWAY from your body.

◆ Check your first cut strip to make sure the strip is straight.

◆ Check straight of grain every few strips as you continue to cut. Re-square the fabric as needed.

◆ If the strip of fabric to be cut is wider than your ruler, use two rulers to get the desired width.

◆ Do not cut through more than four layers of fabric. Cutting accuracy diminishes with each extra layer of fabric. Also, more stress is placed on the hands and wrists when cutting through increased layers of fabric.

◆ Many quilt blocks include triangles, which have extra large seam allowances at the tips. Unless otherwise directed, trim these "dog ears" even with the 1/4" seam allowance of adjacent pieces after pressing and before stitching the next seam.

Pinning Pressing

Machine Piecing Techniques

Place two pieces of fabric with right sides together and raw edges aligned. Stitch the length of the raw edge in a scant 1/4" seam. Back-stitching is unnecessary because the seams will be crossed by other seams.

Begin and end each sewing sequence with a "starter." Stitch a small scrap of fabric under the presser foot, stopping at the front edge. This scrap is your starting point for the next seam. It saves time and thread while preventing small units from being drawn down into the throat plate.

Starter scrap saves time.

Slow down when stitching over intersecting seams

To make perfect points

When assembling units where one piece has intersecting seams, always pin before stitching.
Put the piece with the intersection on top so you can see clearly to sew exactly through the X intersection, even if the seam allowance will not be exactly 1/4".

Strip-Piecing Techniques

Several quilts in this book call for piecing of fabric strips which are then crosscut into strips that become components of the final block.

1. Begin by arranging the pieces of fabric in the sequence stated in the pattern directions.

2. Line up the first two strips, matching the cut edges. Stitch.

3. Set the seam and press according to the directions.

4. If called for, add the next strip of fabric.

Chain-Piecing

Whenever possible, stitch all similar units in sequence, using the chain-piecing method:

1. Place fabric pieces to be joined under the presser foot and stitch the seam.

2. Take a few stitches with no fabric, then slide the next fabric pair under the toe of the presser foot. Do not lift the presser foot or clip the thread.

3. Take another few stitches with no fabric, then repeat with the next unit.

4. When all units have been sewn, end with your starter scrap.

5. Cut the stitched units from the starter and move to the ironing board for pressing.

6. Set and press the seams following the pressing arrows in the pattern.

7. Clip the units apart.

To repair stitching errors

Use your seam ripper to "unsew" a seam when you've made a mistake.

◆ "Rip" every third stitch on one side of the fabric. Then gently lift the thread off the other side of the fabric.

◆ Remove ALL thread snippets before restitching the seam. If snippets do not come off easily, try masking tape.

Pinning

It is not necessary to pin long straight seams. However, it is advisable to pin when encountering seams and intersections that need to be lined up precisely.

To match intersecting seams

◆ Make sure seams are pressed in opposite directions.

◆ Wriggle the pieces together until the opposing seams nestle or "butt" together snugly. Peek to make sure the pieces are lined up.

◆ Place a pin in both sides of the intersecting seams.

◆ Stitch the seam slowly, removing the pins just before they come under the needle. Do not stitch over pins; doing so can bend or break the pin, cause broken needles, or throw off the timing of the sewing machine.

SEAM ALLOWANCE →
SEAMS MEET →
SEAM ALLOWANCE →

To match diagonal or multiple seams exactly

◆ Stab a pin vertically through the exact match point. Keep this pin standing upright to hold pieces in place. Do not pin it down.

◆ Pin the pieces together with a pin on both sides of the center pin. Remove the center pin.

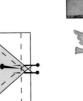

Pressing

Pressing is the third secret to precision piecing. Press every fabric before cutting. Press each seam as you go. Look for the pressing arrows in the pattern diagrams and follow them for every step so that seam allowances at intersections are pressed in opposite directions to lie flat.

To press sewn units

◆ Start by "setting" the sewn seam. Place the sewn units or blocks on the ironing board with the seam facing away from your body. The fabric being "pressed toward" should be on top.

◆ Gently press the sewn seam, using a zigzag motion.

◆ Separate the two fabrics and fold the top fabric back over the seam allowances. Press gently.

For complicated designs, make a pressing plan so all seams butt if possible and you know which way to press them before you start. Within and between complex blocks, several seams may come together and prevent butting. If necessary, press these seams open.

135

Choosing a Setting

Read all instructions completely before beginning.

Making quilt blocks is only one-third of the quiltmaking process. The second phase is to decide on an attractive arrangement for the blocks and then assemble them into a quilt top. Blocks can be arranged into many settings:

◆ **Straight (horizontal) set:** blocks side by side in horizontal rows.

◆ **Straight set with sashing:** blocks side by side in horizontal rows with sashing (lattice) strips between the blocks.

◆ **Diagonal (on-point) set:** blocks turned 45° on their points and arranged in diagonal rows.

◆ **Diagonal set with sashing:** diagonal rows of blocks set on point with sashing (lattice strips) between the blocks.

◆ **Alternate block setting:** a plain block or a simple pieced block is substituted, checkerboard fashion, for half the blocks in a straight or diagonal setting.

◆ **Strip setting:** horizontal or vertical side by side placement of blocks in strips with plain fabric or strips of different blocks set between.

◆ **Overall setting:** single blocks placed in an arrangement so the pattern covers the entire quilt top.

◆ **Medallion setting:** large single block or group of blocks in the center of quilt.

Most of the quilts in this book use a straight set pattern, but even within this simple setting there are unlimited possibilities for arranging blocks. Diagonally divided

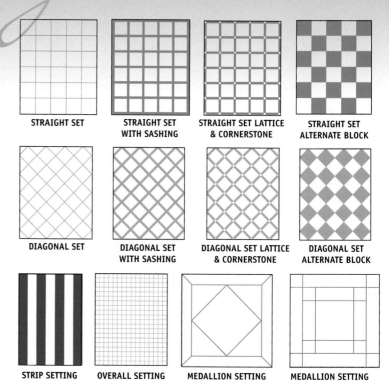

STRAIGHT SET

STRAIGHT SET WITH SASHING

STRAIGHT SET LATTICE & CORNERSTONE

STRAIGHT SET ALTERNATE BLOCK

DIAGONAL SET

DIAGONAL SET WITH SASHING

DIAGONAL SET LATTICE & CORNERSTONE

DIAGONAL SET ALTERNATE BLOCK

STRIP SETTING

OVERALL SETTING

MEDALLION SETTING

MEDALLION SETTING

light/dark blocks are especially versatile in creating intriguing designs across the quilt top. See pages 28–33, 84, 91.

For design inspiration, study examples of other settings scattered throughout this book. Pay attention to the settings in quilts you see and like. Then try them out with your latest project.

Experiment before Deciding

Use a design wall to play around with different block orientations and arrangements until you find one that fits your fabrics and artistic sensibilities. The results can be amazing.

Try turning your blocks diagonally for a lively design. Hen and Chicks on point looks like a totally different block. Experiment with sashings between your blocks. Consider alternate block settings to show off very complex blocks, to make a larger quilt from a small number of blocks, or when you want to feature intricate machine or hand quilting in the plain blocks.

Don't be surprised if a different setting begs for a sashing fabric or border you didn't imagine beforehand. Stay open to the creative inspirations that emerge in this important second design phase of quiltmaking.

Sashings

Settings with sashing (lattice) strips were rare before the advent of the sewing machine which could stitch the long straight seams with ease. Today, quilters typically consider sashings as a design element in four situations:

◆ To provide unity in a quilt whose blocks are of varying sizes or disparate fabrics, especially in sampler quilts or when setting antique, appliquéd, or embroidered quilt blocks.

◆ To "stretch" a quilt to a larger size.

◆ To frame larger blocks for a "country" feel.

◆ To echo design elements in the quilt block, as with Children's Delight, Bear's Paw, Hen and Chicks, or Follow the Leader.

Sashing strips can be set with squares at block intersections, or treated as quilt-wide strips. Sashing strip width should be proportional to the elements in the blocks and replicate some feature in the block, if possible. See Bear's Paw (pages 68-73) for step-by-step instructions to make sashings with setting squares. For a smooth, flat quilt top, press seams of setting squares toward the sashing.

Plan Ahead

Quilts that are set diagonally or with lattice strips take some extra planning before purchasing and cutting fabric. See instructions opposite for determining fabric requirements and cutting the essential corner and side setting triangles for on-point quilts.

Quilt Assembly

Once you have decided on a setting arrangement, it is time to assemble the quilt top. A design wall is helpful to keep blocks in order.

Straight (Horizontal) Set Quilt Assembly

◆ Lay out the blocks side by side in rows.

◆ Sew the blocks together in horizontal rows. Butt and pin all intersecting seams before sewing.

◆ Press as you go. Press all seams between blocks in the EVEN rows to the right and all seams between blocks in the ODD rows to the left.

◆ Lay out the completed rows.

◆ Sew the rows together from top to bottom. Butt and pin all seams before sewing.

◆ To prevent distortion when sewing the rows together, reverse the sewing direction row by row. Sew Row 1 and Row 2 together from left to right. Sew Row 3 to Row 2, from right to left. Continue in this manner, alternating directions until all the rows are sewn together.

◆ Press as you add each row. Press all seams in the same direction.

Diagonal (On-Point) Set Quilt Assembly

To finish the edges of quilts set on point (diagonally), side setting triangles and corner triangles are needed. These triangles can be half blocks from the pattern or cut from squares of the background fabric (see below).

◆ Lay out the blocks diagonally (on point) using the setting triangles to fill in the spaces around the edges of the quilt.

◆ Pin and sew the blocks and setting triangles together, one diagonal row at a time, pressing as you go. Press all seams between blocks in the EVEN rows to the right and all seams between blocks in the ODD rows to the left.

◆ Once the rows are assembled, sew the rows together from one corner to the opposite corner. Leave the corner triangles for last. Butt and pin all seams before sewing. Side setting triangles may be a bit larger than needed, but do not trim them until the whole quilt is assembled.

◆ To prevent distortion when sewing the rows together, reverse sewing direction row by row. Sew Row 1 and Row 2 together stitching from left to right. Sew Row 3 to Row 2, stitching from right to left. Continue in this manner, alternating stitching direction until all the rows are sewn together.

◆ Press seams between rows as you go. Press toward shorter row.

◆ Add the corner triangles last.

◆ Trim edges of the quilt evenly, maintaining a $1/4$" seam allowance at the corners of blocks for adding the border.

Setting Triangles for Diagonal Settings

To stabilize the edge of the quilt, CORNER setting triangles are cut as half-square triangles, straight grain of the fabric on the short, outer legs of the triangle. Quilts of all sizes need four corner triangles, cut from two squares.

SIDE setting triangles are cut as quarter-square triangles, straight grain of the fabric on the long edge of the triangle, which becomes the edge of the quilt. The number of side setting triangles needed is determined by the number of blocks in the quilt.

Calculating corner and side setting triangle sizes

The size of the corner and side setting triangles is determined by the block size, using the magic geometric formulas to the right.

CORNER Setting Triangles

◆ DIVIDE the FINISHED size of the block by 1.4142. Round up to the nearest $1/8$".

◆ Add $7/8$" for seam allowances.

◆ Cut a square of your chosen fabric to that size. Cut the square in half diagonally ONCE to make half-square triangles.

◆ The straight of the grain will be on the short sides of the triangles, the outside of the quilt.

SIDE Setting Triangles

◆ Determine the number of side setting triangles needed. Divide this number by four and round up to calculate the number of squares required.

◆ MULTIPLY the FINISHED size of the block by 1.4142. Round up to the nearest $1/8$".

◆ Add $1 1/4$" for seam allowances. This is the size square you will need for setting triangles. Calculate how much of your chosen fabric you will need to cut the number of squares required for your quilt size.

◆ Cut the required number of squares of your chosen fabric to that size. You may need two rulers side-by-side to cut these large squares. Cut the squares in half diagonally TWICE to make quarter-square triangles.

◆ The straight of the grain will be on the long side of the triangles, the outside of the quilt.

◆ Depending on the number of blocks in the quilt, there may be side setting triangles left over.

137

Borders

The last step in making the quilt top is adding one or more borders to frame your creation. Many quilters do not decide on border treatment until the top is finished and they can see the total effect of the overall design.

Consider what type of borders might enhance your quilt. Choose one or more border types.

Inner borders are usually narrow ($1/2$"–2" finished). The first inner border frames the quilt and gives it definition. Consider a dark color or bold accent.

The **outer** border has nearly as much visual impact as the entire quilt top, so choose carefully. If you use the focus fabric from your blocks as a border, keep the border narrow (3"–5") so it doesn't overwhelm the top.

Plain, straight-set borders (the easiest for beginners) are attached to the sides first and then top and bottom. They are the most economical, especially when they are set with contrasting cornerstones.

Mitered borders take a bit more fabric and sewing expertise to make the Y-corners.

Pieced borders incorporate patchwork elements that coordinate with pieced blocks in the top. Pieced borders require considerable advance planning and may take as much time to assemble as the entire top.

For simplicity of presentation, instructions for all of the quilts in this book call for plain, straight set borders, cut on the crosswise grain for economy. The inner border is usually 1"–2" finished. The outer border is usually 5" finished.

Making Plain (Straight-Set) Borders

Add side borders first

◆ Measure the quilt from top to bottom at the midpoint. Spread it out on the floor or a large table. Pull taut, but do not stretch.

◆ Cut two borders to this measurement. For borders longer than 42", join two or more border strips together with diagonal seams.

◆ Pin the side borders. Divide the quilt side edge and the border strip into four equal sections, placing pins to mark the measurements: one in the midpoint, and one each, halfway between the midpoint and the ends of the border. Match the center pin of the quilt top to the center pin of the border strip and match the other two pins in a similar manner. Use as many other pins as necessary.

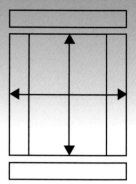

◆ Stitch the side borders to the quilt. For the innermost border, sew with the quilt on top so you can see to stitch through intersecting seams in the blocks. For subsequent borders, stitch with the border piece on top.

◆ Press the seams toward the border strips.

Add top and bottom borders

◆ Measure the width of the quilt at its center, including the side borders.

◆ Cut two borders to this measurement. If necessary, piece long strips with diagonal seams.

◆ Pin and sew borders to top and bottom, following the process outlined for side borders.

Any additional borders are added in this same manner.

Finishing the Quilt

Once the borders are attached, the quilt top is finished and the final phase begins: making a quilt sandwich of top, batting, and backing, attaching the layers together with decorative hand or machine stitching, and finishing the quilt with binding and label.

Backing

For the backing layer, use all-cotton fabric, cut according to the backing layouts included with each pattern. Preshrink the backing fabric and cut off the selvage edges before cutting the backing. Use a $5/8$" seam allowance when combining pieces for the backing and press the seam open.

Batting

Batting provides stability, depth, warmth, and dimension to a quilt. There are many different materials and brands of batting available. Ask for advice from experienced quilters. Open batting and allow it to relax overnight before sandwiching it in the quilt.

Professional Quilters

Many quilters enjoy designing and piecing tops more than quilting the layers together. In most areas of the country, professional machine quilters with special equipment offer their services to busy quilters. Check your local quilt shop for people in your region who will be happy to finish your quilt for you. Expect a six-month or more wait to get on the schedule. There are also many mail-order machine quilting services.

When you send a quilt out for machine quilting, be sure to cut the backing at least 4" larger than the top on ALL sides. Industrial machines need the extra inches to secure the quilt.

Karen McTavish hand guides her Gammill quilting machine.

Making the Quilt Sandwich

If you decide to do your own quilting, begin by assembling the three quilt layers. If you have access to a quilt frame and experienced helpers, layer and baste your quilt that way. If not, try this homestyle method.

◆ Cut batting and backing at least 3" larger than the quilt top on ALL sides.

◆ Lay the backing fabric, right side down, on a large, clean flat surface. Use masking tape to hold the backing tautly to the work surface.

◆ Spread the batting on top of the backing, smoothing it to make sure all the wrinkles are out.

◆ Lay the quilt top, right side up, on top of the batting. Smooth out any wrinkles and remove any stray threads

The quilt sandwich is ready to baste.

Basting

Basting holds the three layers of the quilt together to prevent shifting during the quilting process.

For hand quilting, baste use a light colored thread, a long needle and a long running stitch. Start at the center of the quilt and baste in a grid horizontally and then vertically. The basting rows should be evenly spaced and about 4" apart.

For machine quilting, pin baste using #2 size safety pins. Start at the center of the quilt and work out, placing the pins approximately every 4".

Pin-basting for machine quilting.

Quilting

Quilting is the process used to hold the three layers of the quilt together without slipping. The simplest form of quilting is to **tie the layers together** with decorative thread, spacing the double square knots six inches apart or less. This process is much easier with a quilt frame, but quilters over the years have used the backs of chairs as supports.

Hand and machine quilting enhance the beauty of a quilt by adding texture and design. If you have never tried quilting, here are a few guidelines to get started.

Hand quilting features evenly spaced stitches in a predetermined pattern or design across the quilt top and/or within blocks. Use 18" lengths of 100% waxed cotton thread made especially for hand quilting in a color that matches or compliments your quilt design.

Always work from the center of the quilt to an outside edge. Try to make even stitches rather than small ones. See page 143 for excellent books on hand quilting methods.

Decorative hand quilting in alternate blocks.

Machine quilting requires the use of an even-feed or walking foot for straight line quilting. A darning foot is used for free-motion quilting. Consult your machine instruction manual for information on tension settings. Use 100% cotton or one of the myriad of specialty threads on the market today.

Start in the center of the quilt and work toward the edges, rolling and unrolling the quilt as needed. For beginners, try straight lines 3" or less apart in a horizontal/vertical or diagonal grid. Or stitch in the ditch following seam lines between or within blocks. For more sophisticated machine quilting ideas, read one of the outstanding books on quilting recommended in the resources section, page 143.

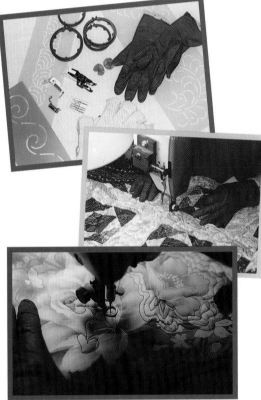
Machine quilting tools and techniques.

Adding a Sleeve

If your quilt will be displayed on a wall or in a show, it needs a hanging sleeve made of muslin or leftover backing fabric

◆ Cut fabric 9" wide and 1" shorter than the width of the top edge of the quilt.

◆ Hem the short ends by turning under 1/2", than 1/2" again. Stitch.

◆ With WRONG sides together, fold the fabric in half lengthwise. Stitch with a 1/4" seam allowance.

◆ Baste the raw edge of the sleeve to the top edge of the quilt back BEFORE the binding is added. The sleeve will be secured when the binding is sewn onto the quilt.

◆ To finish the sleeve, push the bottom edge of the sleeve up about an inch and blind stitch the bottom of the sleeve to the quilt back.

more →

Binding

Binding finishes the edge of the quilt after it has been quilted. Trim the excess batting and backing from the quilt sandwich first. The quilts in this book all used straight grain strips cut 2 1/4" wide. If available, use your machine's walking foot to sew on binding.

1. Measure the perimeter of your quilt to determine the needed length of binding. Add 12" for a safety margin.
2. To get the desired length of binding piece several 2 1/4" strips together using diagonal seams. Press the seams open and trim.
3. Fold the strips lengthwise with wrong sides together. Press.
4. At one end, unfold the binding and turn under 1/4" at a 45° angle. Pin to secure temporarily.

5. Beginning 2" from the pinned starting point, stitch the binding to the quilt with a 1/4" seam allowance.

6. Stitch to within 1/4" of the first corner. Stop and backstitch.

7. To miter the corner, fold the binding up and away from the quilt, forming a 45° angle.

10. Repeat this process at each corner.

11. When you reach the beginning of the binding, cut the end you are sewing about 1" longer than needed and tuck the end inside the beginning. Complete the final stitching.

8. Fold the binding down.

9. Begin stitching from the fold of the binding along the second edge of the quilt.

12. Turn the binding to the back, folding it over the raw edges of the quilt. Blind stitch in place on the quilt back.

13. At each corner, fold the binding to form miters and blind stitch to secure.

Preserving Your Quilt

To preserve and prolong the life of your quilts, treat them with TLC.

◆ Keep them out of direct sunlight.

◆ Refold quilts often to prevent creases and fabric strain.

◆ Beware of changes in temperature and humidity.

◆ Never store quilts in plastic bags.

Quilt Label

When the quilt is finished, sign and date it on the back, lower right-hand corner, using a permanent pen. Or make a label that can be hand stitched to the back.

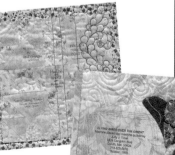

Suggested Reading

Basic Quilting

Doak, Carol. *Your First Quilt Book (Or It Should Be!)*. Bothell, WA: That Patchwork Place, 1997.

Kough, Lynn G. *Quiltmaking for Beginners: A Stitch-by-Stitch Guide to Hand and Machine Techniques*. Lincolnwood, IL: The Quilt Digest, 2000.

Martin, Nancy J. *Simply Scrappy Quilts*. Bothell, WA: That Patchwork Place, 1995.

Martin, Nancy J. *Two Color Quilts*. Bothell, WA: That Patchwork Place, 1998.

Scholley, Peggy. *The Quilter's Pocket Reference*. Milwaukee, WI: PS Publications, 1994.

Young, Blanche and Dalene Young Stone. *Tradition with a Twist*. Lafayette, CA: C&T Publishing Inc, 1996.

Borders and Settings

Hanson, Joan. *Sensational Settings: Over 80 Ways to Arrange Your Quilt Blocks*. Bothell, WA: That Patchwork Place, 1993.

Kime, Janet. *The Border Workbook: Easy Speed-Pieced & Foundation-Pieced Borders*. Bothell, WA: Martingale & Company, 1997.

Martin, Judy and Marsha McClosky. *Pieced Borders: The Complete Resource*. Grinnell, IA: Crosley-Griffith Publishing Company Inc, 1994.

Schneider, Sally. *Painless Borders*. Bothell, WA: That Patchwork Place, 1992.

Color and Fabric Selection

Anderson, Alex. *Fabric Shopping with Alex Anderson*. Lafayette, CA: C&T Publishing, 2000.

Barnes, Christine. *Color: The Quilter's Guide*. Bothell, WA: That Patchwork Place, 1997.

Beyers, Jinny. *Color Confidence for Quilters*. Lincolnwood, IL: The Quilt Digest Press, 1992.

rces

Beyer, Jinny. *Jinny Beyer's Color Confidence for Quilters*. Lincolnwood, IL: The Quilt Digest Press, 1992.

Combs, Karen. *Optical Illusions for Quilters*. Paducah, KY: American Quilter's Society, 1997.

Penders, Mary Coyne. *Color and Cloth*. Lincolnwood, IL: The Quilt Digest Press, 1995.

Seely, Ann and Joyce Stewart. *Color Magic for Quilters*. Emmaus, PA: Rodale Press Inc, 1997.

Finishing

Dietrich, Mimi. *Happy Endings: Finishing the Edges of Your Quilt*. Bothell, WA: That Patchwork Place, 1987.

Mazuran, Cody. *A Fine Finish*. Bothell, WA: That Patchwork Place, 1997.

Hand Quilting

Kimball, Jeana. *Loving Stitches*. Bothell, WA: That Patchwork Place, 1992.

Simms, Ami. *How to Improve Your Quilting Stitch*. Flint, MI: Mallery Press, 1996.

Machine Quilting

Hargrave, Harriet. *Heirloom Machine Quilting*. Lafayette, CA: C&T Publishing, 1990.

Noble, Maurine. *Machine Quilting Made Easy*. Bothell, WA: That Patchwork Place, 1994.

Townswick, Jane, ed. *Easy Machine Quilting*. Emmaus, PA: Rodale Press Inc, 1996.

Piecing

Soltys, Karen Costello, ed. *Perfect Piecing*. Emmaus, PA: Rodale Press Inc, 1997.

Thomas, Donna Lynn. *A Perfect Match: A Guide to Precise Machine Piecing*. Bothell, WA: Martingale & Company, 1998.

Pressing

Giesbrecht, Myrna. *Press for Success: Secrets for Precise and Speedy Quiltmaking*. Bothell, WA: That Patchwork Place, 1999.

Quilt Block Construction and History

Brackman, Barbara. *Encyclopedia of Pieced Quilt Patterns*. Paducah, KY: American Quilter's Society, 1993.

Finley, Ruth E. *Old Patchwork Quilts and the Women Who Made Them*. McClean, VA: EPM Publications, 1929, 1957.

Kansas City Star. *One Piece at a Time: A Selection of the Legendary Kansas City Star Patterns*. Kansas City, MO: Kansas City Star Books, 1999.

Kiracofe, Roderick. *The American Quilt: A History of Cloth and Comfort 1750-1950*. New York: Clarkson Potter Publishers, 1993.

Martin, Judy. *The Block Book*. Grinnell, IA: Crosley-Griffith Publishing Company Inc, 1998.

McCloskey, Marsha. *Marsha McCloskey's Block Party*. Emmaus, PA: Rodale Press Inc, 1998.

Rotary Cutting

Anderson, Alex. *Rotary Cutting*. Lafayette, CA: C&T Publishing Inc, 1999.

McCloskey, Marsha. *Guide to Rotary Cutting*. Seattle, WA: Feathered Star Productions, 1990, 1993.

Thomas, Donna Lynn. *Shortcuts: A Concise Guide to Rotary Cutting*. Bothell, WA: Martingale & Company, 1999.

Selected Publications

American Patchwork and Quilting (bi-monthly)
800-677-4876
www.bhg.com/crafts

American Quilter (quarterly)
270-898-7903 www.aqsquilt.com

McCall's Quilting (bi-monthly)
800-944-0736
www.mccallsquilting.com

Quilter's Newsletter Magazine (monthly except Jan/Feb, Jul/Aug)
800-477-6089
www.quiltersnewsletter.com

Quilting Today (bi-monthly)
570-278-1984
www.quilttownusa.com

Quiltmaker (bi-monthly)
800-477-6089
www.quiltmaker.com

Traditional Quiltworks (bi-monthly)
570-278-1984
www.quilttownusa.com

Recommended Internet Resources

www.QuiltmakersGift.com

Puzzles, projects, and educational resources related to the award-winning picture book by Jeff Brumbeau and Gail de Marcken.

www.abcquilts.org

ABC Quilts Project: Get into the spirit of *The Quiltmaker's Gift*. Make a comforting quilt and give it to a worthy cause: at-risk babies and children.

www.spingola.com.ds

Deanna Spingola's gateway to all the internet quilting resources you could want.

Quilting Organizations

American Quilter's Society

PO Box 3290, Paducah, KY 42002
270-898-7903
aqsquilt@apex.net

National Quilting Association

PO Box 393,
Ellicott City, MD 21041
410-461-5733
www.his.com/queenb/nqa

International Quilting Association

7660 Woodway, Suite 550,
Houston, TX 77063
713-781-6864 iqa@quilts.com

Professional Machine Quilters

Merry Ellestad
& Rosemary Walsberg
Quilting Up North
218 Third Ave
Two Harbors, MN 55616
218-834-3268

Angela Haworth
Catalyst Threads
513 8th Ave East
Superior, WI 54880
715-392-5133

Bonnie Jusczak
Pine Needle Quilting
3992 W Tischer Rd
Duluth, MN 55803
218-728-6950

Rolinda Langham
15209 Langham Rd
Stone Lake, WI 54876
715-865-4732

Karen McTavish
Superior Custom Machine Quilting
1748 Wildwood Rd
Duluth, MN 55804
218-525-0103

Sue Munns
Sue's Quilt Studio
2002 Tyrol St
Duluth, MN 55811
218-727-3835

Carolyn & Charles Peters
Runs with Scissors
1640 Quail Ridge Circle
Woodbury, MN 55125
651-735-0053

Helen Smith Prekker
Skyline Quilting
415 E Skyline Parkway
Duluth, MN 55805
218-722-9880

Debra Lussier Quinn
Deb's Quilting
1317 N 21st St
Superior, WI 54880
715-394-9645

Pam Stolan
Mission Creek Quilting
13107 W 9th St
Duluth, MN 55808
218-626-3344

Award-winning gift books with messages that matter

The charming companion to Quilts from The Quiltmaker's Gift

The Quiltmaker's Gift
Author: Jeff Brumbeau
Illustrator: Gail de Marcken
$17.95

This is the book that inspired us all—a charming fable for our times that celebrates the joy of giving.

You've seen samples of the glorious art and read portions of the inspired story sprinkled among the quilt patterns here. Nominated for the American Booksellers Association Booksense Book of the Year Award, *The Quiltmaker's Gift* has consistently been on the Publisher's Weekly bestseller list. If you don't have your copy yet, now is the time to do yourself the favor! Here are a few comments from fans:

> *You will wish it were Christmas again, so you would have an excuse to buy a copy of this book for every child and most of the adults you know!*

—Quilter's Newsletter Magazine

> *What a different world this would be if* The Quiltmaker's Gift *were on a required reading list for humanity. I know of no other book that promotes the spirit of giving more than this one.*

—Chinaberry Books

> *The story and illustrations are incredible. I want to shout out from the roof top. This is the very best children's book with a quiltmaking theme I have ever seen.*

—Jeanne Glenfield, East Coast Quilters Alliance

You are also invited to visit the book's website at **www.QuiltmakersGift.com**, where you will find puzzles and games, stories of generosity, quilting activities, and conversations with the author and the artist.

Reach for another of Gail de Marcken's artistic gems

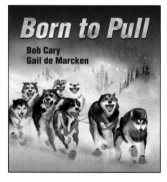

Born to Pull
Author: Bob Cary
Illustrator: Gail de Marcken
$26.95

This collection of fascinating stories and vivid watercolors is beautifully combined into a volume about the world's greatest athletes—sled dogs. A great gift for anyone who loves dogs, for the adventurous at heart, for families, for hard-to-satisfy preteen boys. You can almost smell the "puppy breath" in the amazingly detailed illustrations. Winner of the Minnesota Book Award and a Ben Franklin Medal.

More values-based classics with quilting appeal

Every year, from the more than a thousand manuscripts received, we select one values-based picture book with a message that has moved us greatly—one that we feel will make a positive impact for generations to come. These books blur the line between child and adult—expressing the wisdom and vision of young people and celebrating the child that lives within every adult. Several of these have special appeal for quilters.

A powerful message for girls

Grandmother's Alphabet
Author and illustrator: Eve Shaw
$14.95

Q is for Quilter in this unusual version of the ABCs. Featuring grandmothers of all ages and races in both traditional and nontraditional occupations, this alphabet book shows that "grandmother can be anything she wants to be—and so can I." Encourages girls (and boys) to become whatever they want to be.

Winner of the National Parent Council Outstanding Children's Book citation and the Benjamin Franklin medal for Best Occupational Book.

An inspiring message for all ages

Reach for the Moon
Author: Samantha Abeel
Illustrator: Charles Murphy
$17.95

This remarkable book of poetry and breathtaking art, reflects thirteen-year-old Samantha Abeel's journey of growth and self-discovery as she deals with her learning disability. A powerful testament to the fact that LD does not mean "lazy and dumb," *Reach for the Moon* provides inspiration for all ages and for people dealing with any life challenge.

Winner of the International Reading Association's Book of Distinction Award, the prestigious Margo Marek Award, Best Book for the Teen Age, and several other national citations.

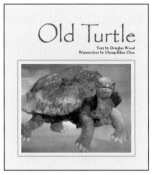

A prophetic fable for the new millenium

Old Turtle
Author: Douglas Wood
Illustrator: Cheng-Khee Chee
$17.95

The beauty and power of this fable has enchanted people around the globe. Chee's evocative watercolors, blending Eastern and Western tradition, provide the perfect setting for Doug's moving message of international understanding and environmental caring.

Winner of the International Reading Association Award, the American Booksellers Association Book of the Year Award and numerous other national and international citations.

The subject of several plays and a world-class choral/symphonic composition, *Old Turtle* is nearing a million copies in print. If you haven't yet experienced the magic of this book, you are missing something important for your heart.

To obtain any of these fine gift books—

Contact your local quilt shop or your favorite bookstore.

Quiltmaker's Gift Generosity Fund

Scholastic Inc. along with author Jeff Brumbeau and illustrator Gail de Marcken have joined in dedicating a portion of the revenue from *The Quiltmaker's Gift* to projects that implement the spirit of generosity portrayed by the quiltmaker and the king.

Acknowledgements

Our heartfelt thanks and gratitude to those who made this book possible:

Quiltmakers (page number of quilt)
Marcia Bowker (108), Michelle Bowker (10), Carol Jean Brooks (43, 68, 105), Lynne Chilberg (33), Jeanette Christensen (15), Gail de Marcken (62, 73, 76, 96), Ann Degen (98), Barb Engelking (49, 86), Jena Engelking (61), Betty Firth (31), Toni Gotelaere (102, 114), LaVonne Horner (61, 112, 124), Elizabeth Benson Johnson (16), Sarah Anne Elizabeth Johnson (16), Shirley Kirsch (20), Christa Knudsen (24), Ferne Liberty (33), Joanne Larsen Line (28, 44, 70, 92, 106, 118), Barbara McKeever (56, 64, 88), Diane Nyman (22, 46), Stephanie Orlowski (120), Ann Ketcham Palmer (54), Judy Pearson (79), Cindy Provencher (85), Lonnie Randall (33), Kelly Sauer (20), Judy J. Timm (24, 34, 80), Jessica Torvinen (50, 94), Spencer Torvinen (50), Nancy Loving Tubesing (38, 74), Kim Hoffmockel Wells (14), Vonn Wien Wells (36).

Machine quilters (page number of quilt)
Marcia Bowker (10, 108), Merry Ellestad (54, 73), Angela Haworth (28, 34, 49, 76, 106, 114), Bonnie Jusczak (62, 112), Joan's Quilting (31, 33, 79), Rolinda Langham (98), Karen McTavish (16, 24, 38, 74, 92, 118), Sue Munns (33, 43, 70), Claudia Clark Myers (50, 86), Carolyn and Charles Peters (44, 61, 96, 105, 124), Helen Smith Prekker (20, 102), Cindy Provencher (85), Debra Lussier Quinn (14, 33, 56, 64, 88), Pam Stolan (15, 22, 46, 120), Judy J. Timm (80), Rosemary Walsberg (54, 73), Vonn Wien Wells (36), Sue Brooks Wiitanen (68).

Pattern testers
Carol Jean Brooks, Carolyn Dean, Claudia Dodge, Betty Firth, Judy Gillen, Stephanie Gudmunsen, Pat Hartley, Peggy Hayes, Rose Heideman, Jane Herstad, Jennifer Isley, Lorraine Kellerman, Stephanie Lemenowsky, Patty Lipe, Bonnie Malterer, Marge Martin, Barbara McKeever, Judy Pearson, Linda Pfuhl, Maree Seitz, Margaret Whalen, Dawn Wicklund, Delores Wojciehowski, Connie Zakula, Barb Zapp.

Mini-quilt makers
Nancy Andreae, Ruth Barsch, Arlene Birchem, Kelly Bogrien, Mary Boman, Marcia Bowker, Michelle Bowker, Jean Brehmer, Carol Jean Brooks, Kristine Campbell, Jeanette Christensen, Patty Christensen, Mary Corbin, Mary Coy, Linda Dally, Marian Degnan, Claudia Dodge, Mary Eblom, Jill Ellsworth, Barb Engelking, Retta Fifo, Gail Fisher, Betty Firth, Donna Fleetwood, Toni Floyd, Linda Ford, Edna Georgious, Judy Gillen, Carol Goman, Joyce Gonzalez, Toni Gotelaere, Sharri Guimont, Susan Gustafson, Cindy Hagen, Julie Hartmann, Peggy Hayes, Linda Johnson, Marlene Johnson, Rita Johnson, Rose Johnson, Shirley Kirsch, Joyce Knapp, Diane Knudson, Eileen Korpi, Cindy Koski, Ann Marden Krafthefer, Penny LaBerge, Agnes Lammi, Donna Lease, Ferne Liberty, Susan MacLennan, Bonnie Malterer, Susan Manning, Carol Maupins, Kim McFarlin, Barbara McKeever, Karen McTavish, Janet McTavish, Lisa Mesedahl, Jan Messner, Claudia Clark Myers, Laura Nagel, Mona Nelson, Diane Nyman, Kim Matteen Orlowski, Ann Ketcham Palmer, Mary Ann Pelletier, Carolyn Peters, Clyda Prosen, Cindy Provencher, Mary Richard, Karren Robinson, Gail Ruuhela, Dorothy Schuknecht, Bev Solseng, Carol Soular, Eileen Sugars, Sandy Thomson, Judy J. Timm, Judy Trempe, Cheryl Wallace, Velda Weeks, Kim Hoffmockel Wells, Vonn Wien Wells Sue Brooks Wiitanen, Elizabeth Wilhelmson, Vickie Youngquist-Smith.

Friendship Star quilt makers
Nancy Andreae, Ami Bieurance, Jean Bouen, Marcia Bowker, Jeanette Christensen, Mary Coy, Gail de Marcken, Marion Degnan, Pat Doran, Nancy Elmore, Jill Ellsworth, Donna Fleetwood, Toni Floyd, Linda Ford, Toni Gotelaere, Shari Guimont, Susan Gustafson, Cindy Hagen, Mavis Harmon, Julie Hartmann, Ann Higgins, Maxine Jacks, Liz Benson Johnson, Rose Johnson, Shirley Kirsch, Joyce Knapp, Cindy Koski, Karen Lamppa, Susan Manning, Kim McFarlin, Lisa Mesedahl, Mona Nelson, Sharon Nemec, Ann Ketcham Palmer, Clyda Prosen, Judy Rich, Pearl Riesgraf, Barb Rinne, Gail Ruuhela, Melodee Schreffler, Doroty Schuknecht, Brenda Shock, Karen Skraba, Bev Solseng, Carol Soular, Vicki Strommen, Eileen Sugars, Judy Trempe, Velda Weeks, Vickie Youngquist-Smith.

Quilt shop professionals
Staff and quilting teachers at Fabric Works: Mary Eblom, Barb Engelking (owner), Julie Ford, LaVonne Horner, Shirley Kirsch, JoAnn Landwehr, Joanne Larsen Line, Claudia Clark Myers, Diane Nyman, Carolyn Peters, Danna Swenson, Sandy Thomson, and Judy J. Timm for their enthusiasm and assistance in all phases of this project, and for being such wonderful models of quiltmentoring.

Wellness for quilters
Marcia Bowker, OTR, CHT, for her consultation and Jessica Torvinen for modeling healthy stretches.

Graphic artist
Joy Morgan Dey for her book and cover design, diagram drafting, flexibility, creativity, and personal support throughout the process of creating *Quilts from The Quiltmaker's Gift*.

Snapshot photographers
Joy Morgan Dey, Toni Gotelaere, David Johnson, Barbara McKeever, Tom Myers, Charlie Ross, Barbara Skogg, Brian Timm.

Proofreaders
Lila Taylor Scott, Jennifer Isley, Susan Gustafson, Barb Engelking, LaVonne Horner.

Glossary & Index
(page references in parentheses)

Accent
Small amount of unexpected color in a block or quilt. Usually one of the colors nearly opposite the main color on the color wheel. (133)

Alternate Plain Block
Block made out of a whole piece of fabric that is placed between stitched blocks. (136–137)

Alternate Design Block
Pieced or appliquéd block that is placed between the main stitched blocks. (136–137)

Backing
Large piece of fabric that covers the back of a quilt. Bottom layer of the quilt sandwich, Backing may be seamed together from more than one piece of fabric. (138–139)

Background Fabric
Fabric of contrasting value to fabric of main design elements in quilt block. Usually a neutral or light color, occasionally dark.

Batting
A layer sandwiched inside the quilt, between the top and the backing. Usually made of a fluffy polyester, cotton, or wool which adds warmth and texture to the quilt. (138–139)

Bias
The diagonal of a woven fabric, which runs at a 45° angle to the selvage. Bias is very stretchy. Pieces cut on the bias need to be handled and pressed carefully to prevent stretching. (132)

Binding
A doubled strip of fabric, cut on either the straight of grain or the bias. Stitched to the edge of a quilt to cover the raw edges of the three layers. (140)

Block
Usually a square or rectangle design unit that is pieced or appliquéd. Typically, quilt tops are made by repeating one or more quilt block designs in a pleasing arrangement.

Border
One or more strips of fabric or patchwork surrounding the main body of the quilt top like the frame on a picture. May be pieced or appliquéd. Many quilts have borders of varying widths. (140)

Botanicals
Fabrics featuring actual or abstract images of nature: leaves, grass, trees, wood grain, etc.

Butting
When seam allowances of intersecting seams fall in opposite directions so they nestle closely together and seams line up on the right side. Sometimes referred to as nesting. (135)

Chain Piecing
Technique used to sew units together, one after another, without lifting the presser foot or cutting the thread between them. (135)

Complement
Color directly opposite on the color wheel. (133)

Corner Square
A square of fabric sometimes used to join adjacent border strips. (10, 50, 106)

Corner Triangle
A half-square triangle used to fill in the four corners of a diagonally set quilt before borders are added. (67, 137)

Cornerstone
See Setting Square.

Crosscut
In rotary cutting, the second cut, dividing a fabric strip or strip set into squares, rectangles, or strips of precise measurement. (134)

Crosswise grain
Threads of a fabric that are woven from selvage to selvage. Crosswise grain has some stretch. (132)

Cutting Mat
Special protective surface specifically designed for use with a rotary cutter. (130, 134)

Diagonal (On-Point) Set
Quilt design arranged so the blocks, turned on their points, are pieced together in diagonal rows with side setting and corner triangles added to complete the rows. (62, 67, 94, 136–137)

Dog Ears
Tips of triangles extending past seam allowances after pieces are stitched. (53, 78, 83, 111)

Focus Fabric
Fabric, usually multi-color, that serves as the major focal point in a quilt. Often used as a border as well as in blocks. (89, 132)

Geometrics
Fabrics with stripes, plaids, dots, checks, or other geometric shapes.

Half Block
Half of a design unit used to fill in at the side, top or bottom of a diagonally set quilt to create a straight edge. (137)

Horizontal Set (Straight Set)
A design arranged so that the blocks and other components are oriented horizontally and vertically. Nearly all the quilts in this book use a horizontal set. (136–137)

Lattice
See Sashing Strip.

Layering
Constructing the quilt sandwich by assembling the three layers (quilt top, batting, backing) together. (138–139)

Lengthwise Grain
Fabric threads that run parallel to the selvages. This straight of grain has little or no stretch. (132)

Machine Quilting
Fast and effective way to stitch the three layers of a quilt together in a functional and decorative manner. May be done on a home sewing machine, long-arm machine, or room-size quilting machine. (139)

Mitered Corner (Set-In Corner)
Point where three seams intersect at an angle to form a "Y." Many of the quilts pictured in this book have diagonal, mitered corner borders. (139)

Neutral
White, off-white, beige, gray, black fabrics. (132–133)

Novelty Prints
Fabrics featuring graphic thematic images such as cars, cartoon characters, sports insignias, balloons. Sometimes called juvenile prints or conversation prints. (132)

On-Point
See Diagonal Set.

Pieced Block
Small pieces of fabric in various shapes stitched together by hand or machine to form a larger design. (front cover)

Pieced Border
A design made up of small shapes stitched together into long strips that form the border of the quilt. (112, 138)

Pin Basting
Using safety pins to secure the three layers of the quilt. Method of choice for machine quilting done on a home sewing machine. (139–140)

Pressing
Lifting and placing an iron to flatten fabric and seam allowances. Can be done with or without steam. (135)

Quilt Top
Upper layer of a quilt, made of appliquéd or pieced blocks, sashing, setting squares, and/or borders. (136–141)

Rotary Cutter
Tool shaped like a pizza cutter with an extremely sharp round blade. Used to cut strips and shapes from multiple layers of fabric. (127, 130, 134)

Rotary Cutting
Technique for cutting strips and shapes from several layers of fabric at the same time, using a rotary cutter. For its accuracy and speed, this method is used in all the instructions for quilts in this book. (127, 130, 134)

Sashing Strip (Lattice Strip)
Strip of fabric sewn between two rows of blocks or within a block to divide quadrants. (16–21, 22–27, 68–73, 74–79, 92–96, 136–137)

Sashing Square
See Setting Square.

Seam
Line of stitches joining two fabrics together.

Seam Allowance
Portion of fabric between the stitched seam and the cut edge of the fabric. Usually a scant 1/4" for successful quilting. See page 131 for testing instructions.

144